THE ARTS OF
ASIA

MEHER McARTHUR

THE ARTS OF
ASIA

MATERIALS • TECHNIQUES • STYLES
With 435 color illustrations

Thames & Hudson

To all Asian artists working to keep traditional
materials, techniques and styles alive.

1 (half-title): Seated Buddha, lacquered wood, Vietnam,
19th century
2 (opposite title page): Dish with longevity (*shou*)
characters and floral scrolls, wheel-thrown porcelain with
underglaze blue, clear glaze, and overglaze painted enamel
decoration (*doucai*), China, Jiangxi Province, Jingdezhen,
Qing dynasty, Guangxu mark and period, 1874–1908
3 (title page): Taoist immortal, porcelain, China, early
19th century

© 2005 Thames & Hudson Ltd, London

First published in 2005 in hardcover in the United
States of America by Thames & Hudson Inc.,
500 Fifth Avenue, New York, New York 10110

thamesandhudsonusa.com

Library of Congress Catalog Card Number
2005923470

ISBN-13: 978-0-500-23823-3
ISBN-10: 0-500-23823-5

Printed and bound in Singapore by Craft Print
International Ltd

ACKNOWLEDGMENTS

So many people have generously contributed their time, expertise and photographs. Without them, this book would surely not have materialized, and I am deeply grateful for their kind support.

I would like to thank the following museums, galleries, art dealers and publishers for providing many of the mag-nificent images in the book: Aizen Kobo, Kyoto; the British Library, London; Brooklyn Museum of Art; Denver Art Museum; Huntington Library, Art Collections and Botanical Gardens, California; Sam Fogg Ltd, London; the Fowler Museum of Cultural History, UCLA; Francesca Galloway Ltd, London; Hiromi Paper International; the Kelton Foundation, Los Angeles; Kim 3 International Furniture; Los Angeles County Museum; the Metropolitan Museum of Art, New York; National Folk Museum of Korea; Norton Simon Museum, Pasadena; Pacific Asia Museum, Pasadena; Percival David Foundation, London; Ruth Chandler Williamson Gallery, Scripps College, Claremont; Silk Roads Design Gallery, Los Angeles; Smith-Gibbs Publishers; Tai Gallery, Santa Fe; Victoria & Albert Museum, London; Warisan, Los Angeles.

Certain individuals were instrumental in helping me to obtain images, most notably Julian Bermudez of Pacific Asia Museum and Giselle Arteaga Johnson of the Los Angeles County Museum of Art, to whom I offer my sincerest thanks. I would also like to thank the following individuals who were also extremely helpful in obtaining images for the book: Nancy Allard, Giancarlo Avancini, Susan Sayre Batton, Yvonne Chang, Rob Coffland, Don Cole, Terry Davis, Martin Durrant, Lisa Griffin, Roy Hamilton, Elizabeth Jackson, Ruth Janson, David Kamansky, Hiromi Katayama, Christine Knoke, Marty Lee, Donna Luehrmann, Melanie Lum, Jon and Cari Markel, Joan Marshall, Sally McKay, Linda Nimori, Ayami Oishi, Marcia Page, Aaron Rath, Sue Scheimann, Lyssa Stapleton and Julie Zeftel.

The following collectors, artists and designers generously lent images from their private collections and their homes, and I would like to express my gratitude to them for sharing their treasures, art work and study pieces with us all through this book: Barefoot Elegance, Lloyd Cotsen, Donal and Althea Bassett, Dale Gluckman, Ruth Sutherlin Hayward, David Kamansky, Kenneth Lapatin, Mona Lutz, Richard Manness, Beverley Messenger, Yamataka Ryoun, Colleen and Shoichi Sakurai, Michael Stevenson, Rae Terk, Ayomi Yoshida, Shohachi Umakoshi.

I am also grateful to the following photographers for lending their spectacular and informative photographs: Luca Corona, Christopher Covey, Hollis Goodall, Gale Beth Gordon, Douglas Hill, Richard Hughes, Rochelle Kessler, Dana Levy, Alan McArthur, Daniel Stiles, Art Streiber, June Takahashi, Sharon Takeda.

This book tackles a broad range of material, and I could not have faced the task without the guidance of the following specialists who read through different sections of the book to check for accuracy: Dana Boehnlein, Bruce Coats, Dale Gluckman, David Humphrey, Julia Hutt, Hiromi Katayama, Rochelle Kessler, Kenneth Lapatin, June Li, Stephen Markel, Andrew Mitchell, Stacey Pierson, Ann Richardson, Sonya Rhie Quintanilla. Any errors or inaccuracies that have slipped through are entirely my responsibility.

Finally, I would like to thank Jamie Camplin of Thames & Hudson for believing in this book, and my patient and thoughtful editor Philip Watson for making the process an enjoyable one. My family and friends and especially my husband David Marsh have also been a great source of support, and I thank them all for staying by my side.

CONTENTS

INTRODUCTION 8

1 JADE
24

2 SILK
44

3 PORCELAIN
66

4 LACQUER
90

5 IVORY
112

6 BAMBOO
134

9 WOOD
198

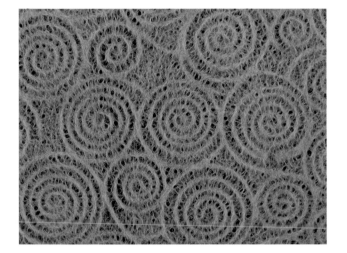

7 PAPER
156

10 STONE
220

Illustration credits   244
Bibliography   246
Museums   249
Buying Asian art   252
Index   254

8 GOLD
176

INTRODUCTION

THE ARTS OF ASIA have been the object of fascination and admiration in the Western world for many centuries. The silks of China and India, Chinese porcelains, lacquers from Japan and jade and ivory jewelry and ornaments have featured among the treasures of the wealthy and powerful throughout the world. Often considered 'mysterious' and 'exotic', Asian art objects have long been imported from Eastern countries as luxury items. They have been collected and displayed in palaces and homes, and eventually museums, often without being well understood by their Western owners. Over the last one hundred years or so, the study of Asian art has grown significantly. Now, most major Western museums house collections of Asian art, numerous academics specialize in Asian art history at universities and museums, and art galleries, antique shops, design galleries and furniture shops sell Asian-style furnishings and accessories.

This book adopts a new approach to the arts of Asia by using the artistic materials themselves as the starting point for each chapter. It is intended as an introduction to some of the principal materials used in Asian art – jade, silk, porcelain, lacquer, ivory, bamboo, paper, gold, wood and stone – and to the most significant ways in

INTRODUCTION

ABOVE: *Ginger jar with design of plum blossoms, porcelain with underglaze cobalt blue decoration, China, 19th century.*

ABOVE RIGHT: *Green jade wine vessel inlaid with gold and enamel, 17th century, Mughal period, India.*

which artists throughout Asia have transformed these materials into art objects over the centuries.

Each chapter begins with an introduction to the material itself, its physical make-up, origins and cultural significance, followed by an examination of some of the major techniques used to transform the material into an art object. Photographs of artists at work help elucidate the often complex methods to create art from these raw materials. Each chapter also features a brief survey outlining the principal artistic styles from particular regions of Asia over the centuries.

There are several reasons for choosing this material-based approach. First, when embarking on a study of Asian art, many students are required to study the history and geography of Asia before actually learning about the objects themselves. Many introductory books and college courses on Asian art are chronological or geographical in structure, introducing an array of dynastic titles, complex place names and terminology

LEFT: *Porcelain lidded ewer with lion and floral panels, with powder blue glaze, overglaze painted enamel decoration and gilding, China, Qing dynasty, Kangxi period (1662–1722).*

BELOW: *Porcelain dish with gardenia spray, lotus, pomegranates, peaches and grapes in underglaze blue with clear glaze and overglaze yellow enamel ground, China, Ming dynasty, Hongzhi mark and period (1488–1505).*

BOTTOM: *Porcelain vase with tea dust glaze, China, Qing dynasty (1644–1911).*

OPPOSITE: *Chinese Ming dynasty carved and painted wood Buddhist figures, Vietnamese painting of the Buddha and Chinese calligraphic inscription reading 'long life'.*

LEFT: *Marble sculpture of a Jain saint, India, in an interior in Los Angeles.*

BELOW: *Head of the Buddha, ivory, India, mid-20th century.*

that can be intimidating to the beginner. This volume begins with the very substance of the art so that the student can become familiar with the basic information about the art objects themselves before embarking on a study of their cultural context.

Secondly, many of these materials have an important spiritual significance in the cultures that use them. Jade, for example, because of its hardness and durability, has long been associated with immortality in China, so jade objects are often valued in part for their association with immortality and longevity in China and other cultures under China's influence. Long associated with imperial authority, jade also connotes wealth and power. Similarly, bamboo, which bends and sways in the strongest winds, symbolizes flexibility in East Asian cultures, a quality that is greatly admired in human beings and one which often infuses the bamboo artifact. An understanding of the spiritual and symbolic significance of these materials can lead to a more profound understanding of the art created from them and of the respect shown to the artists who create them. It is important to note that, while, in Western cultures, the highest praise is traditionally

ABOVE: *Pendant made from Chinese jade archer's ring of the Song dynasty (960–1279), set in 18-karat gold with Burmese cabochon rubies, designed by David Humphrey, Los Angeles.*

reserved for the 'fine arts', namely painting, sculpture and architecture, and other art forms are categorized as 'decorative arts' or 'crafts', this distinction does not exist in Asia. In Japan, for example, a maker of bamboo baskets can be considered a Living National Treasure and sell his baskets for considerable prices.

Thirdly, most of the materials featured in the book — jade, silk, porcelain, lacquer, ivory, bamboo and paper — were actually discovered, invented or first worked in Asia, so they can be considered 'Asian materials'. In fact, many of these materials have historically pervaded all aspects of the life — practical, religious and artistic — of the peoples of Asia. Bamboo has been employed as a building material, used to make containers, sculptures, clothing and musical instruments, so it is part of the fibre of life, as it were, to

INTRODUCTION

ABOVE: Netsuke *toggle in the form of a dragon, carved wood with staining, Japan, 18th century.*

RIGHT: *Shoulao, the God of Long Life, carved wood, China, 19th century.*

many Asians. Lacquer, which is now a luxurious decorative finish, was originally a protective coating on food vessels made of wood or bamboo. Porcelain has long been used to make food vessels as well as vases and furnishings for the home and garden, tools for the scholar's desk and objects of worship in temples. When these materials were first encountered by Westerners, they were considered mysterious and exotic, and, hence, highly desirable. Both lacquer ('japon' or 'japanning') and porcelain ('china') were named for their places of origin, indicating their strangeness and also preciousness. The European appetite for silks from China stimulated international overland trade as early as 2,000 years ago, and later, European maritime traders made their fortunes shipping Chinese porcelains and Japanese lacquer to the West. Asian ivories and jades have also

nerld

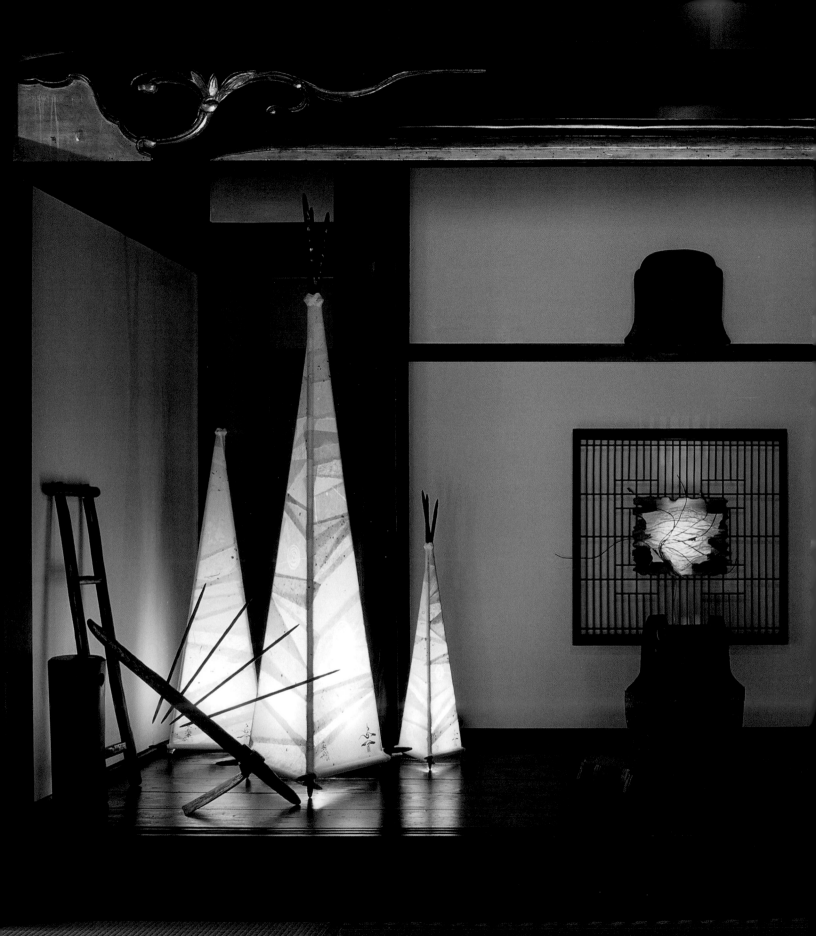

LEFT and ABOVE: *Illuminated paper sculptures by Shoichi and Colleen Sakurai, made from traditional Japanese paper, inside a converted Japanese farm house, Akiya, near Kamakura, Japan.*

INTRODUCTION

BELOW: *Throne cover made of cut-velvet silk, China, Qing dynasty, Qianlong period (1736–95).*

LEFT: *Indian silk cushions and hangings with wooden Burmese elephant, design by Kim 3 International Furnishings.*

ABOVE RIGHT: *Detail of kesa, or Buddhist priest's robe, made of silk brocade, Japan, 19th century.*

OPPOSITE: *Indian and Thai cushions on Chinese day bed, design by Warisan, Los Angeles.*

had a great appeal over the centuries, though the limited supply of these materials has meant that, traditionally, objects made of these materials have not been exported in such large quantities. Paper, a material invented in China and produced in various regions of Asia before reaching the West, has undeniably had an impact on the entire world beyond the realms of art.

Although the last three materials examined in this book – gold, wood and stone – are not uniquely Asian materials, there are many uniquely Asian ways in which they have been used to create art. Gold leaf is applied to Japanese folding screens as a surface

INTRODUCTION

RIGHT: *Bamboo chair and wardrobe, private collection, California. Bamboo is one of the most versatile materials used in Asia today.*

BELOW LEFT and RIGHT: *Bamboo basket by Living National Treasure Hayakawa Shokosai V (b. 1932), Japan, 21st century.*

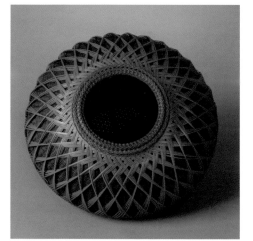

OPPOSITE ABOVE: *Burmese lacquered wood Buddhist figures and Vietnamese lacquered dishes and bowls, design by Kim 3 International Furnishings.*

OPPOSITE BELOW: *Origami crane on origami papers, Japan/USA, 21st century.*

for painting and to Thai and Burmese temple buildings; it is also used to coat many religious sculptures, lending them a brilliance that befits their spiritual luminescence. Wood is not only crafted into religious statuary and objects throughout many regions of Asia, but it is also carved into blocks to produce colourful woodblock prints and printed books. Stone is also significant in both religious and secular architecture such as Angkor Wat in Cambodia and the Taj Mahal in India, and garden design, such as the famous rock gardens of Japan's Zen temples.

Finally, many of the materials presented in this book are misunderstood in the West. What is often called 'rice paper' is actually made from mulberry wood pulp; 'cinnabar' refers to a lacquer coloured red with mercuric sulphide, or cinnabar. Lacquer itself is not the base material of a vessel or sculpture, but merely the hard, glossy coat-

ing. In the world of Asian ceramics, it is not always clear that the term 'porcelain' refers to the clay body of a vessel, while 'celadon' refers to the glaze. Jade is actually 'abraded' rather than 'carved' since it is too hard to cut with a blade. In Chinese silk embroidery, a wonderful, exotic myth exists about the so-called 'forbidden stitch', supposedly banned by the Chinese government because it was so intricate that embroiderers went blind.

This book is a celebration of the materials themselves as the very essence of Asian art. It is intended to serve as a useful source of information for students and collectors of Asian art alike; it is hoped that the book will inspire enthusiasts to delve deeper into the world of Asian art.

INTRODUCTION

LEFT: *Gold vessel and cover on stand in the shape of a sacred goose, decorated with filigree work, inlaid with rubies, Burma, 19th century.*

BELOW: *Ivory brisé fan with pierced decoration, China, Qing dynasty. Copyright 2005 The Kelton Foundation.*

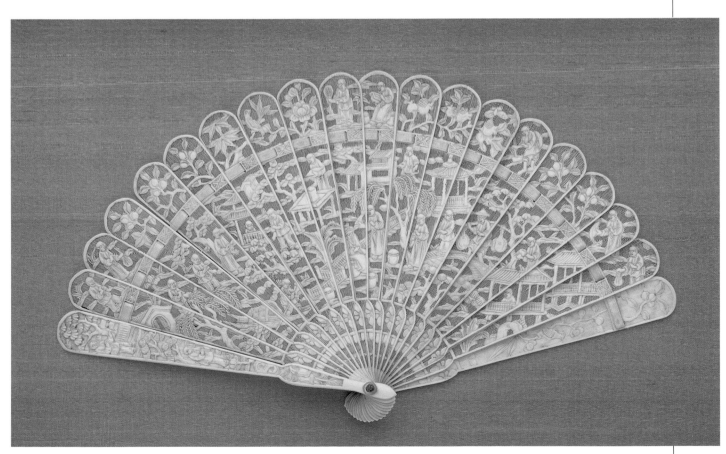

OPPOSITE: *Perforated disc (bi). See p. 33.*

LEFT: *Snuff bottle. See p. 40.*

BELOW LEFT: *Chimera. See p. 37.*

BELOW: *Crab claw ear pendants, China, Qing dynasty, 19th century.*

JADE

JADE IS CONSIDERED by many to be the most powerful and mystical material used in Asian art. Admired for its sheen, strength and durability, jade has long been associated with imperial authority, heaven and immortality, particularly in China, where the stone has been worked for thousands of years. In various Asian cultures, jade has been the stone of emperors and kings and has embellished their palaces, adorned their bodies and even accompanied them to their graves to join them in the afterlife. The Chinese have a saying: 'one can put a price on gold, but jade is priceless.' Today, the finest jade is exceeded in price only by diamonds, and is a desirable commodity all around the world.

JADE

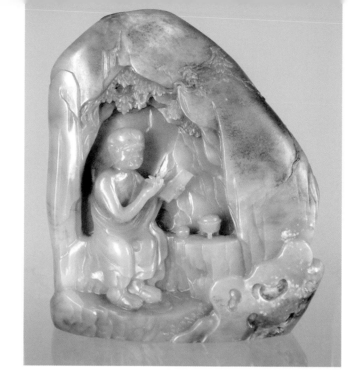

THE MATERIAL

THE TERM 'JADE' is correctly used to refer to two stones, nephrite and jadeite, which are actually clusters of minerals, each with very distinct chemical compositions. The difference between the two types of jade was only discovered by a French mineralogist in the mid-19th century. Nephrite is translucent with a matt surface that is often

ABOVE: *Luohan (Buddhist sage) in a grotto (detail), nephrite, China, 18th or 19th century. Nephrite's colours, generally softer than those of jadeite and derived mostly from iron, include black, brown, yellow and green, for which it is most celebrated. In its purest form, nephrite contains no iron and is a soft white. It is this pure white nephrite, known by the Chinese evocatively as 'mutton fat', that is most highly prized in China. Nephrite belongs to the amphibole group of minerals and is a silicate of calcium and magnesium, made up of interwoven fibrous crystals. It is a fairly hard stone, reading 6–6.5 on the Mohs' scale of hardness (chalk is 0, diamond is 10).*

The Stone of the Kidneys

The word jade *travelled into the English language from Spanish via French. It was first used in reference to the jades of Meso-America, then later the jades of China. In the late 15th to early 16th century, when the Spanish were in Central America, they noticed the local custom of wearing green stones around the waist. According to the Native Americans, these stones had the power to cure kidney disorders. The Spaniards too began to wear these stones around their waists for medicinal reasons and called them* piedra de los riñones, *'stone of the kidneys', or* piedra de ijada, *meaning 'stone of the loins'. The latter term travelled with the stones to Europe and was mistranslated into French. What should have been* pierre de l'éjade *became instead* le jade, *which then crossed into English as 'jade'. When the stone was given a Latin name, the association with the kidneys remained in* lapis nephriticus, *or 'stone of the kidneys'. This term,* nephrite *in English, was applied to all jades from Meso-America and China.*

Then in 1863, French mineralogist Alexis Damour discovered that there were two distinctly different types of jade. He called one type, the Meso-American jades in particular, jadeite. *Ironically, the Chinese stone continued to be called* nephrite, *even though it had never been associated with the kidneys in China.*

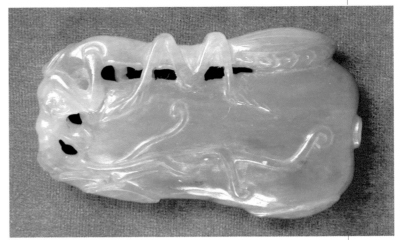

described as waxy or oily. Most Chinese jades until the 18th century are nephrite, after which time jadeite from Burma was widely used. Jadeite, often referred to as gem jade, has a glassier, more gem-like appearance and stronger colours than nephrite. In Asia, jadeite is mined primarily in Burma and has been exported from there for centuries.

The Sources of Jade

HISTORICALLY, JADE HAS either been gathered from rivers or mined from the mountainsides. In ancient times, China appears to have had its own sources of jade, in particular around the Lake Tai area in the eastern province of Jiangsu. Over the centuries, however, China's main sources of nephrite were Khotan (Hotan) and Yarkand in eastern Turkestan, now within the province of Xinjiang in the far west of China. Khotan was the primary source until the 16th century. There, the stones were gathered from the beds of the nearby Black Jade River or the White Jade River that flowed down from the Kunlun Mountains. For much of China's jade working history, water-worn pebbles and boulders of jade like this one were collected and transported over 2,000 miles to central China, through much treacherous terrain. From the 17th century, nephrite was also collected from Yarkand, and later still, spinach-green jade in particular was imported from the area around Lake Baikal in Siberia.

The source of all Asian jadeite is Burma, and traditionally it has been mined in and near Hpakan, the 'jade capital' in the state of Kachin in northern Burma. The jadeite here is mainly situated in a low-altitude plateau and is deposited in dykes that cut

JADE

RIGHT: *Breaking the jadeite apart in a dyke at Tawmaw, Burma. Once dikes containing jadeite are exposed, miners break into them with dynamite or jackhammers to access the jadeite within.*

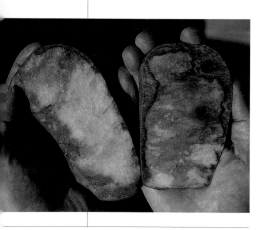

ABOVE: *The 'show points' of bright green jadeite on a boulder (top); a jadeite boulder split open (bottom). The colour is derived from various oxides: green is from chromium, yellow from iron, and lilac usually from manganese.*

across the plateau at various depths. Fairly close to this area, jadeite is also found in conglomerates of boulders that are buried under a layer of alluvial soil. These boulders are excavated by digging. Often, these boulders can be identified as containing jadeite by the 'show points' on their skin that reveal glimpses of the jadeite inside.

Creating the Basic Form in Jade

WE OFTEN REFER to jade 'carving', but both nephrite and jadeite are actually too hard to be carved. Instead, jade is actually abraded by friction using abrasive sands in conjunction with tools, the earliest being of stone and bamboo. Since around the 5th century BC, when bronze tools were first employed in jade working, metal rotary discs, string saws, solid awls and tubular drills have been the principal implements. The abrasive sands are made of ground-up materials with a higher reading than jade on the Mohs' scale of relative hardness: jade measures 6.5–7 points, compared to, for example, quartz (7), garnets (7.5) and most commonly black corundum sand (9). In the 1920s, corundum was replaced by the man-made material carborundum, an abrasive made from carbon and silicon. Nowadays, much jade carving is done in factories using metal tools, specialized machinery and workers on a production line.

Historically, the first stage in the jade working process was to cut down the large river boulders and quarried stones into more workable pieces. This was done using a two-handled metal saw that was kept moist with wet abrasive sand. The jade boulder was

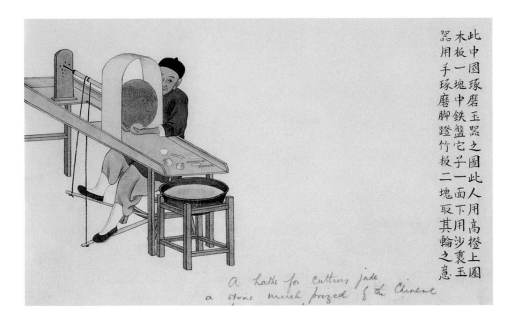

此中國琢磨玉器之圖此人用高橙上圈木板一塊中鐵盤它一面下用沙裹玉器用手琢磨脚蹬竹板二塊取其輪之意

A lathe for cutting jade a stone much prized by the Chinese

placed on a solid wooden base, and two men at either end of the saw would steadily wear away at the surface. It could take several weeks to cut the boulder into two halves.

After the stone was cut down into a workable size, it was then cut into the desired shape and form using a lathe, which consisted of a table with cutting tools attached to a horizontal bar fixed parallel to it. The worker continuously applied abrasive sands and water to the edge of the cutting tool to abrade the jade. To polish the jade at the end of the process, tools made from leather and wood could also be attached to the lathe and used with a paste made of ruby dust and water. By polishing the stone, the jade worker removed any scratches and created a smooth surface.

Decorating the Surface of the Jade

To decorate the surface of jade with fine details, the jade worker traditionally used lap wheels, plates that resemble nail heads that are attached to the main bar and rotated using the treadles. With these tiny discs, more detailed patterns, such as spirals, floral scrolls, or animal forms, could be abraded into the surface of the stone. The jade worker often worked with the colour of the stone to create interesting designs in the surface. For example, in the case of jadeite, which can be both green and lavender, he might carve the green part of the stone into leaves and the lavender part into a flower. Sometimes, the skin, or outer coating of the jade, was left and incorporated into the carved design, resulting in a two-colour image, such as a brown design against a pale green background.

TECHNIQUES

JADE

ABOVE: *Bowl with painted gold decoration (right: detail), nephrite, China, Qianlong mark and reign (1736–95), Qing dynasty.*

BELOW: *Abrading openwork designs in jadeite, China. Many Chinese jade vessels are incredible feats of technical virtuosity, featuring not only openwork, but suspended rings and chains that have all been created by abrading the jade using this method.*

OPPOSITE: *Mouthpiece for a water pipe (mukhnal), white nephrite with diamonds, rubies and emeralds set in gold, India, Mughal, c. 1675–1700. Inspired by the gold and jewel inlay on metal and rock crystal objects of the Ottoman Turks and other Islamic cultures, the Mughal jade artists of India set gold wires into scrolling patterns incised into the surfaces of jade vessels and inset precious gems such as rubies, emeralds and sapphires into the gold.*

One of the most remarkable accomplishments of the jade worker is openwork carving. The surface of the jade is first pierced along the lines of the design using a narrow drill with a diamond tip, and then worked with a small bow saw to open up the hole. The blade of the saw is inserted through the drilled hole before being attached to the other end of the bow, and the saw is moved back and forth to enlarge the hole, with the jade held in a vice to prevent it from moving.

Decoration has also been applied to the surface of jades in China and India. For example, in China in the Qing dynasty in particular, jade vessels with smooth surfaces were occasionally decorated with designs painted in gold, usually scrolling flowers and leaves, but also images of human and animal figures. Perhaps the most spectacular decoration applied to jade was the inlay with gold and precious gems created in the workshops of India's Mughal craftsmen of the 17th to 19th centuries.

CHINA

To the Chinese, there is probably no material as valuable as jade. The stone has been admired for its strength and worked into tools for thousands of years. Its durability has led to the association of jade with immortality, heaven and imperial power, and its beauty and smoothness have made it a desirable material for ornaments, jewelry and fondling pieces. In Chinese, jade is known as *yu*, a term that traditionally referred to a number of hardstones that have been carved in China for many centuries. Until the 17th century, the principal type of jade worked in China was nephrite, brought to central China from Khotan. This type of jade is often regarded by the Chinese as 'old jade' or 'soft jade'. From the 18th century, jadeite was imported from Burma and worked into jewelry and decorative and ceremonial objects. This gem-like jade was considered a 'new jade' or 'hard jade', and today is preferred by many Chinese to the old jade.

Jade has been worked in China since the Neolithic period (*c.* 5000–1500 BC), when the area that we know as China was inhabited by a number of distinct cultural groups. Fortunately, because it is such a hard stone, examples of worked jade from some of the cultures of this period have survived. During the Neolithic period, metal working had not yet been invented, so most tools and weapons were made out of stone and bamboo. From at least 4500 BC, some of the early inhabitants of China are known to have made higher-status, and sometimes ceremonial, versions of utilitarian tools such as axes and knives, out of nephrite. In the Neolithic cultures around the Yangzi River and the Liao

WANG

king

YU

jade

ABOVE: *There has long been a connection in China between jade and royalty. Wang, the Chinese character for 'king' (top), is written with three horizontal lines connected with a vertical line. The character for yu, jade (bottom), represents three pieces of jade connected with a cord. To distinguish it from the character for* wang, *a dot was added.*

The Symbolism of Jade in Daoism and Confucianism

Jade features prominently in China's ancient belief systems: the mystical Daoism, which explains the structure and forces of the universe, and the practical Confucianism, which advises on social and political conduct. According to Daoist beliefs, jade was an attribute of the creative principle of the universe, Qian. In Daoist cosmology, Heaven was presided over by the Jade Emperor, who ruled over the Jade Universe from the Jade Capital. The earthly emperor was also associated with jade. The Chinese character for jade, yu, was originally the same as the character for king, wang, which symbolized the emperor linking the three realms of Heaven, Earth and Man. The Chinese emperor wielded a jade seal of state and other ceremonial jade items, and references to his speech and appearance were prefixed with the word 'jade', as in 'jade sounds' and 'jade visage'. Ancient Daoists also believed that jade conveyed health and even immortality, so employed the stone in burial rituals to prevent the vital essence from leaking out of the corpse. Also, jade was considered to be a yang material, associated with the male force and the sun, and since yin is drawn to yang, Chinese myths abounded of naked women (yin) swimming in rivers at night to attract jade rocks and pebbles.

In the Confucian tradition, exemplary behaviour and virtues such as loyalty, intelligence, justice, humanity and truth were considered to be jade-like characteristics that should be cultivated by gentlemen. White nephrite jade, in particular, was associated with purity.

River in northeastern China, jade ornaments and sculptures of birds, animals and fantastic creatures were also made as early as *c.* 3500 BC, marking the beginnings of jade as a material for artistic expression in China. Most Neolithic jades have been excavated from burial sites of high-ranking members of society and are believed to have served a ritual function as well as denoting social rank.

From about 2500 BC, in the Liangzhu culture in southern Jiangsu and northern Zhejiang provinces, two very distinctive types of jade objects were being buried in large numbers with the deceased. The first type are the jade discs known as *bi*, which were generally plain, though later ritual discs were often decorated, for example, with a raised

ABOVE: *Perforated disc* (bi) *with unfinished relief spirals, nephrite, China, Late Eastern Zhou dynasty, Warring States period, or early Western Han dynasty, c. 481–100 BC. Perforated jade discs such as this one have been found in many ancient Chinese burials, placed around the corpse. They served a ritual purpose, but their significance has not been fully understood.*

JADE

spiral curl pattern. The second major type are the cylinders known as *cong*, which comprise a square cross-section and a round hole. The purpose of these two forms is unclear, but they are thought to have had a ceremonial function, one theory being that they symbolize Heaven (the circle) and Earth (the square). In the Hongshan culture in the Liao River region, pendants in the form of coiled dragons, often referred to as 'pig dragons', were also created from about 3500 BC onwards.

China's Bronze Age began in the Shang dynasty (*c.* 1500–1027 BC), and some jade ceremonial objects were made at this time in imitation of bronze artifacts. By the Eastern Zhou period (*c.* 770–256 BC), significant technological and artistic advances resulted in more advanced jade working done with bronze tools. Typical of the objects created in jade were sword fittings, plaques and flat pendants, known as a *huang*, often covered with elaborate surface patterning. All three of these early jade forms were often decorated with

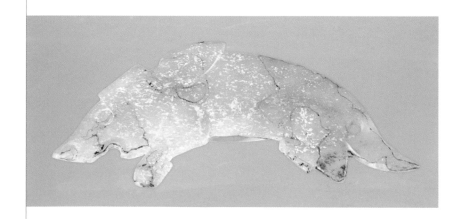

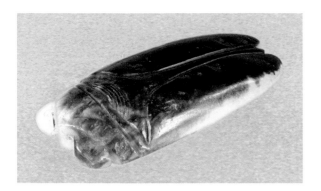

incised lines or designs and patterns in relief and have continued to be created for burials. These forms have also inspired later Chinese ornaments and vessels, both in jade and other materials such as ceramic.

By the Han dynasty (206 BC– AD 220), Daoist beliefs required the dead to be preserved from disintegration so that their souls would have a permanent home. By this time too, jade was accorded the power to heal and even to confer immortality, and jade objects were commonly used in burials to preserve the corpse from decay. Entire jade suits, made of thousands of plaques of nephrite and other stones sewn together with gold and silver wires, were used to dress the highest ranking members of royalty. In this period, jade was also used to make items of personal adornment as well as ornaments. In addition, an increasing number of jade objects and vessels were worked in the round, making full use of the shape of the jade stone. Squatting animals such as pigs, dogs or buffalo, depicted with their legs tucked underneath them, were hewn out of jade as compact figurines that fit snugly into the palm for the owner to fondle.

By the Six Dynasties (265–589) and Tang dynasty (618–906), many figures of animals and humans were being created out of jade, with a greater attention paid to three-dimensionality and realism in the form, modelling and surface treatment. The prominence of Buddhism during these periods also led to the creation of jade Buddhist figures for use in temples and in the residences of wealthy believers. Contact with the Near East at this time resulted in the influence of vessel forms such as the *rhyton* (a drinking vessel in the shape of an animal's head) and decorative schemes inspired by Persian metalwork and textile design. Decorative techniques used to work jade in this period included engraving, carving in relief, polychrome painting and gilding, all of

ABOVE LEFT: *Body plug in the shape of a cicada, nephrite, China, Ming dynasty or earlier. Carved jades, often in the form of cicadas, had been employed as body plugs since the Zhou dynasty, and by the Han dynasty, these had become prevalent in burials. These plugs were placed in the nine body orifices to prevent the vital essences from escaping from the corpse. Many of these plugs were in the form of cicadas, symbols of regeneration.*

ABOVE: *Shield-form pendant with dragons with russet markings, nephrite, China, Han dynasty (206 BC–AD 220). From the Han dynasty, many pendants, belt-hooks and other accessories were created out of jade and decorated with dragons and other animal forms.*

ABOVE: *Hare, nephrite, China, Tang dynasty (618–906).*

which were used to created more pictorial designs, often of figures in natural settings, on the surface of the jade.

During the Song dynasty (960–1279), jade working followed two principal trends that characterize many of the decorative arts of the period. The first was a preference for refinement, simplicity and a love of nature, all dictated by the aesthetic tastes of the Imperial Court. Jade vessels often featured simple lines and minimal surface decoration, and many were made in the form of flowers, lotus leaves, birds and animals. Under the Liao (907–1125) and Jin (1115–1234) dynasties, nomadic peoples who ruled northern

China during roughly the same period, jade figures of mythical animals, birds and hunt scenes were created with a particular dynamism. The other major trend in Song China was a reverence for antiquity, demonstrated by both the Imperial Court and the scholars of the period. Both groups collected Chinese antiquities, including ancient jades and bronzes and used jade brush pots, brush washers and book weights, both in archaistic and naturalistic forms.

During the Yuan dynasty (1279–1368), China was ruled by the nomadic Mongols, and many of the nomadic themes and designs of hunt scenes and wild animals, popular under the Liao and the Jin, continued to appear in the jades of this period. Many Yuan jades feature dragons, fantastic beasts, aquatic creatures and birds rendered in a vigorous manner while also exhibiting the smooth overall modelling and finely incised decorative lines characteristic of this period. Buddhist motifs also entered the jade repertoire from Nepal and Tibet, and some traditional Chinese motifs took on a Tibetan flavour, with Chinese mythical creatures, including fish, being depicted with wings.

In the Ming dynasty (1368–1644), many of the trends of earlier jade working continued, including the imitation of ancient forms in jade. However, while the Song archaistic jade forms copied ancient jades and bronzes, Ming examples tended to copy the Song, so were further removed from the original forms and decoration, becoming instead more heavily stylized. In addition, many copies and fakes of ancient Chinese jades from the Eastern Zhou and Han periods were made. Many of the jades made in this

ABOVE: *Chimera, nephrite, Ming dynasty or earlier, possibly Song dynasty. Song dynasty jade figures of animals were often realistically rendered with attention to the actual movement of the creature and the texture of its skin, feathers or fur.*

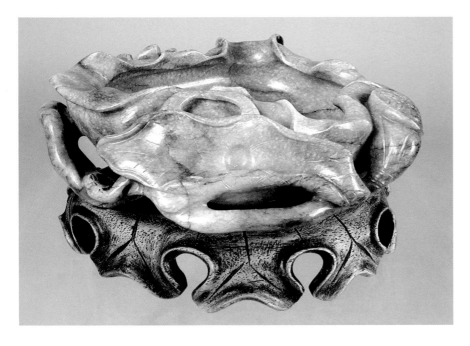

JADE

period were objects for the scholar's desk, such as brush pots, brush washers and personal seals. Some of the forms and decorations used were inspired by the paintings and other decorative arts of the period, which flourished under the patronage of the Ming Court. Although China lost access to some of the finest quality jade stones during this period, Ming jades display the high quality craftsmanship of jade workers of the period.

During the Qing dynasty (1644–1911), jade working flourished and reached its peak of technical virtuosity. China under the Qing dynasty was stable and prosperous and its emperors, though foreign Manchus, were enthusiastic patrons of jade and other traditional Chinese art forms. The finest quality nephrite from Khotan was available in abundance, and at the end of the 18th century, large quantities of jadeite were imported from Burma for the use of the Imperial Court and other wealthy Chinese. Imperial jade workshops were established, employing the country's best craftsmen to produce technically perfect jades for the Imperial palace. Qing nephrite jades range in colour from the pure 'mutton fat' white to pale green and yellow with touches of brown, and spinach-green. More personal items included small animal carvings for fondling and tiny bottles made to hold snuff, or powdered tobacco.

OPPOSITE: *Mandarin duck with scrolls (detail), nephrite, China, Yuan or early Ming dynasty, 1279–1450. Many Yuan period jades feature birds and animals of the type that the nomadic Mongol rulers enjoyed to hunt; geese being attacked by falcons were particularly favoured.*

ABOVE LEFT: *Brush washer in the form of a lotus leaf, nephrite, China, Ming dynasty (1368–1644).*

ABOVE RIGHT: *Seal blank in the form of a dragon, nephrite, China, Ming dynasty. Personal seals used in official documents, painting and calligraphy were also made of jade, and incised with the owner's name in ancient seal script.*

CHINA   39

JADE

ABOVE: *Marriage bowl in 'mutton fat' nephrite jade, China, Qing dynasty, 18th century. In the Qing dynasty, some of the most exquisite jade bowls, vases and ceremonial objects with delicate surface designs were created to decorate palaces and the residences of the wealthy.*

RIGHT: *Snuff bottle, nephrite with jadeite stopper, China, Qing dynasty, 19th century. Introduced by the Europeans in the 18th century, snuff was taken for stomach ailments and the like. It was carried in small bottles made of glass, porcelain, and stones such as jade and agate.*

Emperors often exerted their artistic taste on the art of the day, and the Qianlong Emperor (1736–95) more than any other had a great influence on the arts of his time. His taste was highly elaborate in all the arts, but he is known to have been particularly obsessed with jade. He encouraged his jade workshops to create new vessel forms in jade as well as more elaborate versions of traditional forms. The Qianlong Emperor was especially enamoured with the new type of jade that was being brought into China from Burma. More glassy and gem-like, this jade was available in a wider range of colours that were often stronger than nephrite. In the 18th century, considerable amounts of jadeite were used to create jewelry for the Imperial Court, and from the 19th century, figurines and elaborate vessels were also made. One of the rarest types of jadeite was the deep green that became known at this time as *feizui*, or 'kingfisher feathers', and is known by some collectors as 'Imperial Jade'.

LEFT: *Palace censer, nephrite, China, Qing dynasty, Qianlong period (1736–95). This censer, for burning incense in the imperial palace, is a fine example of the technical virtuosity of Qing dynasty jade workers.*

Burma is famous as a producer of jadeite and for the last 250 years has been the primary source of the world's top-grade material. However, because it has exported most of its jadeite, the country does not have a tradition of jade working. Officially, all jadeite mined in Burma today belongs to the State of Burma, and the jadeite boulders are supposed to be taken to the capital to be sorted into grades and auctioned to international traders. Some of the country's jadeite is sold this way, but much of it is smuggled out of the country and into China, Laos and Thailand. Much Burmese jade ends up in China, where it is worked by Chinese craftsmen and factory workers into jewelry and ornaments and then sent to the jewelry shops of Hong Kong.

Thailand does not have a history of jade mining, as most of the jade in Thailand also originates in Burma. However, it is worth noting that excavation of archaeological sites of the ancient Ban Chiang culture of Thailand (*c.* 3600 BC–2nd century AD) have revealed nephrite jade burial objects similar to Neolithic Chinese objects. These burial jades may have been worn by the people of the Ban Chiang culture, but it is also likely that they served a ceremonial function in the burial.

INDIA

Jade working has a brief history in India under the reign of the Mughals, Islamic rulers who were descended from the Mongols and the Timurids. The Mughals ruled India from 1526 to 1857, and during that time built many notable Islamic monuments and patronized many new and traditional art forms, including the working of jade. It is not clear exactly when the Mughals first encouraged their artists to work in jade. In the Islamic cultures of the Ottoman Turks and the Safavid Persians, jade working was a relatively recent practice, dating back only as far as the 15th century. In India, the carving of rock crystal and other hard stones was known to Mughal artists, and it seems likely that the same artists who worked rock crystal turned their skills to jade. This transition to jade working occurred sometime during the 16th century, possibly in the workshops of Emperor Akbar (r. 1556–1605), but maybe even earlier.

The jade used in India was primarily nephrite from Khotan and Kashgar in Central Asia. Whereas the Ming Chinese admired soft pale green jades with subtle russet markings on the original skin of the stone cleverly worked into the decoration, the Mughal patrons preferred an even tone, either white or pale green, with no strong markings. Dark green, almost black, jade was also popular. These stones were worked into elegant, organic forms, often reminiscent of Ming Chinese jade vessels modelled after flowers or gourds. The most famous example is the white jade cup that belonged to Shah Jahan (r. 1628–58) and now in the Victoria and Albert Museum, London. This translucent cup in the shape of a shell or melon curves gracefully to one side, ending in a naturalistically rendered goat's head finial. The cup bears the inscription Shah Jahan and the date 1657. Such imperial

JADE

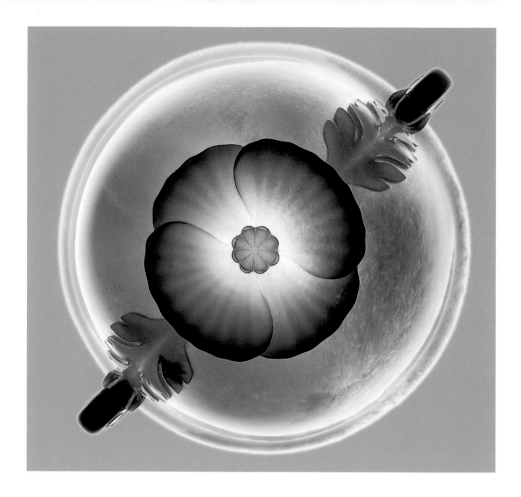

ABOVE: *Bowl with handles, nephrite, India, Mughal, c. 1640–50. This translucent jade bowl features a raised floral pattern abraded into the surface.*

OPPOSITE: *Dagger hilt with triple bud pommel, white nephrite inlaid with rubies, diamonds and emeralds set in gold, India, Mughal, c. 1700–50. Many Indian Mughal jades are inlaid with precious stones. In this technique, the gold inlays were fitted into grooves cut into the surface of jade and jewels such as rubies, emeralds, sapphires and diamonds were set into the gold and held into place by crimping the gold with a hammer.*

inscriptions were common on early Mughal jades, suggesting that these items were rare and valuable. After this date, however, imperial inscriptions were no longer added, indicating that jade had become more widely available.

Vessels such as wine cups, ewers and bowls are some of the most common Mughal jade forms. Water containers for *huqqa*, or hubble-bubble pipes, pipe handles, archers' rings and dagger hilts were also made from jade. Some of the early Mughal jades featured incised decoration, but throughout most of the 17th and 18th centuries, perhaps under the influence of European relief modelling in stone, designs were raised above the surface of the vessel in modelled relief. Ancient European motifs such as the acanthus leaf, which travelled from Roman Europe via the Silk Road to China and India in the 1st millennium, were also used prolifically on bowls, dagger hilts and other Mughal jades. Many dagger hilts feature elements such as animal heads, rendered with a great elegance and naturalism. These details are often accompanied by decoration in gold inlay and inset jewels, a typical decorative technique of the Middle East. These elaborately embellished jades were admired as far as China, and in the 18th and 19th centuries, under the direction of the Qianlong Emperor, were copied, sometimes by Hindustani craftsmen, as 'Hindustan Jades'.

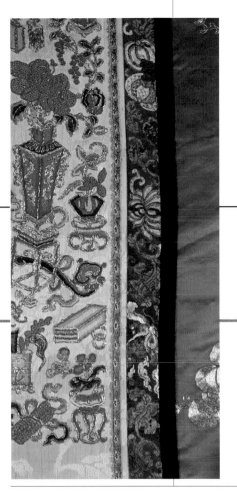

SILK

SILK IS A STRONG, lustrous cloth woven from threads produced by the silk worm, or more correctly, caterpillar. Throughout Asia, the cloth has been considered the 'queen of fibres' and for centuries has been the preferred fabric of members of royalty. Not only is it smooth to the touch and gorgeous to look at, this fibre is also absorbent, rot-resistant and possesses isothermal properties, meaning that it keeps the wearer warm in the winter and cool in the summer. It has also served as a delicate ground for paintings in several Asian cultures. The combination of the beauty and functionality of this material has made it one of the world's most desirable commodities for trade.

OPPOSITE: *Brocade weave, India. See p. 50.*

ABOVE LEFT: *Rank badge, Korea. See p. 58.*

ABOVE CENTRE: *Detail of silk panel, embroidered using Peking knot stitches ('forbidden stitches'), China, Ming dynasty.*

ABOVE RIGHT: *Detail of sleeve band of bridal robe, China, 19th century. See p. 57.*

SILK

THE CHINESE FIRST produced silk as early as the 5th millennium BC and around 2,000 years ago began to export it widely, jealously guarding the secret of its manufacture. Word of this wondrous fabric quickly reached Roman Europe, and demand for silk led to the establishment of a trade route that spanned 4,000 miles from the eastern Mediterranean to central China. The 'Silk Road' became a major international thoroughfare along which not only exotic Asian silks, but religious, cultural and artistic traditions spread for centuries afterwards. In the 6th century AD, spies for Emperor Justinian of Byzantium smuggled silk worm eggs and mulberry leaves out of China and back to Constantinople (modern Istanbul). Nonetheless, China continued to dominate the silk export market for many centuries.

THE MATERIAL

SILK IS THE ONLY material in this book that is created by an animal. It is produced by the caterpillar of the *Bombyx mori* moth, the only silk-making moth that can be domesticated since it can feed on both living and cut mulberry leaves. The female *Bombyx mori* lays roughly 200–500 eggs at a time on the leaves. From these eggs hatch tiny larvae

ABOVE: *Eggs of the domesticated* Bombyx mori *moth, which will hatch larvae that become caterpillars; the caterpillars will each spin a cocoon from a single filament. It is this silk thread that is collected to be woven into a naturally lustrous fabric.*

or worms. Each worm eats voraciously for about thirty days, consuming as much as twenty times its own weight in leaves. During this time, the worm sheds its skin several times, finally transforming into a caterpillar. The caterpillar stops feeding and excretes filaments from glands on both sides of its body, joining them together with a gummy substance called sericin. It then spins the single thread around itself for several days and forms a cocoon. Under normal circumstances, the caterpillar remains inside the cocoon and sheds its skin, transforming into a pupa, or chrysalis. After another fifteen days or so, it breaks open the cocoon, damaging the silk thread, and emerges as a moth.

Techniques for processing the silk threads vary from country to country. Typically, to obtain the unbroken silk thread from the cocoon, the cocoon is steamed or boiled, killing the creature inside. The threads from the cocoons are loosened and the silk worker then picks up the ends with a comb or a stick and, using the remaining sericin as an adhesive, joins together several threads, to create a single silk thread. As each thread nears its end, another thread is carefully joined to it. In the case of raw silk, such as Indian *tussah* silk, the silk thread is produced by wild silks moths that break through their cocoons. The shorter, thicker threads are knotted together, leaving bumps on the surface of the fabric.

RIGHT: *A silk worker separating strands from cocoons, Chiang Mai, Thailand. The thread from a single cocoon can measure up to a mile in length. Typically, it takes the thread of several thousand cocoons to make one silk garment.*

BELOW: *Dyeing cloth with indigo, Aizen Kobo, Kyoto, Japan. When an overall colour is required, the silk threads or the bolt of cloth are immersed in the vat; the longer the immersion, the darker the hue.*

TECHNIQUES

SILK HAS TRADITIONALLY been dyed with colours derived from plants, animals and minerals (see some examples below), although from the late 19th century onwards, chemical dyes have been used on many Asian silks. The dyes are usually prepared in a vat into which the cloth may be submerged. When resist-paste is used to create patterns on the threads or on the cloth, the dye is applied with a brush. In the case of the majority of natural dyes, metallic salts called mordants are added to the solution to bond the dye with the fabric.

Some Sources of Asian Dye Colours

A wide range of vegetable, mineral (and later, chemical) dyes are used on Asian silks. The following are samples of colours and their common natural sources:

White – *natural colour of bleached silk threads*

Red – *madder, safflower petals, the lac insect, cochineal*

Blue – *indigo*

Yellow – *philodendron, gardenia, turmeric, myrobalan flowers with mango bark, pomegranate skins, jackfruit*

Purple – *gromwell roots, indigo combined with sappanwood chips*

Green – *yellow dye source combined with indigo*

Grey – *tannin from woods*

Black – *indigo and ink, logwood*

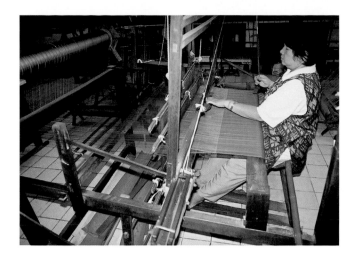

(1) The Woven Design

IN MANY CASES, the silk threads are dyed first and then woven on a loom. The weave is determined by the order in which the warp (vertical) threads and the weft (horizontal) threads are interlaced. In general, the warp threads are set on the loom, and the weft threads are woven through using one or more of a variety of weaves. Shown on the following pages (pp. 50–51) are some of the most common weaves. Two examples, brocade and velvet, employ secondary or supplemental warp or weft threads.

(2) The Dyed Design

DYEING A DESIGN on cloth usually involves protecting the cloth from the dye. There are two main methods: tie-dyeing, in which the cloth is bound tightly where the dye is not needed, and resist dyeing, in which a paste is applied to areas to be left undyed.

Tie-dyeing is a widely used method of creating dyed patterns on silk. Typically, areas of the silk cloth are bound using string or sewn together tightly, so that the bound sections will not absorb the dye. To create circles or dots on the silk, the silk is pulled up and then tied around the protruding section. The smaller the dots required, the smaller the section bound. The cloth may also be folded and sewn to create more linear patterns.

A tie-dyeing technique known as *ikat*, from a Malay word meaning 'tied,' is used in many parts of Asia, most notably in Indonesia, Japan and Central Asia. *Ikat* involves dyeing the threads before weaving to create a pattern once the threads are woven. First, the bundles of warp or weft, or sometimes both, threads are measured carefully and

ABOVE LEFT and RIGHT: *Weaving silk cloth on a standard treadle loom, Chiang Mai, Thailand. The treadle loom is operated with foot pedals that raise and lower the warp to allow the shuttle holding the weft thread to pass through. This type of loom was brought late to Thailand, and contrasts with the traditional backstrap looms, in which the weaver's body serves as a frame and controls the tension of the threads.*

SILK

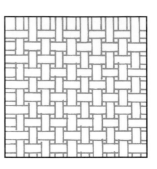

RIGHT: Plain weave. *The weft thread is passed over one warp and under the next in one row, and then the order is reversed in the next row, and so on. Detail: Japan, 20th century.*

RIGHT: Gauze weave. *Pairs of adjacent warp threads are twisted around each other before the weft is passed through them. The wide gaps between the warps produce a light, airy cloth suitable for summer clothing. Detail: Japan, 20th century.*

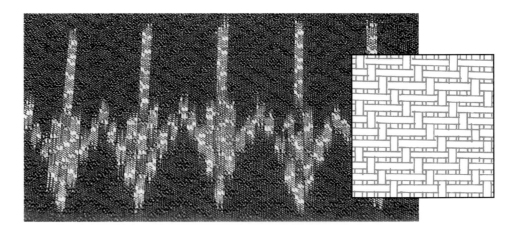

RIGHT: Twill weave. *The weft is passed over two or more warps and then under two or more warps on one row, and continuing this on the next row, starting one warp to the left or right. This creates a simple diagonal pattern, which can be varied to produce diamonds and other diagonal designs. Detail: Cambodia, 20th century.*

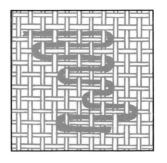

RIGHT: Brocade weave. *The main ground of the cloth is created with the warp and the primary weft thread, and the pattern is created by passing the secondary, or supplemental, weft threads over a number of warps to form the desired design. Detail: India, 19th century.*

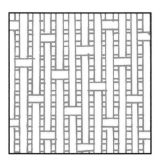

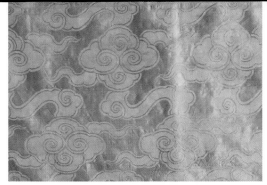

LEFT: Satin weave. *Cloth is created by passing the warp thread over at least four weft threads and then anchoring it under one weft. The cloth's sheen is created by the rows of floating warp threads. Detail: China, 18th century.*

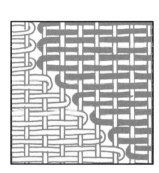

LEFT: Damask weave. *In silk damask, patterns are created using two contrasting weaves, such as twill and satin weaves, or the two faces of satin weave. Typically, the main design is created in satin weave with widely spaced weft threads, which appear dull in contrast with the shinier, more closely set warp face. Detail: Japan, 20th century.*

LEFT: Tapestry Weave. *Weft threads of different colours are woven with a plain or twill weave only in the areas where that colour is needed, rather than across the entire width of the cloth. Where one colour of weft meets another, it turns back on itself and goes back in the opposite direction along the next row. If this meeting point runs vertically for more than two rows, a vertical slit, or 'cut', appears in the cloth, hence the Chinese name for this technique, kesi, or 'cut silk'. Detail: China, 19th century.*

LEFT: Silk velvet. *A secondary warp thread wraps around several rods that span the width of the cloth at regular intervals. When the rods are pulled out, they leave a row of loops (the pile of the velvet). The loops are cut, leaving soft tufts of silk, which are held in place by the main ground weave of the cloth. Patterns may be created by leaving areas of the pile uncut, in contrast to the cut, fluffy areas. In voided velvet, the pile is not pulled up in the desired background areas. Detail: China, 19th century.*

SILK

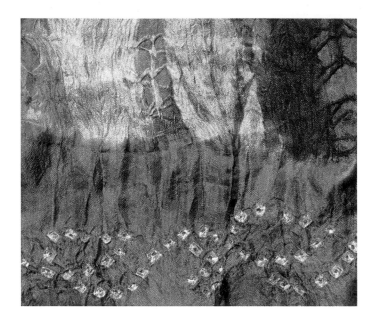

OPPOSITE: *Weft-ikat silk (detail), Thailand, 20th century.*

OPPOSITE BOTTOM LEFT: *Paper stencil, or katagami, for resist dyeing fabric, Japan, 20th century. The resist paste is applied through a stencil so that the areas covered in paste will remain undyed, while the areas with no paste will be coloured in the design of the stencil.*

OPPOSITE BOTTOM RIGHT: *Batik dyed (selendang lok can) ceremonial shoulder cloth (detail), made in Java for Bali, c. 1900. In batik dyeing, some of the most elaborate designs on silk are painted in pigments using a brush or sharpened stick. The resist is applied over the painted design and then the ground colour is applied to the rest of the cloth with a brush.*

ABOVE: *Silk cloth tie-dyed using folding and wrapping techniques (detail), Pakistan, 20th century.*

BELOW: *Woman wrapping threads for ikat dyeing, South India.*

bound tightly at the points where the dye is not needed. After dyeing, great care is taken to keep the all the threads in position, especially in double *ikat*, when both the warp and weft are dyed. As the warp and weft threads are woven together using a plain or twill weave, a contrasting design emerges.

Resist dyeing follows a similar principal to tie-dyeing, but instead, a substance, such as hot wax, clay, mud or rice paste, is applied to areas of the fabric, sometimes using a stencil, to protect them from the dye. One notable type of resist dyeing is Indonesian and Malaysian *batik*, in which designs are rendered on cloth (mainly on cotton but sometimes on silk) with wax before dyeing.

(3) The Applied Design

MANY SILK COSTUMES and accessories from East Asia and India in particular feature designs embroidered with silk threads. Embroidery may cover the entire garment or simply enhance a section such as the collar, cuffs or hem. In preparation for embroidery, the artist stretches the silk taut by stitching the sides to a bamboo or wooden frame, creating a firm surface. A variety of stitches are used to create numerous textural and visual effects on the surface of the cloth. For example, with satin stitch, long silk stitches run parallel to create the sheen of satin, while seed stitches (or Peking knots) that sit on

SILK

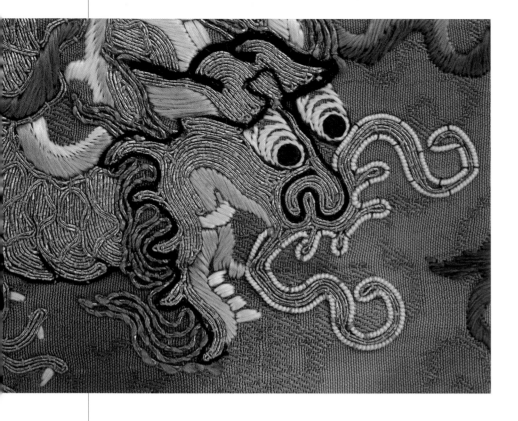

ABOVE LEFT: *Woman's skirt with embroidered and couched design of a dragon (detail), China, 19th century.*

ABOVE RIGHT: *Painting on silk, China, Qing dynasty. Traditionally, the painting surface is a smooth, whitish ground of plain weave silk, and designs are applied either in black ink only or with additional vegetable and mineral pigments and sometimes gold. These paintings are usually mounted onto a paper backing, framed with patterned silk brocade and then attached to wooden rods at the top and bottom to form a hanging scroll. When not being displayed, these paintings are rolled up and stored.*

the surface of the silk create the effect of clusters of flowers or the scales of a dragon.

Various techniques are used to apply gold to silk cloth. To embellish an embroidered design, for example, gold sheets may be stuck onto paper, cut into strips and then wound around silk threads. These threads are not sewn into the fabric but are instead laid onto the surface of the cloth and attached with tiny stitches in a technique known as couching. Larger designs in gold leaf may also be applied to the cloth using adhesive (see p. 182). In some cultures, in particular China and India, precious stones, pearls, glass beads and mirrors are sewn into the silk for costumes and accessories worn on special occasions.

It is important to note here that silk is also used as a ground for painting and writing in many Asian cultures, particularly China, Korea and Japan. Before painting onto the silk, the surface of the cloth has to be sized, or primed, usually with a coating of alum to prevent the ink from running along the lines of fibres and blurring the image.

ALTHOUGH LEGEND ONLY attributes its invention to the 3rd millennium BC (see 'Legends of the Origins of Silk', p. 47), silk may have been produced in China as early as the 5th millennium BC. The earliest surviving Chinese silk garments come from tombs dating to the 5th century BC. It was also around this time that documents were first written on silk. Its smooth surface made it easy to write on, and its lightness made the documents easy to transport. Silk was probably also used as a ground for painting around the same time. A number of silk fragments have survived from the 1st century BC in Han dynasty (206 BC–AD 220) tombs and military posts. These early silks featured woven and embroidered designs of animals surrounded with scrolling clouds and flowers. By the Tang dynasty (618–906), silk workers were producing most types of woven silk cloth, including tapestries, gauzes, damasks and brocades, as well as resist-dyed silks.

During the Song dynasty (960–1279), some of China's finest silk brocades and damasks were created for religious and secular use and featured elaborate designs of birds, animals and flowers, as well as geometric motifs, auspicious Chinese characters and religious symbols. Arguably the most important silk cloth of this period is the *kesi*, or 'cut silk' tapestry, which may have been introduced to China from Central Asia by the Uighurs of western China, who wove woollen textiles using this method. Buddhist devotional silk images and texts made with this technique have also been excavated from cave temples such as Dunhuang in Gansu province.

The Buddhist and Daoist temples and Imperial palaces of the Ming (1368–1644)

ABOVE: *Panel with bird and flower design, kesi or 'cut silk', China, Song dynasty (906–1279). Emperors of the Song dynasty commissioned silk weavers to create kesi tapestries that resembled contemporary paintings on silk.*

LEFT: *Rank badge with phoenix, China, 19th century. Rank badges were worn to identify the rank of the wearer: animals signified military officials, while birds identified civil officials.*

SILK

ABOVE: *Dragon robe, kesi or 'cut silk' weave, China, 19th century. These robes were named for the nine dragons on the front, shoulders and back of the robe. Symbols of the Emperor and the creative energy of the universe, the dragons are shown flying through the clouds above swirling seas, representing the Earth. When the Emperor, who represented Heaven, wore such robes, he symbolically united Heaven and Earth.*

LEFT: *Man's ceremonial robe (chaofu), silk with embroidered and couched gold dragons, China, Qing dynasty (1644–1911). The chaofu was worn during important court ceremonies and in the presence of the emperor.*

and Qing (1644–1911) dynasties, too, were lavishly decorated in luxurious silk furnishings. Wall hangings and cushions made of silk velvet first appeared in China during the 16th or 17th century, most likely introduced by Portuguese Jesuit priests. The robes and accessories of the Emperor and his court were even more extravagant. Most spectacular are the dragon robes of the Chinese emperor and his family. Over dragon robes, male members of the Court wore plain outer coats decorated with square badges on the front and back to identify the rank of the wearer.

Women's silk robes were no less elaborate. In particular, the bridal robes worn by Qing dynasty Chinese noblewomen were remarkably sumptuous silk garments, combining embroidered or woven designs of peonies and other symbols of feminine beauty with bold golden dragons applied using gold-wrapped couched threads often weighing several pounds.

KOREA

ABOVE RIGHT: *Embroidered rank badge with crane, Korea, 19th century. Embroidery is probably the most popular decoration on silk in Korea. By the 11th and 12th centuries, embroidery was so popular that the government attempted to prohibit the overly ostentatious use of embroidery on clothing and accessories. Traditionally, the embroidery was executed by women, and all high-class Korean ladies were expected to master the skill.*

AROUND 200 BC, silk cultivation was first introduced to Korea from China. Early Korean paintings on tomb walls depict noblewomen wearing long, striped skirts made from strips of silk of different colours. According to early Chinese and Korean historical records, many of these silk robes were embroidered with birds and flowers and other designs. Around the 8th and 10th centuries, under the influence of Tang China, silk cloth was woven with elaborate brocade and damask patterns, often floral scrolls or roundels containing dragons and phoenixes. Embroidered garments and accessories also continued to be favoured by aristocracy, and show the decorative technique at which the Koreans have excelled.

Most surviving Korean silk garments and accessories date to the late Joseon or Yi dynasty (1392–1910) and feature sophisticated weaving techniques, such as brocade and damask, as well as intricate embroidery. Traditional Korean clothing, or *hanbok* – a jacket and skirt for women, and a jacket and trousers for men – is bold in colour but reserved in decoration. However, the robes created for formal occasions, weddings and court ceremonies display spectacular woven, embroidered and applied gold leaf designs. A princess's bridal robe, for example, was primarily red for celebration, with stripes on the sleeves of yellow, blue, and white, and was laden with auspicious symbols.

LEFT: *Painting of three young women by Miyagawa Shunsui (worked c. 1740–55), ink, colours and gofun on silk, Japan, 18th century. These three young women are wearing kimono of different types. The women standing are wearing the standard kosode, or short sleeved kimono, while the seated woman wears a furisode, or 'swinging sleeved' kimono, usually reserved for younger, unmarried women.*

The Japanese *Kimono*

The kimono is a long, T-shaped robe with no darts, gathers, or curves to tailor it around an individual's figure. Worn by men and women, it is made up of seven main pieces, all cut from a single length of cloth 36 cm (14 inches) wide. The left side is folded over the right. A man's kimono is ankle-length and is tied with a narrow sash called an obi. A woman's kimono is longer and is bunched up over the obi, which is tied at the back. The sleeves of a woman's kimono may be short (kosode) or long and swinging (furisode).

In the Heian period, the kimono was a voluminous garment with long, full sleeves. The highest ranking noblewomen wore as many as 20 layers of kimono at a time, and the weight of so much silk made their movement slow and laborious. The many layers were arranged carefully so that the resulting gradation of colours – seen at the neck, hem and ends of the sleeves – matched the season, the occasion and each other perfectly. A mistaken matching of colours could destroy a lady's reputation.

IT IS NOT CERTAIN exactly when silk was first made in Japan. Chinese texts record silk fabrics in Japan in the 1st century BC and a gift of silk worms from a Chinese ruler to the Japanese emperor in the 2nd century AD, although silk cultivation is believed to have been introduced to Japan by Korean immigrants prior to that. For centuries, the silk robes of the upper class Japanese resembled Korean or Chinese robes; many were made by Korean and Chinese weavers in Japan. Under the influence of Tang China, imperial courtiers and Buddhist priests in the 8th and 9th century wore silk brocade and damask robes, often dyed using techniques such as *kanoko-zome* (deer spot dyeing), a tie-dyeing technique characterized by dense areas of tiny spots.

During the Heian period (794–1185), Japanese culture was dictated by the Imperial Court in Kyoto, the historic centre of Japan's silk industry. The Japanese *kimono*, literally,

JAPAN

SILK

'the thing one wears', began to evolve distinctly from any other Asian dress form. *Kimono* in the Heian period were made of the finest silk brocades and damasks and were worn in layers, with long, flowing sleeves (see 'The Japanese Kimono', p. 59). In the following periods of military government, the *kimono* became a more practical garment, namely the short-sleeved *kosode*. Despite their simple form, *kosode* were often made of lavishly decorated Chinese-style patterned silks and tapestry, as well as more native-style dyed and embroidered silks.

Some of the most spectacular silk robes of the 16th century onwards are those made for the Noh theatre. These robes often feature bold brocade and embroidered designs that are symbolic of the dramatic action or emotion, as well as applied gold leaf details that reflect the light as the actors move across the stage. Some of Japan's most elaborate silk cloths are the sashes, or *obi*, used to tie the *kimono*. Made of finely woven silk brocade, with gold and silver threads, the *obi* is often the focal point of a woman's dress. Silk brocades have also been used widely in Buddhist temples, either as robes for the clergy or as cloths used in Buddhist rituals. One particular type of silk cloth is a type of priest's outer robe called a *kesa*, a rectangular cloth resembling a patchwork of different silk brocades (see p. 18).

Painted and dyed decoration is also important in the history of Japanese silk. One technique, known as *tsujigahana*, developed in the 16th century and combined areas of solid, dyed colour with delicate painted designs of natural motifs. In the 17th century, silk dyers in Kyoto developed a resist dyeing process called *yuzen*, in which a design is painted onto the silk and then outlined in resist paste, leaving a characteristic narrow white line.

महा रावरा जाजी श्री बसतसीधंजी   माराजा साहबपर ता सीय्ती

INDIA

ALTHOUGH THE WEAVING and dyeing of cotton dates back as early as the 3rd millennium BC in India, silk does not have such an ancient history, and very little Indian silk can be dated to before the 15th century. Early Indian texts describe fine silk cloth worn by the aristocracy. This cloth may have been imported Chinese silk, but it could also have been silk produced in India by indigenous silk-producing moths. Most of these moths are wild and break through their cocoons tearing the silk threads, producing the textured silks known as *tussahs*, still a specialty of Bengal today. By the 6th century AD, Buddhist monks are believed to have brought Chinese silk-reeling techniques and the eggs of the *Bombyx mori* moth to India, making domestic silk cultivation possible.

Silk has been produced in many regions of India for use by members of its upper classes. Some of India's most exquisite silks were produced in the royal workshops, or *karkhanah*, of

its Muslim rulers. For example, the Delhi Sultans, who ruled north and central India from the late 12th century, employed thousands of silk weavers to produce the hundreds of thousands of silk robes of honour for the sultan to bestow upon worthy followers.

From the 16th century, under the Mughal emperors, the royal workshops of India's various kingdoms produced lavish silk cloths for clothing and to decorate the interiors of palaces, silk tents and carpets. These silks were woven and embroidered with silk and metallic threads, with floral and geometric patterns often derived from Persian designs. India's silks also attracted attention overseas. Europeans not only admired the cloths for their rarity and beauty, but seized the opportunity to trade India's silks for the precious spices of Southeast Asia. The royal courts of Thailand, Indonesia, and other Southeast Asian countries willingly exchanged nutmeg, cinnamon and cloves for India's finest silks.

Of all India's exquisite silk textiles, the *sari*, the traditional dress of Hindu women, is probably the most varied. Worn by Indian women for hundreds of years, the *sari* is a long unsewn cloth that is usually wrapped around the hips to form a slightly pleated skirt and then draped over one shoulder on top of a short blouse. *Saris* are made of some of the finest silk cloth in India; many feature exquisite brocade borders or embroidered motifs. Others are embellished with embroidery or minutely tie-dyed spotted patterns, created by tying the cloth over hundreds of tiny nails. The most elaborate and expensive *saris* are the double-*ikat patola saris* of Gujarat, in which both the warp and the weft threads are dyed before weaving. Red *saris*, in particular, are worn by brides and are often embellished with gold ribbon and auspicious symbols such as elephants, representing wealth. One notable type of embroidery from the Indian subcontinent is *phulkari*, or 'flowered work', which shows colourful, shining geometrical patterns on shawls and wedding veils.

OPPOSITE: *Painting of Maharao Basant Singh and Maharaja Sahab Prithivi Singh, watercolour on paper, Rajasthan, India, c. 1775. Robes of fine silk were an important part of the lavish decoration enjoyed by India's royalty.*

ABOVE: *Woman in patola double-ikat sari, Gujarat, India.*

ABOVE LEFT: *Phulkari embroidery (detail), first half of the 20th century, India/Pakistan. In phulkari work, the speciality of silk workers in the Punjab in Pakistan, designs made up of horizontal and vertical lines are sewn with untwisted silk threads often of a single colour onto a cotton ground. The stitches reflect the light in different directions, suggesting more than one shade of colour in the design.*

SOUTHEAST ASIA

SOUTHEAST ASIA CURRENTLY has one of the world's great silk-weaving industries and is renowned for its colourfully patterned silks. However, since silk cultivation was first introduced to the region in the 1st millennium AD, it has not been widely practised here, in part because many of its peoples are Theravada Buddhists and oppose the destruction of living creatures. Traditionally, most of the textiles of the area have been made of cotton and other vegetable fibres. Silk threads for weaving were imported from China, while luxurious silk cloths were often imported from India. The main area of silk cultivation in Southeast Asia is northeastern Thailand. The silk from this region tends to be rougher than Chinese and Japanese silk, and higher sericin content in the threads makes them stickier and harder to weave. Often, a warp made of imported silk threads is combined with a weft of local Thai silk thread to make weaving easier.

In most Southeast Asian cultures, the traditional dress has been a variation of a rectangular cloth that is wrapped around the hips and secured with a belt or sash or tucked into the waist. These hip wrappers may also be sewn at the ends to form a tubular skirt, or *sarong*, which is also wrapped around the hips and tucked in at the front. A longer variation of the *sarong* was traditionally worn by members of Cambodian royalty. The

BELOW: *Silk with kain songket gold supplementary weft decoration (detail), Thailand, 20th century.*

rectangular cloth was wrapped around the hips and one end was pulled between the legs and tucked into the waist to create trousers. In contrast, perhaps the most tailored of all the traditional garments of Southeast Asia is the *ao dai* of Vietnam, a variation of a Chinese dress with a mandarin collar and side fastening. The dress fits neatly at the waist, has long side splits and is worn over loose trousers.

The majority of Southeast Asian *sarongs*, head scarves, sashes and other silk garments are woven using a plain weave and feature stripes and plaid patterns. In most regions, *ikat* decoration is a favoured decorative technique on these plain weave silks. The *ikat* of Thailand, known as *mud mee*, is typically a weft *ikat* and features geometric motifs, especially diamond-shaped patterns. The silk *ikat* of the Shan states of Burma, made traditionally with imported silk threads, is known for its intricate weft *ikat* designs of tiny scrolls and flower patterns. The many islands of Indonesia boast the greatest diversity of textiles, and its weavers have traditionally excelled in cotton and silk *ikat*. The complex double *ikat*, similar to the *patola* double-*ikat* silks of India, is even produced in a small area of Bali.

The most common woven decoration used in Southeast Asian silks is supplementary weft patterning, in which weft threads of a contrasting colour are floated over selected warps to create designs. Throughout the region, the designs are typically repetitive geometric patterns, built up with abstracted natural motifs such as flowers, animals, and trees. In a technique known commonly by the Malay name *kain songket*, supplementary wefts of gold or silver threads provide a dazzling contrast with a dark ground. Some of the most spectacular examples are made in Malaysia, Cambodia, Thailand and Sumatra in Indonesia for royalty and for special occasions, such as weddings.

ABOVE LEFT: *Young woman wearing ikat-dyed blouse and* sarong, *Chiang Mai, Thailand. In Southeast Asia, silk hip wrappers and sarongs have traditionally been worn with tailored tunics, blouses or jackets, varying in form and design depending on the culture.*

ABOVE: *Bride in songket ensemble, Palambang, Southern Sumatra, Indonesia.*

OPPOSITE: *Kakiemon dish, Japan. See p. 85.*

FAR LEFT: *Dish with underglaze blue design of a dragon and waves, China, Ming dynasty, from the Xuande reign (1426–35) – the apogee of Chinese blue-and-white porcelains.*

LEFT: *Detail of early Qing dynasty jar, China. See p. 79.*

BELOW: *Detail of old Kutani dish, Japan. See p. 86.*

PORCELAIN

THE FINE HIGH-FIRED white ceramics known as porcelains were truly born in Asia, although they are now made in many countries throughout the world. The Chinese were the first to produce and export porcelains around the 6th or 7th century AD. China jealously guarded the secret of porcelain manufacture and for many centuries remained the only country producing and exporting these fine white ceramics. It is not surprising, therefore, that high-quality ceramics have come to be referred to in English as 'china'.

PORCELAIN

ABOVE LEFT and RIGHT: *Two figures of the bodhisattva* Guanyin, Dehua ware *blanc de chine* porcelain, China, 18th century. Although figures such as this were made primarily for religious use in Chinese homes, they had great appeal to Westerners who admired the warm whiteness of the porcelain and the well sculpted forms of these 'exotic' Chinese gods.

PORCELAIN WAS MADE initially for the Chinese elite who admired its purity and durability. The material soon caught the attention of members of the upper classes in other parts of the world. For centuries, the Chinese have exported porcelains to the Middle East, Southeast and East Asia, Europe and, more recently, North America. In Korea, porcelains may have been first produced as early as the 9th century, but were only made in significant quantities for the royal court from the 15th century onwards. Unlike in China, porcelains were produced in small numbers in Korea and were not exported in significant numbers. In Japan, porcelain clay was discovered around 1610, and from that time onwards, Japan has competed with China to export fine blue and white and polychrome porcelains to Europe and the rest of the world.

European aristocrats were so taken by porcelain that they encouraged potters in their own countries to discover how to make porcelain. The first European kiln to produce porcelain was the Meissen kiln in Germany in the 18th century, followed by kilns in France, the Netherlands and the United Kingdom. Many of the early porcelains produced in European kilns were copies of porcelains from China and Japan.

What is Porcelain?

THE TERM 'PORCELAIN' refers to the clay body of the vessel, rather than its glaze or decorative style. Porcelains are high-fired white ceramics that are translucent and give off a ringing sound when struck. In East Asia, they are generally made of a combination of a fine clay known as kaolin and porcelain stone. Porcelains contain quartz (silica) and mica or feldspar, and are fired to at least 1300°C, which is higher than the firing temperature for earthenwares (700–800°C) and stonewares (1000°C).

ABOVE: *Cowrie shells, known in Italian as porcellana. When the Italians first encountered Chinese fine white ceramics, they believed that they were made from these shells.*

From Pigs to Porcelain

The word 'porcelain' has one of the most fascinating origins of any art term in the English language. According to tradition, the Italians encountered unusually sturdy vessels made of a pure white material when they visited China in the 13th century. They could not believe that they were made of clay, since no clay in Europe at that time was as hard or as pure white. Instead, they guessed that the vessels were made of ground-up white cowrie shells, called porcellana, *or 'little female pigs', in Italian. These shells, in turn, had been given this name because the mouth-like opening on one side of the shell was thought to resemble the sexual organs of a female pig.* Porcellana *went into French as* la porcelaine *and then English as* porcelain.

In China since around the 10th century, porcelains have been produced chiefly at the southern city of Jingdezhen in Jiangxi province, a ceramics centre long controlled by the Imperial government (see 'Porcelain City, Jingdezhen', p. 74). At Jingdezhen, porcelain is made from kaolin and porcelain stone. Kaolin is named after the Gaoling, or 'High Ridge' granite mountain range of Jiangxi province, where large deposits of this clay are found. A high-firing pure white clay, it does not contain iron or other colouring mineral oxides. The kaolin is added to the second ingredient, porcelain stone, or *baidunzi*, 'little white bricks', a volcanic rock made up of quartz and mica. The quartz, or silica, is a 'glass-former' that fuses and hardens like glass during firing, while the mica acts as a flux to lower the fusing temperature. Typically, silica melts at 1700°C. A flux enables the silica mixture to melt at around 1300°–1400°C. Korea and Japan share a geological base with the Jingdezhen area, so their porcelains are also made from a combination of kaolin and porcelain stone.

Preparing the Clay

Porcelain clay is washed out from granite rocks and is purified, dried and transported to the workshops. It is finely ground, mixed with the porcelain stone and water, and then kneaded until it is soft and pliable enough to be worked into a form. This clay is relatively soft and plastic and is particularly suitable for building smaller forms.

Creating the Form

There are several ways to create a ceramic form out of porcelain or other clay. The main techniques are wheel-throwing, hand-building, slab-building, and mould-casting. Sometimes, a combination of two or more of these techniques is used. For example, a basic round form may be thrown on a wheel, and moulded elements applied to it.

Glazing

Glaze is a glass-like coating that is applied to a ceramic vessel to render it waterproof and to allow for decoration. Glazes are made from the same ingredients as the body of the vessel, but they contain more glass-formers such as quartz or feldspar, and more fluxes, the substances that make the glaze melt at an attainable kiln temperature. The Chinese porcelain glaze is known as an acid-rock glaze because it contains a high proportion of porcelain stone, which is an acid rock.

Although some Asian porcelains have coloured glazes, most are covered with a transparent glaze to show off the white body and the under- or overglaze decoration. Typically, after a vessel form has been created, it is left to dry in the sun, although some vessels are fired once in what is known as a *biscuit*, or *bisque*, firing (from the French *bis cuit*, 'twice cooked'). Both of these processes remove all the water from the vessel's body. After the vessel is dry, the potter either applies glaze to its surface with a brush or dips the vessel into the wet glaze. When the glaze is dry, the vessel is fired, and the glaze hardens into a smooth, glass-like coating. Coloured glazes derive their hue from cobalt, iron, copper, manganese and other mineral oxides that are added to the glaze. Glaze colours vary according to the quantity of the mineral oxide in the glaze solution and the atmosphere inside the kiln.

Underglaze and Overglaze Decoration

Often, decoration is applied to porcelains before the glazing, so is known as underglaze decoration. The principal underglaze colour is blue, derived from cobalt oxide, although occasionally copper red and iron brown are used. The pigment is mixed with water and painted onto the surface of the dry vessel. After the pigment has dried, the vessel is coated with transparent glaze and fired. In major ceramics-producing centres, the painting is done by skilled artists whose work is as fine as any painting on paper or silk.

ABOVE: *Mould-casting porcelain bowls, Arita, Japan. Arita is Japan's principal porcelain-producing region. Here, in c. 1610, the potter Ri Sanpei discovered tôseki, or 'ceramic stone'. The potters of Arita produced large quantities of porcelain for domestic use and export, bringing considerable wealth to the region.*

Some porcelains are decorated with overglaze enamels, which are essentially low-firing glazes fluxed with lead. Added to these glazes are mineral oxides such as copper, iron, and cobalt, which produce vivid colours such as green, yellow, and blue respectively. Enamelling occurs after the vessel has been glazed and the glaze has had time to cool and dry. The vessel may already be decorated with underglaze blue designs or it may be plain. The enamels are used like paints and applied to the surface of the glazed vessel. When the enamels are dry, the vessel is fired again at a lower temperature (about 800°C). Gold leaf and gold enamel are sometimes added to the array of overglaze colours.

Firing

The kilns used for firing porcelains reach a higher temperature than most other ceramic kilns. At Jingdezhen, porcelains are fired in large 'egg-shaped' kilns that are wood-firing and reach temperatures of around 1300°C. In Japan and Korea, porcelains may be fired in 'dragon kilns', or 'climbing kilns' that ascend the side of a gentle hill. Porcelains are placed inside containers called *saggars* to protect them from kiln debris and then stacked on top of each other inside the kiln. The amount of oxygen in the kiln is crucial to the firing, as it dictates the colours of the glazes and the under- and overglaze painted decorations. For example, in an oxidation firing (an oxygen-rich atmosphere), mineral pigments such as iron and copper will fire a warm brown and dark green respectively, while in a reduction firing (an oxygen-starved atmosphere), the same pigments will fire a cool green and red. The firing usually takes a day or two, followed by another day of cooling before the porcelains are removed from the kiln.

ABOVE: *Applying overglaze enamel pigments onto a glazed pot, Jingdezhen, China. Since the 11th century, the city of Jingdezhen in Jiangxi province, southern China, has been the world's largest centre for porcelain production.*

BELOW: *Climbing kiln, I Chon, Korea. Several arched chambers rise one above the other. These kilns can fire a large number of ceramics at once and can reach the high temperatures required for porcelain. The Chinese used them to develop early porcelains.*

RIGHT: *Pair of early porcelain 'Samarra' dishes, China, late Tang dynasty, 9th century. These simple porcelain dishes, characterized by a thickly rolled lip, were made in northern China and were found in such large numbers at the site of Samarra in Iraq that they are known as 'Samarra dishes'.*

OPPOSITE LEFT: *Ding ware dish with incised lotus decoration, China, Northern Song dynasty, 12th century. This dish from the Ding kilns in northern China has a characteristic warm ivory tone that derives in part from an oxygen-rich kiln atmosphere. Simple designs such as this lotus motif were incised or combed into the leather hard clay. Later, more complex designs were applied using moulds.*

CHINA

THE WORLD'S FIRST porcelain was produced in northern China in the 6th or 7th century during the Tang dynasty (618–906) at the kilns at Gong xian in Henan province and at the Xing and Ding kilns in Hebei province. Some porcelains from the Gong xian kilns have been excavated at the site of the Daming palace at Xi'an, the Tang capital of Chang'an, so were likely to have been tributes to the Tang emperors. Many of these early porcelains were modelled on glass and metalwork vessels from Iran and Central Asia that had arrived in Tang China along the Silk Road. Some of these early white porcelains have also been excavated in the Middle East.

The Ding kilns in Hebei province continued to produce porcelains well into the Northern Song dynasty (960–1127) and became one of the preferred ceramics of the Northern Song emperors. These fine porcelains were made primarily of kaolin clay and are characterized by their light weight and soft ivory tone. As most Ding bowls and dishes were fired upside down, their rims were left unglazed and were later finished with

ABOVE: *Qingbai ware bowl with incised floral decoration, China, Southern Song dynasty, 13th century. Similar in form and decoration to the Ding wares of the north, southern qingbai wares, however, are characterized by a faint blue tinge to the glaze that is very evident in the incised lines where the glaze pools. The blue derives from a tiny amount of iron in the glaze that fires a cool blue tone in an oxygen-starved kiln atmosphere.*

decorative metal bands, a distinctive feature of these wares. In the Southern Song dynasty (1127–1279), production of porcelains shifted with the Imperial court to Southern China, where the porcelain kilns of Jingdezhen soon began their long history of large-scale porcelain manufacture. The first porcelains produced at these kilns were the *qingbai*, or 'bluish-white' porcelains made for both for Imperial and domestic use as well as for export, primarily to other parts of Asia.

During the Yuan dynasty (1279–1368), when the Mongols controlled China, the potters at Jingdezhen produced large numbers of porcelains painted with underglaze blue designs, primarily for export to the Middle East, where Chinese porcelains were admired for their purity and durability. Yuan dynasty blue and white porcelains are characterized by high quality painted designs of dragons, fish, lotuses and other auspicious motifs.

The kilns of Jingdezhen continued to produce blue and white porcelains under the Ming dynasty emperors. The finest blue and white porcelains were made for the Imperial

PORCELAIN

OPPOSITE: *The 'David Vases' decorated with underglaze blue designs of dragons, China, Yuan dynasty, dated 1351. Designs on Yuan porcelains were generally arranged in bands – one central design bordered by decorative bands. On vases and other closed wares, a large central design – here spectacular dragons – were bordered by six or seven smaller bands of lotuses, banana leaves or clouds. On large dishes made for banquets held at Middle Eastern palaces, a central design was surrounded by bands of motifs around the rim.*

Porcelain City, Jingdezhen

Since the 11th century, the city of Jingdezhen in Jiangxi province in Southern China has been the world's largest centre for porcelain production. The hundreds of kilns at Jingdezhen have for 800 years produced porcelains for both domestic use and for export all around the world. Traditionally, the kilns were run by government officials who oversaw hundreds of craftsmen specializing in throwing, mould production, underglaze design painting, overglaze enamelling and calligraphy, as well as less skilled workers who prepared the clay and transported the finished pots to the river for shipping. During the Ming and Qing dynasties, certain kilns were designated Imperial kilns, and there the finest craftsmen produced the highest quality porcelains for the Imperial court. If pieces did not meet the high standards, they were destroyed immediately, as is evident from the many porcelain fragments with flawed designs that have been excavated from early imperial kiln sites at Jingdezhen.

court, and their designs often reflected the taste of a particular emperor or empress. Many of these pieces bear reign marks on their bases that date them to the reign of a particular emperor; these marks, however, are not always to be trusted. The Imperial blue and white porcelains of the Xuande (1426–35) and Chenghua (1465–87) Emperors are considered to be the most refined Ming porcelains and were often copied for the later Qing dynasties emperors. The blue and white porcelain bowls, bottles, and dishes of the Jiajing (1522–66) and the Wanli (1573–1620) reigns were among the first porcelains to be shipped in large quantities to Europe. The European hunger for Chinese porcelains led to orders from Europe for porcelains in European forms, such as soup tureens and wide rimmed plates, and with European coats of arms and other motifs. These forms and

decorations soon entered the repertoire of the Chinese porcelain makers.

In the Ming dynasty (1368–1644), many polychrome porcelains were created using overglaze enamels, a decorative technique that may have begun in the Yuan dynasty. During the Chenghua reign, a refined type of enamelling was invented known as *doucai* or 'joined colours'. *Doucai* consisted of underglaze blue outlines, filled in with red, yellow, aubergine, green enamels applied over the transparent glaze and fired again at a lower temperature. Another, more lively style that emerged in the Ming dynasty was *wucai*, or 'five colour', enamelling, in which certain elements of the design were painted in underglaze blue, while others were added over the glaze in red, green, yellow and black enamels.

In addition to these polychrome porcelains, monochrome porcelains in white, red, blue and yellow were produced during the Ming dynasty. At the Dehua kilns in Fujian province, a fine ivory-white porcelain with a clear glaze was also made from the late Ming dynasty onwards. Commonly known as *blanc de chine*, or 'Chinese white', this distinct porcelain tradition includes plain white vessels and figures of popular gods (see p. 68).

The Qing dynasty (1644–1911) saw a continuation of the blue and white, polychrome and monochrome porcelain traditions, often produced using more sophisticated materials

OPPOSITE: *Dish with underglaze blue designs of Buddhist emblems, China, Ming dynasty, Chenghua reign (1465–87). Compared with the vigorous cobalt blue designs of the Xuande reign, the fine blue and white porcelains of the Chenghua reign feature designs more carefully painted in dark blue outlines and then neatly coloured in with a pale blue wash.*

ABOVE: *Bowl with underglaze blue design of boys playing, China, mid-Ming dynasty. Many mid-Ming dynasty porcelains feature lively designs in deep cobalt blue of children playing – representing fertility – as well as flowers, birds, and other symbols of long life and good fortune.*

PORCELAIN

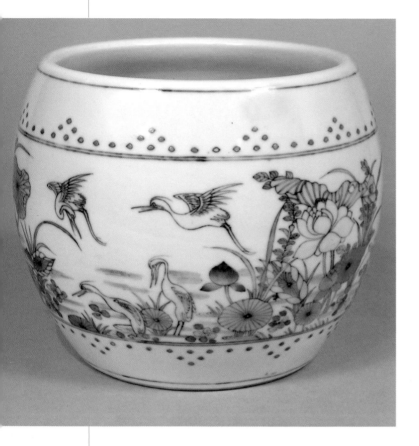

ABOVE LEFT: *Goldfish bowl with doucai decoration in underglaze blue and overglaze enamels, China, Qing dynasty, Yongzheng reign (1723–35). The elegant* doucai *('joined colours') style of colouring in underglaze blue outlines with overglaze enamel pigments began in the 15th century during the Xuande reign, but was revived to great effect in the 18th century during the Yongzheng and Kangxi (1662–1722) periods, and then in Japan at the Nabeshima kilns.*

and styles. The porcelains of the reigns of the Kangxi (1662–1722) and Yongzheng Emperors (1723–35) are generally considered the most elegant, while those of the Qianlong (1736–95) are the most ornate. Overglaze enamelled porcelains reached new artistic heights in the early Qing dynasty. At that time, many porcelains were painted in the *famille verte*, or 'green family' palette, consisting of greens and an overglaze blue. Slightly later, the *famille rose*, or 'pink family' palette, was developed, featuring a pink enamel, possibly brought from Europe by Jesuit missionaries, and an opaque white enamel that could be mixed with other colours to create pastel shades. Monochromes also reached their peak during the Qing dynasty, with many spectacular new glaze colours being invented and perfected. The quality of these glazes was admired so much in Europe that legends spread of Chinese potters who threw themselves into the flames of the kiln in the quest to achieve a perfect glaze.

OPPOSITE RIGHT: *Cup with underglaze blue floral decoration, China, Qing dynasty, Kangxi reign (1662–1722). Porcelains of the 18th century feature expertly painted designs of natural motifs and landscapes, often with a poem or calligraphy.*

LEFT: *Jar with underglaze blue and overglaze enamels in the* famille verte *palette, China, Qing dynasty, Shunzhi (1644–61) or Kangxi reign (1662–1722). Green is the dominant colour in the* famille verte *palette, established in the Qing dynasty and used for many designs on porcelains for domestic use and export.*

ABOVE: *Vase with overglaze enamels in the* famille rose *palette, China, Qing dynasty, Daoguang reign (1821–50). The pink enamel and an opaque enamel enabled ceramic artists to create the effect of a European oil painting on the porcelain surface.*

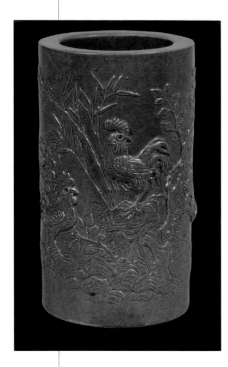

KOREA

ABOVE: *Brush pot with rooster and cockscomb motif under coffee-coloured glaze, Qing dynasty, China.*

PORCELAIN APPEARS TO have been first made in Korea in the Goryeo dynasty (918–1392), though it may have been produced as early as the 9th century. At this time, only small quantities of porcelain were made, alongside the fine green-glazed stonewares known as celadons, for which Korea is more famous. Widespread production of porcelain began in Korea in the Joseon dynasty (1392–1910). In the early 15th century, the Korean court was forced to provide gold and silver as a tribute to China's more powerful Ming emperors. To replace the gold and silver previously used at court functions, Korean rulers decreed that ceramics and lacquer should be used by the court, and the Korean aristocracy began their patronage of porcelains.

Probably inspired by the Chinese imperial porcelain kilns at Jingdezhen, the Korean government established an official government-controlled factory, or *punwon*, in the Kwangju district near Seoul. This kiln produced fine white porcelains for the Korean court, while other porcelain kilns provided wares for the rest of the aristocracy. Many of the early Korean porcelains were simple in form and completely undecorated, their primary feature being the creamy white colour of the porcelain body.

From the 15th century, Korean porcelains were also decorated with underglaze cobalt blue, an expensive pigment imported from China. The blue and white wares of the 15th century, with their Chinese-inspired natural motifs, are often said to represent the peak

PORCELAIN

LEFT: Bottle with underglaze blue design of flying cranes, Korea, Joseon dynasty, 18th century. Many Korean blue and white porcelains feature auspicious motifs such as cranes and turtles, which symbolize long life. The flying crane motif appeared first on the green celadons of the Goryeo dynasty, and is common to Korean ceramic design.

ABOVE: Porcelain jar, Korea, Joseon dynasty, 19th century. The natural simplicity of these Korean porcelains was in keeping with the sensibilities of the Joseon dynasty, who embraced Neo-Confucianist ideals of austerity, simplicity and humility.

of Korean blue and white porcelain production. However, the 18th century was a time of great technical innovation as well as a 'Koreanization' of porcelain decoration and style. During this period, blue and white porcelains were embellished with delicate, native natural designs as well as auspicious symbols such as cranes and turtles. Also appearing in the late 17th and 18th centuries were porcelains with designs painted in underglaze copper red and underglaze iron brown designs.

In general, Korean porcelains are not as densely decorated as their Chinese counterparts, and white is often the most dominant colour. Decoration in blue, red or brown underglaze pigment is usually fairly sparse on the surface, leaving large areas of white visible. Overglaze enamels were never used on Korean porcelains. This is probably due to the Korean aristocracy's preference for subdued colours in keeping with their Neo-Confucian beliefs that emphasized austerity, simplicity and humility.

JAPAN

JAPAN BEGAN PRODUCING porcelain in the early years of the Edo period (1600–1868), following several remarkable events involving Korean potters. At the end of the 16th century, Japanese armies kidnapped many of Korea's best potters under the orders of the military dictator, Hideyoshi (1537–98). These potters were employed by the feudal lords of Japan's southern provinces, particularly on the island of Kyushu. According to legend, the potter Ri Sanpei (Korean: Yi Sam P'yong, d. 1655) of Hizen province (modern Saga prefecture) was commanded by Lord Nabeshima to search for porcelain clay within his territory. Eventually, around 1610, he discovered *tôseki*, or 'ceramic stone', at Izumiyama in the region of Arita. This stone was combined with kaolin clay to make porcelains similar to Chinese wares. The potters of Arita went on to produce large quantities of porcelain for domestic use and export, bringing considerable wealth to the region. As the father of the Japanese porcelain industry, Ri Sanpei was deified, and a shrine was built to him in the city of Arita.

Although porcelain is now made in several regions, including Kyoto and Seto in central and eastern Japan, Arita is still Japan's principal porcelain-producing region. Porcelain produced here is broadly known as 'Arita ware' after the town where the kilns are located. Unlike Chinese porcelains, which were produced for centuries at the same kilns of Jingdezhen, and so are distinguished by their date and decorative styles, Japanese porcelains are usually referred to by their kiln name.

PORCELAIN

Blue and White

THE EARLIEST ARITA porcelains featured simple underglaze cobalt blue designs of flowers and grasses, geometric patterns, and landscapes. Known as *shoki Imari*, or 'early period Imari' wares, after the nearby port of Imari, these porcelains bear a strong resemblance in design and form to slightly earlier Chinese and Korean porcelains. In the 1640s, the Chinese kilns at Jingdezhen, which had been exporting large quantities of porcelains to Europe, ceased production due to the collapse of the Ming dynasty. The Dutch, aware that the Japanese had discovered porcelain, turned to the island nation for supplies of porcelain. The kilns at Arita obliged by producing large quantities of blue and white porcelains, many of which were almost exact copies of Chinese porcelains of the early to mid-17th century. Some of the early blue and white wares were also modelled on European forms such as beer tankards, medicine bottles, beaker vases, and even incorporated European inscriptions.

Kakiemon

IN THE MID-17TH CENTURY, Japanese potters mastered the art of overglaze enamelling. According to tradition, overglaze enamelling on porcelains was pioneered in Arita by Sakaida Kakiemon (1596–1666), and a style of overglaze enamel decoration is named after him. Kakiemon wares are characterized by a creamy white ground decorated with designs of landscapes, bird and flower motifs painted entirely in red, green, blue, yellow,

ABOVE LEFT: *Kraak ware blue and white dish, Japan, Edo period, mid-17th century. After the collapse of the Ming dynasty in the 1640s, the Japanese produced porcelains for export to Europe. Many of these early Japanese porcelains were almost exact copies of Chinese porcelains, as in the case of the kraak wares.*

ABOVE RIGHT: *Kakiemon dish with overglaze enamel decoration, Japan, late 17th century. Some Kakiemon designs show Chinese elements, as in the case of this dish with a kraak-style pattern and Chinese floral motifs. Other Kakiemon porcelains are Japanese in inspiration, featuring asymmetrical compositions, large areas of empty white space and native landscapes or flora.*

PORCELAIN

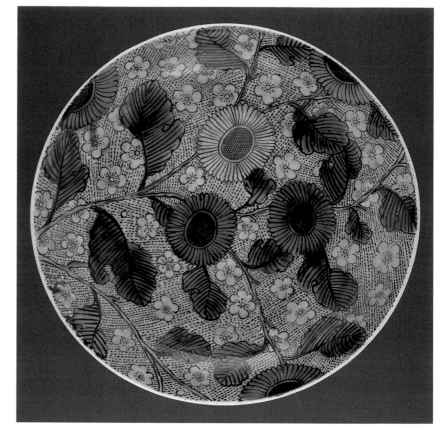

purple and black overglaze enamels. These Kakiemon wares were greatly admired in Europe, and many of the first European porcelains from the kilns in Meissen (Germany), Chantilly (France), and Chelsea (England) were almost exact copies of these Kakiemon porcelains.

Imari

PROBABLY THE BEST-KNOWN of Japanese porcelains, Imari wares have been exported continuously since the mid-17th century. Named after the port of Imari near Arita, from where most of the local porcelain was shipped, these ornate porcelains were specifically made for export to Europe, and later North America. Imari wares are usually decorated in a palette of underglaze blue and overglaze black, red and green enamels and gilding.

Kutani

ANOTHER GROUP OF Japanese polychrome porcelains, Kutani wares, were reportedly made from the mid-17th century at the Kutani kilns in Ishikawa prefecture on Honshu island, although early Kutani wares were probably made at Arita. These porcelains were

generally made for the domestic market and feature a similar palette of overglaze enamels to Kakiemon wares but with bold, uniquely Japanese designs, such as close-up details of plants, birds or rice fields.

Nabeshima

ARGUABLY THE MOST refined Japanese porcelains are the Nabeshima wares produced near Arita. In 1628, Lord Nabeshima established private kilns to produce elegant porcelains for his own use and for presentation to the shogun (military dictator) and other feudal lords. Nabeshima ware is best known as round, high-footed dishes featuring neatly rendered designs that were first drawn on paper, transferred to the surface of the dish and then retraced in underglaze blue pigment. Nabeshima wares often feature overglaze enamels in the Chinese *doucai* style.

Hirado

THE HIRADO WARES of the 18th and 19th centuries are extremely refined. Produced near Arita at the Hirado kilns of Lord Matsuura, these porcelains were initially made for

ABOVE: *Nabeshima ware dish with design of five jars in underglaze blue and celadon glaze, Japan, late 17th to early 18th century. Nabeshima wares typically feature carefully drawn motifs, such as flowers or other natural forms, usually arranged in an asymmetrical composition. As in this dish with a witty design of five ceramic jars, textile patterns are incorporated into the design of many Nabeshima wares.*

his private use or as gifts to other lords, and were often used in such refined pursuits as tea drinking and incense connoisseurship, or as ornaments in the home or scholar's studio. Hirado wares are characterized by a pure white body and Chinese-style designs expertly painted in underglaze blue.

Satsuma

SATSUMA WARES, with their colourful overglaze enamel decorations of natural motifs, Japanese legends, or Buddhist deities, are often mistakenly called porcelains. These wares are actually made of low-firing earthenware clay.

Vietnamese blue and whites

MANY VIETNAMESE BLUE AND WHITE and enamelled ceramics closely resemble porcelain and often ring like porcelain, though they do not have the translucency of true porcelains. Northern Vietnam has plentiful deposits of high quality smooth, grey-white clay that can be fired to high temperatures, but it does not have deposits of the porcelain stone, or *baidunzi*, one of the key ingredients of Chinese porcelains. Since the 14th century, Vietnam has produced blue and white ceramics resembling Chinese porcelain. In the 15th century, Vietnamese blue and whites, and later, enamelled wares, began to evolve distinctly from their Chinese counterparts, featuring native forms such as bottles and ewers with long necks, *kendi* water vessels, and globular stem bowls, as well as local decorative motifs.

ABOVE LEFT: *Stem bowl with underglaze blue lotus design, stoneware, Vietnam, c. 1500. Although closely resembling Chinese porcelains, Vietnamese blue and white wares are not porcelain, but stoneware. They often display a distinctive painting style, discernible here in the elaborate treatment of flowers and leaves.*

ABOVE RIGHT: *Large dish with underglaze blue design of mynah birds, stoneware, Vietnam, c. 1550. Vietnamese blue and white wares tend to feature an airier composition than Chinese porcelains, and they often feature local motifs such as parrots and other native birds.*

OPPOSITE: *Hirado ware ewer with underglaze blue landscape design and dragon handle and spout, Japan, late 19th century. The designs on Hirado wares are often derived from Chinese painting manuals or Qing dynasty porcelains. From the 19th century, Hirado wares were produced mostly for export to the West.*

OPPOSITE: *Lacquer painting on wood, by unidentified artist, Vietnam, 20th century.*

FAR LEFT: *Seated Buddha, lacquered wood, Vietnam, 19th century.*

LEFT: *Detail of tray, Japan, 19th century. See p. 103.*

BELOW: *Carved lacquer bird motif, Burma, 19th century. See p. 109.*

LACQUER

LACQUER IS A UNIQUE Asian artistic material as it is not a base material like the other materials discussed in this book. Instead, it is a coating that is applied to an object to make it more beautiful and to render it resistant to heat, water, insects and acid. There are several types of lacquer (see 'True lacquer, lac and japanning', p. 92). This chapter will explore 'true' lacquer, which derives primarily from the sap of the *Rhus* species of tree. Of these, the *Rhus verniciflua* produces the finest quality sap for lacquer-making and has been used to make lacquer in China, Japan and Korea for thousands of years. Later, Burma, Thailand and Vietnam also developed highly sophisticated lacquer-making traditions, using sap from similar trees.

LACQUER

'True' lacquer, lac and japanning

There are three main categories of lacquer: 'true' lacquer, 'resin' lacquer, also known as lac, and various varnishes known as japan work or japanning. 'True' lacquer is made from the sap of the rhus species of trees, primarily the Rhus verniciflua, although other species produce a similar sap.

The second type of lacquer is a dark red, transparent resin that is produced by the female of many species of insects, especially the Tachardia lacca or Coccus lacca, native to India. Often known as lac, this sticky material is extracted from the insects and the twigs they are found on, heated and then purified. It is used as a coating for fabric, wooden objects and furniture and as a base for painting. This lacquer is found in the artistic traditions of India and the Middle East.

The third type of lacquer, known as japan work or japanning, is the European substitute for the Asian lacquered objects that became fashionable in Europe in the 17th century. These varnishes are made from ingredients such as shellac, or thin flakes of lac resin, and give furniture a protective, shiny coating.

THE MATERIAL

THE WORD LACQUER probably derives from the Hindustani word *lac*, or *lakh*, which refers to the insect deposit on certain trees; this word entered Portuguese as *lacca* and then English as 'lacquer'. In the 1600s, Europeans, impressed by fine Japanese lacquer wares, called this material 'japan', in much the same way that fine ceramics were named 'china'. 'Japan' was even used as a verb, so that to 'japan' an object meant to lacquer it. Today, the process of lacquering or varnishing objects is still often called *japanning* (see above).

For centuries, lacquer has been made from the sap of lacquer trees. After the sap is extracted and purified, it is heated and stirred constantly to remove any excess water and gradually thickens into a sticky, caramel-like liquid. The process of applying lacquer to wood, bamboo, paper or cloth, is time-consuming and requires very specific climatic conditions. The application is done in a succession of extremely thin layers. The first layers, or base coats, are generally made of lower-quality lacquer mixed with ash or clay, which seal and strengthen the core and prevent warping. Each layer of lacquer must dry and harden thoroughly before the next is applied, and this can only be achieved at temperatures of between 25°C and 30°C. Curiously, lacquer can only dry in an environment with a humidity level of 80 to 85 per cent. Each coat can take days to dry.

TECHNIQUES

Lacquer: Beautiful but Poisonous

As well as being a complicated material to work with, raw lacquer can also be poisonous. The Rhus verniciflua tree is a member of the genus that includes poison ivy, poison oak and poison sumac. Touching raw lacquer or sometimes just inhaling its fumes will often result in a toxic reaction that causes an external and/or internal rash. However, once lacquer is dry, it is no longer toxic.

Many colouring agents used to decorate lacquer can also be harmful. Red, for example, is derived from cinnabar, or mercuric sulphide. Handling cinnabar powder and breathing its dust can lead to mercuric poisoning, which in extreme cases can be fatal. In certain lacquer-making traditions, yellow is derived from orpiment (arsenic trisulphide), a toxic substance that can enter the skin through cuts and splinters. The addition of colouring agents is done at the early stages of lacquer processing, so lacquer artists do not generally come into contact with these toxins.

After each layer has hardened, it must be polished smooth in preparation for the next coat. Lacquer is usually polished using stones, ash or charcoals.

Colouring agents are added to the main layers of lacquer. In traditional lacquer, the range of colours that can be mixed with lacquer is limited. Red derives from mercuric sulphide (cinnabar) or iron oxide, while black is produced from iron, white from lead or eggshell, and yellow from cadmium, orpiment (arsenic trisulphide), ochre or gardenia extract. Green and brown are usually created by mixing the other colours. Nowadays, chemical colours can also be used to produce any colour except pure white.

Painted and Etched Decoration

PAINTED DECORATION IS probably the oldest type of lacquer decoration but is not widely used in 'true' lacquer, where lacquer is not only the ground coating but also the binding agent for the paint pigments. In Vietnam, however, lacquer painting has been widely used since the early 20th century as a local alternative to oil painting. After much lacquering and burnishing of the wood board, Vietnam's lacquer painters apply their design in a limited palette of colours. Red (cinnabar), yellow (orpiment), or black (iron) are mixed with lacquer; brown is the natural, untreated colour of the lacquer. In the

cultures that produce resin lacquer, painting is the main decorative technique. In India and the Middle East, pigments are mixed with oil and painted onto a lacquered surface. A wider range of these litharge pigments can be used in oil than in 'true' lacquer painting.

The appearance of painted designs is also achieved by etching lines into the lacquer and filling them with colours or gold. In China and Japan, in particular, 'etched gold' (Chinese: *qiangjin*) outlines are created by incising, or etching, fine lines into the lacquer surface and then pressing gold leaf into the incised lines. In the Burmese *yun* technique, lines are etched into a lacquer ground, usually black, and filled in with red, green, yellow and sometimes blue lacquer.

Inlaid and Applied Decoration

ONE OF THE earliest methods of decorating lacquered objects was to inlay other materials into the lacquer coating while it was still sticky. The most common material used for inlay is mother-of-pearl, a term that refers to the iridescent inner layers of a number of freshwater and marine shells. Pieces of the shell are cut using a bow saw into individual shapes and set into the sticky lacquer surface, with additional lacquer being added to fill in any gaps. The thinner the shell slices, the greater the iridescence, and

ABOVE LEFT: *Food box with yun etched decoration (detail), Burma, 20th century.*

ABOVE CENTRE: *A selection of shells used in Japanese lacquer inlay. Shells such as the nautilus, turbo cornutus, and turbo marmortus were used to decorate Chinese lacquer as early as 1000 BC. Traditionally, the outer surface of the shell is removed and the remaining sections are cut into small pieces and then polished to reveal their colour.*

ABOVE: *Rubbing away excess gold leaf used to fill in incised outlines in lacquer, Japan.*

LACQUER

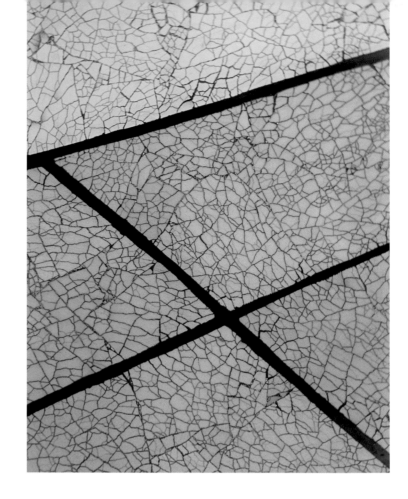

RIGHT: *Detail of chicken and duck eggshell inlay, Vietnam, 20th century. In Vietnam, chicken and duck eggshells are often used to create inlaid patterns in lacquer. Chicken eggshell is white and duck eggshell provides a subtle blue.*

OPPOSITE LEFT: *Carved 'cinnabar' lacquer vase, China, 19th century. Many Chinese carved lacquers are entirely red and are sometimes referred to as 'cinnabar', after the mercuric sulphide from which the colour red is derived.*

colours such as blue, green, pink and purple can be arranged to form kaleidoscopic patterns inset into the lacquer.

Precious materials such as ivory, jade and coral are also inlaid into lacquer furnishings and smaller items, as are more humble materials such as coloured glass, pewter and lead. Even eggshell is used as an inlay in the lacquer traditions of Japan and Vietnam in particular. Gold and silver are also inlaid into or applied to lacquer. In Thailand and Burma, a method known in Thai as *lai rot nam*, or 'designs washed with water', is used to transfer gold leaf designs onto a black lacquer ground using a resist.

Maki-e, *'sprinkled pictures'*

ONE OF THE MOST elaborate and painstaking methods of decorating lacquer is the Japanese 'sprinkled pictures' technique, best known by its Japanese name, *maki-e*. In this technique, gold and silver powders are sprinkled onto the still damp lacquer surface with a tube to create intricate pictures. *Maki-e* designs are either flush with the surface (*togidashi maki-e*, polished out), in low relief (*hiramaki-e*, flat) or in higher relief (*takamaki-e*, raised). These three types of *maki-e* are often combined to create complex designs.

Carved and Moulded Decoration

LACQUER CARVING IS remarkably time-consuming, as it can require as many as 300 layers of lacquer. Assuming each layer requires up to four or five days to dry, a single piece can take as long as two years to prepare before the carver can begin to carve the design through these layers. Traditionally, the wooden base of the object is strengthened with a layer of black lacquer mixed with ash. Then, several layers of yellow lacquer are applied, followed by many layers of red, interspersed with several layers of black lacquer, which serve as depth markers to the lacquer carver. Once all the layers are dry, the carver carves the design into the lacquer, stopping when he reaches certain marker colours.

In Burma, a type of relief-moulded lacquer, *thayo*, also resembles carved lacquer. In this technique, lacquer is mixed with fine ashes, powdered bone, rice husks or even cow dung to form a plastic material, *thayo*, which is moulded into various floral and other forms and stuck onto the surface of the object. The piece is then allowed to dry and coated with lacquer. Many *thayo* pieces are inlaid with jewel-like glass fragments and covered with gold leaf.

TOP: Lai rot nam *technique, Chiangmai, Thailand. The design is transferred onto the black lacquer base coats, protective paint is applied to the areas that are to be left ungilded. Gold leaf is applied to the unpainted areas and then treated with absorbent paper. The protective paint and any excess gold are then washed away with water; lai rot nam means 'washing with water'.*

ABOVE: *Sprinkling gold powder through a tube for maki-e design, Japan. The design is drawn on paper and transferred onto the lacquer surface; the outline of the design is traced with transparent lacquer. Gold and silver powders are sprinkled through a tube onto the wet transparent lacquer, where they adhere.*

LACQUER

CHINA

LACQUER HAS BEEN produced in China for at least 3,000 years, and because of the durability of the material, some ancient objects decorated with lacquer have actually survived from as early as the Shang dynasty (*c.* 1500–1050 BC). Early lacquered material found in tombs of the Warring States (475–221 BC) and Han dynasty (206 BC–AD 220) include wooden coffins and vessels coated with lacquer and painted in red and black with supernatural beings and figures from the spirit world.

During the Tang dynasty (618–906), lacquer vessels were inlaid with birds, dragons and floral details in gold and silver foil or with mother-of-pearl designs. For Buddhist sculptures, the 'dry lacquer' technique was developed. First, a clay core for the sculpture was built. It was then coated with cloth soaked in lacquer and then modelled into the form of the deity. The figure was then painted or gilded and the clay core was removed, leaving a sculpture that was light, easy to transport and insect-resistant.

In the Song dynasty (960–1279), lacquer wares were simple yet elegant. Monochrome cups and bowls in the form of flowers were so admired that they influenced porcelain and metalwork vessels. When decoration was used, the preferred technique was *qiangjin*, or 'etched gold', in which incised lines were filled with gold.

During the Yuan dynasty (1279–1368), under the Mongols, Chinese lacquer decoration once again became ornate. Mother-of-pearl inlay techniques were greatly refined, with shells cut into smaller, thinner slices, resulting in greater iridescence and a variety of colours. Complex scenes of figures and landscapes, modelled after popular contemporary paintings, were rendered in mother-of-pearl inlay. Most significant was the development of carved lacquer, probably China's most important lacquer technique. The

OPPOSITE: *Painted lacquer lidded box, China, Western Han dynasty (100 BC–AD 25). Lidded wooden boxes painted with red and black geometrical designs were among the luxury items buried alongside the royalty of the Han dynasty.*

BELOW: *Carved lacquer round box, China, early Ming dynasty (1368–1644). Carved lacquer reached its zenith during the early Ming dynasty. Examples of lacquer bowls, dishes and boxes show carved scenes of figures in landscapes or dragons and phoenixes painstakingly cut into the lacquer.*

LACQUER

ABOVE: *Coromandel screen (details), China, early 20th century. Coromandel lacquered cabinets, screens and trays are named after the Coromandel Coast of India, from where they were sent to Europe. They feature a combination of carved and painted designs of Chinese landscapes and architectural settings.*

carved lacquer trays, dishes and boxes of this period and the Ming dynasty (1368–1644) feature bold designs of birds and flowers, either black with a hint of a red ground, or more often in cinnabar red only. Etched gold decoration continued to be popular in the Ming dynasty, as did the related *tianqi*, or 'filled-in lacquer', in which designs are cut out of the hardened lacquer surface, filled with lacquer of different colours and polished. The outlines were then incised and filled with gold to create a brilliant polychrome design.

All of these lacquer techniques were continued into the Qing dynasty (1644–1911), enjoying the patronage of such emperors as the Qianlong Emperor (1736–95), an avid collector of fine lacquers. Large elaborate screens and wall panels with carved details of landscapes or inlaid Buddhist and Daoist auspicious symbols graced the walls of palaces and temples and intrigued European visitors to China. In the late 17th century, the Chinese Coromandel lacquers were made with designs carved into the lacquer and filled in with lacquer and oil-painted details. Named after the Coromandel coast of India, from where they were shipped westward, they were created primarily for export to Europe.

RECENT EXCAVATIONS OF tombs in southern Korea have revealed that plain black lacquered ritual vessels were produced in Korea as early as the 1st or 2nd century BC. The tree *Rhus trichocarpa* is native to Korea, and its sap was probably used to make Korea's first lacquer, although *Rhus verniciflua* was probably introduced from China around the 1st century BC. Very little early Korean lacquer has survived, but from the examples that have been unearthed from 5th and 6th century royal tombs, it is evident that red and black lacquered vessels and ornaments, some decorated with gold leaf, were popular.

A small number of exquisite lacquer pieces have survived from the Goryeo period (918–1392), when the Goryeo nobility and the Buddhist clergy patronized many of

KOREA

BELOW: *Lidded box, lacquer inlaid with mother-of-pearl, Korea, 17th century. Many cosmetic boxes in the Joseon period were coated with lacquer and feature inlaid mother-of-pearl designs of scrolling lotuses and peonies, executed in a fluent, representational style.*

Korea's arts. Most of these feature designs rendered in inlaid mother-of-pearl, or *najon*, the most celebrated technique of Korea's lacquer artists. Secular objects include cosmetic boxes in the form of flowers, decorated with mother-of-pearl and tortoise shell. Religious objects are primarily rectangular *sutra* boxes for holding sacred Buddhist texts. These boxes were coated in black lacquer and inlaid with tiny mother-of-pearl chrysanthemum, lotus and peony scrolls, arranged geometrically precise manner to cover the whole box. Inlaid silver and copper wires formed the delicate stems and stalks of the flowers.

During the subsequent Joseon period (1392–1910), lacquer was used predominantly to decorate boxes and furniture for the upper classes. Shell inlay pictorial landscapes with figures and animals appeared very late in the Joseon period, and often embellished the panels of the large chests used for storing clothing in the homes of the upper classes.

JAPAN

ABOVE: *Detail of lacquered clothing chests decorated with mother-of-pearl inlay, Korea, early 20th century.*

BELOW: *Negoro-style sake set, lacquered wood, Japan, 20th century. A two-colour effect is created by rubbing the red surface of the lacquer to reveal the black lacquer underneath.*

ACCORDING TO RECENT discoveries at archaeological sites in Hokkaido in northern Japan, lacquer was used there as early as 9000 BC, even earlier than in China. It is not clear from which species of tree the lacquer was derived, but *Rhus verniciflua* was cultivated in Japan by the middle of the 1st millennium AD. At this time, Japan's lacquer tradition showed much influence from Korean and Chinese lacquer decoration. Some 8th century objects feature bold geometric designs inlaid in mother-of-pearl, or *raden* in Japanese; others have painted designs made with gold and silver powders mixed with glue. Some Buddhist sculptures of this period were made using the Chinese dry lacquer technique.

During the Heian period (794–1185), when native Japanese culture blossomed, the *maki-e*, or 'sprinkled pictures', technique evolved, possibly from the earlier method of mixing metallic powders with glue. Simple gold and silver pictorial designs of birds, animals and flowers and stylized swirling waves embellished the writing boxes, food vessels and furnishings of the upper classes. Since this period, *maki-e* has been Japan's most celebrated lacquer technique.

In the Kamakura period (1185–1333), under the country's first military rulers, gold featured prominently in lacquer decoration. In *maki-e*, varying shades and sizes of gold and other metallic powders were sprinkled to form the main design and the background. In addition, *kirikane*, or 'cut gold', was laid onto a lacquer ground to provide gilded details. In contrast, an austere type of lacquer emerged from the Buddhist temples of this period. Named after the temple in Wakayama prefecture near Kyoto, Negoro lacquers are simple monochrome red vessels that have been worn down in places on the surface to reveal the black lacquer underneath. During the Muromachi period (1333–1573), *maki-e* designs became more painterly, with more elaborate pictorial designs laden with native Japanese poetic or literary references inlaid in mother-of-pearl. At the same time, a strong

interest in Ming dynasty (1368–1644) Chinese culture resulted in the popularity of Chinese carved lacquer in Japan and the evolution of a simpler Japanese imitation known as *Kamakura-bori*, or 'Kamakura carving', after the city where it has traditionally been produced. In these lacquers, the wooden base, and not the lacquer itself, is carved.

The brief but important Momoyama period (1574–1615) gave rise to some of Japan's most sumptuous lacquer decoration, often executed on a large scale, covering temple altars, palanquins and even entire buildings. In a strong native Japanese style, the Kodaiji lacquers of Kyoto are characterized by their stylized *maki-e* designs of autumn grasses and flowers rendered in a bold, diagonal composition. In contrast, Namban (or 'Southern Barbarian') lacquers, with their more exotic designs, bear the influence of Japan's relations with Europeans.

During the subsequent Edo period (1600–1868), the military government patronized the established lacquer styles and techniques, while the increasingly wealthy townspeople patronized the lively new designs of such celebrated lacquer designers as Koetsu Honami

ABOVE LEFT: *Lacquered tray with* maki-e *design of heron and water plants (detail), Japan, 19th century. Most objects that are referred to as lacquer are actually made of wood, bamboo or another core material and then coated with multiple layers of lacquer and decorated using techniques such as* maki-e, *in which gold and silver powders are sprinkled onto the lacquer to create designs.*

ABOVE RIGHT: Kamakura-bori *carved writing box with design of chrysanthemum carved into the wood, rather than into the lacquer itself, Japan, 19th century.*

LACQUER

ABOVE: *Namban-style lacquered frame with mother-of-pearl inlay on Christian oil painting, Japan, 17th century. Namban lacquers, often made for the Portuguese Jesuit clergy living in Japan, typically feature traditional Japanese pictorial gold lacquer designs framed within geometrical borders.*

(1558–1637), Ogata Korin (1658–1716) and Ogawa Haritsu (1663–1747), also known as Ritsuo. Many Edo period artists showed off their lacquer decorating skills on some of the tiniest objects of the day, such as the small *inro* used for holding personal seals and medicine, which were suspended from *kimono* sashes.

During the Edo and later Meiji (1868–1912) periods, Japan exported large quantities of lacquer to Europe, primarily cabinets and screens. This export peaked in the 17th century, with the Dutch exporting hundreds of lacquer cabinets, chests, basins and game boards from Japan to Europe. Most 19th century export lacquers feature *maki-e* landscapes and bird and flower motifs in gold on a black ground. Such Japanese lacquer furnishings graced the rooms of European homes and inspired the Europeans to perfect their own japanning techniques for varnishing wooden furniture.

To the south of Japan are the Ryukyu Islands, which include Okinawa. These islands were an independent kingdom from the 15th century until 1879, and were influenced by the cultures of China, Japan and Southeast Asia. Under China's influence, *qiangjin*-style lacquers decorated with incised lines filled with gold were produced from the 15th century onwards. From the 16th century, painting in gold lacquer and coloured oil paints, or litharge, became popular, particularly on a red ground. Also very typical are the lacquers decorated with inlaid mother-of-pearl and the lacquers known as *tsuikin*, or

ABOVE LEFT: *Writing box with inlaid inro design, basketry, wood, clay, and lacquer, by Ritsuo (Ōgawa Haritsu, 1663–1747), Japan, 18th century. Ritsuo's works feature inlays in ivory, jade, coral and even ceramic, and he is renowned for creating ceramic and lacquer details that resembled stone, wood and metal.*

ABOVE RIGHT: *Lacquered inro with design of ants eating mulberry leaves by Shibata Zeshin (1807–91), Japan, 19th century. Small enough to hold in the hand, inro are composed of three or four sections that slot into each other and are generally made of wood and coated with lacquer decorated with sophisticated maki-e and inlay designs. Shibata Zeshin, a renowned lacquer artist, created some of his most exquisite and remarkable designs on these highly personal objects.*

ABOVE: *Lacquer tray on a high foot with painted gold decoration, Ryukyu Islands, 19th century.*

'piled-up brocade', referring to both the inlay of various hard stones, wood and ivory, and the use of coloured lacquer putty to achieve a similar effect to lacquer carving.

THAILAND

LACQUER IN THAILAND derives from the *Melanorrhea usitata* tree. The history of Thai lacquer is obscure, and probably does not extend back to the 1st millennium. It seems likely that the earliest lacquered vessels in Thailand were made of bamboo basketry bases and used for holding food. It is generally accepted that the greatest period for the development of Thai lacquer was the Ayutthaya period (1350–1767), with the most impressive work dating to the 17th and 18th centuries, when a number of lacquer techniques were used to embellish objects and architectural details.

Mother-of-pearl inlay, made with tiny pieces of green turban shell from southwest

Thailand, may have been used from as early as the 14th century, though no examples remain from this date. Although the technique of inlaying with iridescent shells was used in China, Japan and Korea many centuries earlier, the Thais have used this technique on a monumental scale in temple architecture in particular. From the 17th century, the large doors and other architectural details of Thai Buddhist temples in the capital were embellished with designs inlaid in the finest mother-of-pearl inlay. Even the soles of the Buddha's feet were decorated with mother-of-pearl details. On a smaller scale, domestic items were also inlaid with these luminous shells for royal use.

Probably the best-known Thai lacquer decoration is the *lai rot nam* technique of applying gold leaf to a black lacquer background. From the 17th century, many wooden cabinets, made to hold Buddhist sacred texts, were embellished with gilded designs.

LACQUER

BELOW: *Manuscript cabinet, wood with lacquer and gilding, Thailand, 18th century. Cabinets like these contained sacred Buddhist texts and were gilded with scenes from Buddhist legends and the Hindu epic, the Ramayana.*

BURMA

THE PRODUCTION OF lacquer in Burma may date back to the 1st millennium. It is known from Chinese records that the Pyu, who built Burma's first cities, applied lacquer to their palace architecture by the 9th century AD. The earliest datable Burmese lacquer pieces have been excavated from Buddhist monuments and tombs from the 13th century, during the Pagan period. From what little documentary and archaeological evidence exists, it seems likely that the earliest Burmese lacquer items were plainly decorated bamboo containers for food and drink and Buddhist bowls and ritual vessels.

Widespread lacquer production probably only began in Burma in the late 17th century, and many of the main decorative techniques appear to have been introduced to Burma after several wars with Thailand. In 1767, when the Burmese sacked the Thai capital of Ayutthaya, they captured Thai craftsmen and transported them back to Burma. Lacquer craftsmen who were installed in the Burmese capital of Pagan introduced the engraved lacquer, or *yun*, technique, which has since flourished in Burma.

Around the late 17th or 18th century gold leaf began to be used in abundance on Burmese lacquer. It was often applied to vessels and furniture using a technique similar to the Thai *lai rot nam* technique. However, in Burmese lacquer, a negative design technique is more common. The part of the design that is to remain black (the background) is painted with a water-soluble resist made of yellow orpiment and gum. A thin coat of lacquer is applied to the areas that are to be covered with gold, and then gold leaf is

RIGHT: *Lacquer bowl with yun decoration, Burma, 19th century. One of Burma's main types of lacquerware, yun engraved ware features scenes from legends, human and mythical figures and animals, framed by elaborate floral and geometric borders.*

OPPOSITE LEFT: *Offering vessel (hsun-ok), bamboo with lacquer and thayo moulded decoration, Burma, 19th century.*

OPPOSITE FAR RIGHT: *Seated Buddha, dry lacquer with thayo and gilding, Burma, 18th century. Many late Burmese Buddhist figures were made using dry lacquer. Thayo paste was applied over the temporary clay core of the figure, and the features and details of the Buddha were modelled in it. Many of these Buddhist figures are covered with gold leaf and inlaid glass.*

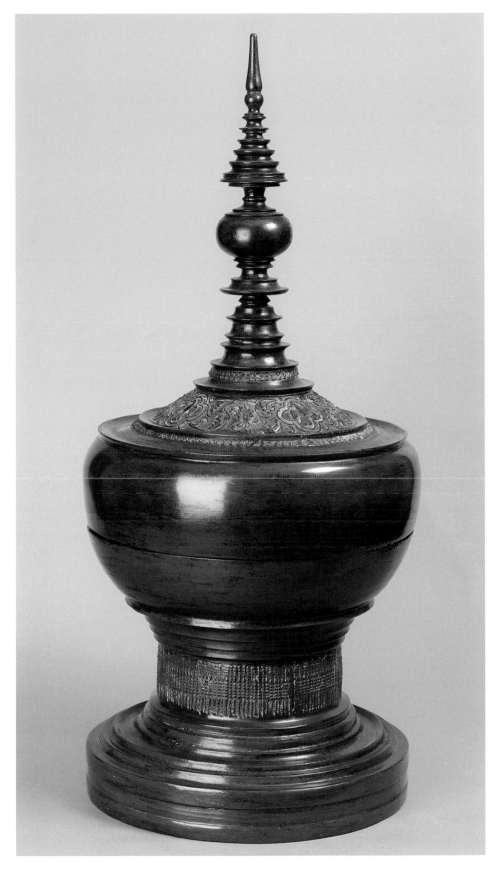

ABOVE: *Buddhist manuscript page, wood with lacquer and gilding, Burma, 19th century. Some of the most exquisite examples of this type of lacquer decoration are found on the Burmese Buddhist books that are made of long, stiff pages, enclosed in teak wood covers. The pages of these sacred Buddhist texts feature Pali script in black lacquer and a gold leaf background often embellished with tiny scrolling designs in red lacquer.*

applied to those areas and pressed down hard. Then the excess gold is washed off leaving gold designs on a black ground.

In the same period, gold leaf was used on *thayo*, relief-moulded lacquers. Although first created in China, relief-moulded lacquer was not popular there, nor was it widespread in Thailand. In Burma, however, it became an important method of decoration for vessels, furniture and Buddhist book covers. In the 18th century in particular, this technique was often enhanced with tiny pieces of coloured mirrored glass and mica inlaid into the lacquer surface. During the Mandalay period (1857–85), improved cutting tools from Europe enabled artists to make smaller, finer glass fragments. In the 18th and 19th centuries, *thayo* was used to create Buddhist imagery using the dry lacquer technique.

VIETNAM

TWO MAIN TYPES of tree provide lacquer sap in Vietnam: *Rhus succedamea* in the north and *Melanorrhea laccifera* in the south. It is not certain when lacquer was first used in Vietnam, but it is possible that lacquer-making began sometime before the 15th century. Early Vietnamese lacquers are believed to have been household objects, such as food vessels and containers, made of wood or bamboo. Vietnamese lacquer vessels are traditionally monochrome, often red, orange, black or green, although silver and gold leaf have traditionally been applied. From the 15th century, lacquer has been used as a coating for Buddhist and Daoist sculptures. The sculptures are made from wood, or sometimes even bronze, and then coated with red, black and gold lacquer.

The 20th century saw a renaissance of lacquer art in Vietnam, in particular in the realm of lacquer painting. In the 1920s and '30s, Vietnamese students of Western oil painting techniques were motivated to experiment with traditional lacquer, and the result was a unique art form that is still vibrant in Vietnam today. Pioneered by such major

LEFT: *Detail of lacquered spun bamboo lidded box, Vietnam, 20th century.*

RIGHT: *Seated Buddha, wood with lacquer and gilding, Vietnam, 19th century.*

LACQUER

INDIA

figures as Nguyen Gia Tri (1908–93), Vietnamese artists created a new type of painting that was neither Western nor traditional Vietnamese. They mixed pigments with pine resin and painted onto wooden canvases, coating the whole work with lacquer and burnishing it for a silky sheen. Many of these paintings have backgrounds brightened with gold leaf and whitish details rendered with inlaid eggshells.

THE LACQUERS OF INDIA are not considered 'true' lacquer, since they are made of a resin produced by insects, rather than the sap of the *rhus* tree. However, they are important in certain regions, so are worth noting briefly. The lacquers produced in India are wooden objects painted with oil or litharge pigments and coated with a transparent resin lacquer. Indian lacquer does not seem to predate the 17th century, when it was introduced to the subcontinent from Persia, under the rule of the Islamic Mughal Court. Made primarily in Kashmir, most surviving examples of Indian lacquer date to the 19th century and are generally small personal items, such as cases and pen boxes, embellished with colourful and minutely executed floral or figural decoration, often in a Persian style.

BELOW: *Pen box, resin lacquer decoration, Kashmir, 20th century. Although not 'true' lacquer, being derived from insects rather than the sap of the Rhus tree, they are popular decorative objects.*

IVORY

IVORY IS THE MOST controversial of all the materials explored in this book, since it is derived from the tusks of mammals that have traditionally been killed for their ivory. This white or near-white material, from the tusks of elephants, walruses, hippopotami and certain types of whales, has been admired for millennia for its clean beauty, sheen and smoothness to the touch. Ivory is soft enough to allow elaborate carving yet hard enough to survive for thousands of years buried under the ground or the sea. In many cultures, the material has also been valued as a medicine, and walrus ivory has been believed to heal wounds and detect poison.

OPPOSITE: *Seated Ganesha, ivory, Orissa, India, 14th to 15th century.*

ABOVE LEFT: *Lacquered wood* inro *with ivory* netsuke *toggle, Japan, mid-19th century.*

ABOVE CENTRE: *Ivory comb, Nepal. See p. 127.*

ABOVE RIGHT: *Ivory carving of Guanyu (the Daoist God of War), China, Qing dynasty.*

IVORY

ABOVE LEFT: *Ivory netsuke toggle depicting Fukurokuju (God of Long Life) and Okame (Goddess of Mirth), Japan, 19th century.*

ABOVE RIGHT: *Three bodhisattvas, carved ivory on wooden stand, China, 19th century.*

THE MATERIAL

IVORY FROM ELEPHANTS, mammoths and walruses has been worked in Asia for at least 4,000 years. Exquisite ritual and religious objects, luxury personal items, religious icons, and gaming pieces have been carved out of this fine substance both for domestic use and for export. Here, we will deal mainly with elephant ivory, the most commonly used.

In Asia, the chief source of ivory has been the Asian elephant, once native to China and still found in India, Thailand, Burma and other regions of Southeast Asia. The tusks of African elephants and walruses have been less commonly used. Tragically, the desire for ivory all over the world has led to the decimation of populations of elephants, walruses and other mammals (see 'Endangered Species', opposite).

What is Ivory?

IVORY IS THE TEETH of certain animals; the name derives from the Latin *ebur*, meaning ivory. True ivory comes from the tusks, or prolonged upper incisors, of the African elephant (*Loxodonta africana*) and the Indian, or Asian, elephant (*Elephas maximus*), as well as their ancestor, the mammoth, whose remains have been discovered in frozen land masses in Siberia and other regions. The Indian elephant is generally smaller than the African elephant, as are its tusks; an African elephant tusk can measure up to 9 ft (2.75 m) in length. Female Indian elephants either have extremely small tusks or no visible tusks at all.

The main part of the tusk is solid except for a small nerve hole that runs all the way to the tip of the tusk. It is not round but oval in cross-section. The root, which measures about one third of the tusk length, is embedded deep in the head, and comprises a conical

Endangered Species

The history of the ivory trade has been full of blood and cruelty. In Africa, from the 17th to the 19th centuries, Europeans traded in 'black and white gold', enslaving black Africans and forcing them to carry the heavy white tusks of elephants. The slave trade was prohibited in the mid-19th century, but trade in ivory continued. In both Africa and Asia, so many elephants have been slaughtered for their tusks that in the 1970s, international restrictions were imposed by CITES (the Convention on the International Trade in Endangered Species of Wild Fauna and Flora) on the killing of elephants for ivory and on the trade of raw ivory and ivory products. Antique ivory is not included in this ban, but it is carefully scrutinized as it is moved around the world, for example, by museums lending art objects internationally. This ban has succeeded in reducing the killing of elephants in certain areas, though poaching still continues. (For information on CITES, see www.cites.org, and on the protection of elephants, see www.savetheelephant.com.)

Although this ban on ivory trade is essential to prevent the extinction of these animals, it has resulted in another predicament in the world of art. As supplies of ivory dwindle, Asian and other ivory carvers, whose families have worked the material for generations, can no longer practice their art and may also die out. As a solution, it has been suggested that the ivory from elephants that have died naturally be given to these artists to work into fine art objects, while factories specializing in ivory souvenir items be restricted to ivory substitutes such as bone. This compromise would prevent either group, elephants or artists, from becoming extinct.

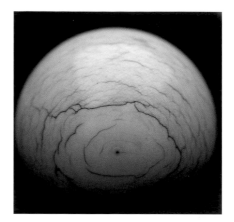

ABOVE: *The tusk is oval in cross-section. Its smoothness, sheen and durability have made it attractive to collectors for centuries.*

ABOVE RIGHT: *Detail of billiard ball showing diamond pattern formed by dentine tubes. The diamond or lozenge patterns that may also be visible in a cross section of ivory, usually towards the outer layers, are formed by the thousands of tiny tubes that carry the dentine from the interior in two well ordered streams that criss-cross around the length of the tusk. The nerve hole of the tusk is also visible here.*

cavity containing soft pulp around a hollow centre. The tusk grows outwards from inside the skull, so the tip is the oldest part. From deep within the pulp cavity, a collagenous substance, dentine, is secreted and hardens in conical layers between the pulp and the ivory, lengthening the tusk, cone under cone. The layered, conical growth of the tusk is reflected in the concentric oval growth lines that can be seen in a cross section of solid ivory. These lines are comparable to the annual growth rings of a tree, but are not determined by age and cannot be used to date ivory. Growth lines depend on nutrition; a diet rich in vitamin D produces the greatest growth. The concentric arcs seen on the surface of certain ivory objects are actually sections of the oval growth lines of a tusk and are sometimes referred to as the 'grain' of the ivory.

On the death of an elephant, the tusk is removed by cutting through the animal's flesh as close as possible to the bone. Almost one third of the length of the tusk is embedded within the jaw, and the hollow inner part is also valuable, since it can be used to make containers. The tusks are transported to the workshops of ivory carvers. The ivory is not carved immediately; it is generally dried or 'seasoned' so that any shrinkage and distortion in form occurs prior to carving. Seasoning the ivory can take several months. Once the ivory is seasoned, the outer layer, or rind, is removed using a knife, chisel or file.

TECHNIQUES

Cutting and Carving the Form

SOMETIMES A TUSK IS LEFT IN ITS entirety and decorated with carved designs. More likely, a number of smaller items are produced from a single tusk. The techniques and tools of ivory carving vary from culture to culture, but the following broad description applies to most Asian traditions. For multiple carvings, the tusk is cut into smaller sections of ivory using a manual or electric saw. Beginners may first learn to carve wood

IVORY

The Distinguishing Features of Ivory

Ivory is similar to bone and teeth, and it is often difficult to tell the materials apart. In many cases, ivory can be recognized by the grain — either concentric lines or criss-crossing diamond-pattern lines visible on the surface. Unlike bones and antlers, tusks have no blood vessel system, so ivory is a denser, heavier material and will not float in water. Unlike teeth, tusks are not coated with enamel, although they are coated with a layer of cementum at the base of the tusk, which is removed before carving. In addition, older tusks generally have a brownish outer layer often referred to as the bark or skin of the ivory. It is also usually removed before carving. When this outer coating is removed, the material can be rubbed with a soft cloth to produce a gloss because of the oil in the dentine of ivory.

Colour can sometimes help differentiate ivory from bone and teeth. Elephant ivory is close to white in colour, but can vary in tone depending on the species and the diet of the animal, which can give tusks a brownish yellow to a gentle pinkish tone. For example, in Africa, it is whiter from animals who fed in the savannah, brownish from those who fed in the forests and pinkish from those who fed in bamboo forests. Ivory can also change colour over time, often turning a warm yellow or brownish hue with age, or turning white due to prolonged exposure to sunlight. Japanese netsuke, such as the example above carved in the form of three frogs on a lotus leaf, were intended to be handled, and over the years, the oils from the owner's hands have given many ivory netsuke a warm, caramel tone.

and other softer materials with these tools before tackling harder ivory. When dividing up the tusk, the carver must keep in mind the solid and hollow sections, the oval circumference of the tusk and the curve of the tusk. Consistency is particularly important when carving a series of objects, such as cutlery or chess sets; all pieces must be carved from the same tusk to avoid discrepancies in colour and texture. Sometimes during the cutting process, cracks, other defects, and even bullets, may be discovered inside the tusk.

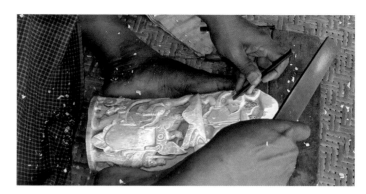

Incised and Carved Decoration

ONCE A SECTION OF IVORY is ready to decorate, a great variety of tools is used to incise or carve designs into the material, including saws, drills, chisels, knives, rasps, files, punches, and scrapers. The simplest way of decorating ivory is to incise motifs or scenes onto the flat or curved surface of the ivory.

The Most Puzzling of Ivory Carvings

Perhaps the most technically intricate carvings are the openwork Chinese puzzle balls, sometimes called 'devil's balls'. They comprise a set of thin ivory spheres carved one within another, and were made as early as the 14th century in the southern Chinese port of Canton. By the 18th century, Europeans were intrigued. S. Wells Williams explains in The Chinese Commercial Guide (1863):

'A fine piece of ivory is chosen and worked to an exact sphere; several conical holes are cut into its body, all meeting in the centre by means of drills working to a gauge, so that each hole will be of the same depth. The centre being bored out an inch or so, the mass of ivory is fixed firm with wedges, and a line is drawn far inside of each conical hole at the same distance from each surface; the workman cuts into this line with knives working on a pivot and passes around the sphere from one hole to another, cutting into the sides of each until the incisions meet and the central sphere is loosened. Its faces are then turned over to the holes, so that they can be smoothed and carved with proper tools, before proceeding to the next. Another line is then drawn outside of this sphere, and the same process is repeated till another is loosened, and the new surfaces polished like the first. In this way all the concentric spheres are cut out; about three months labour is required for a large ball.'

A puzzle ball comprising 28 layers was made for the Panama-Pacific International Exposition in San Francisco in 1915.

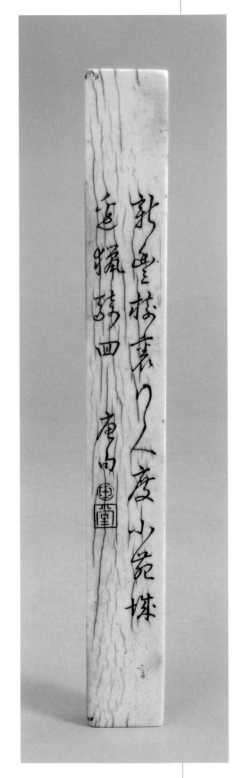

RIGHT: *Seated* bodhisattva, *ivory, Tibet, 18th century.*

FAR RIGHT: *Calligraphic inscription on a plaque, China, 19th century. Thin sheets of ivory have been made into official tablets or pages of sacred books. Incised texts are usually filled with black ink, lacquer or other pigments.*

Many remarkable ivories have designs carved in low relief, high relief or pierced work, either on a single surface or done in the round. To carve smaller pieces of ivory in the round, the piece may be gripped in a vice, while larger pieces are steadied by the carver's feet. The outline of the design is then drawn onto the surface of the ivory, and the carver uses gouges and chisels to carve out the basic shape. Then, the most experienced carvers execute the fine details using chisels, awls, small files, and other tools to create minute details, holes, openwork and lace-like filigree work. After the carving is completed, the piece is smoothed and polished. Finally, ivories are sometimes soaked in a mixture of tea, coffee and/or tobacco leaves to give them the warm patina of antique ivories. This technique has been employed in some cases in the faking of antique ivories, in part to circumvent laws against trade in new ivory.

Ivory has also been used as a material for inlay, especially in Indian and Chinese furniture, boxes and board games made for both the local aristocracy and for export to Europe. Ivory was occasionally the base material into which other materials, including precious and semi-precious gems were inset. In India and Southeast Asia in particular, gold leaf is occasionally applied to further embellish the ivory.

IVORY

Painting and Staining

ALTHOUGH IVORY has long been admired for its natural colour and sheen, it has often been embellished with bold colours. Indian and Chinese ivory religious and secular figurines often feature painted clothing and facial details. Flat sheets of ivory have been used as a painting surface, often for miniature paintings and portraits of important personages. Ivory may also be stained a single contrasting colour to achieve a dramatic contrast with the natural white of the material, as can be seen in 19th century Chinese chess sets, with one white army and the other stained cinnabar red.

INDIA HAS A LONG HISTORY of ivory working, in part due the abundance of elephants in the region. Excavations of sites in the Indus Valley (*c.* 2500–1750 BC) in northwest India and Pakistan have revealed ivory beads, combs, seals, dice and vessels. Ancient Hindu epics such as the *Ramayana* and the *Mahabharata*, written in the 1st millennium BC, refer to ivory carving guilds and ivory court objects, and by this time, India is known to have exported ivory to the court of King Darius I of Persia. Some of the elaborate stone figure carving on the gates of the Great Stupa, or reliquary mound, at Sanchi in central India, is known to be the work of ivory carvers of the 1st century AD, although no ivory carvings have been found at this site. Ivory was also exported to the Roman Empire, and a small Indian ivory carving of a female, dating to around the mid-1st century AD, was found at Pompeii.

Among the most important early Indian ivories are the 600 carved ivory plaques known as the Begram Ivories, after the city of Begram in Afghanistan where they were found. Their incised and carved designs of beautiful ladies enjoying various elegant pastimes and other motifs date to the 1st or 2nd century AD and closely resemble stone

INDIA AND SRI LANKA

ABOVE: *Ebony and ivory chess board with ivory pieces, India, c. 1850. Small pieces of ivory cut out of a flattened sheet are inlaid into darker woods such as rosewood or ebony to create boldly contrasting patterns on beds, cabinets, chairs and gaming boards. This was the first Asian art object purchased by American collector Norton Simon in the early 1970s; his collection of Asian art is housed at the Norton Simon Museum in Pasadena, California.*

IVORY

carvings at contemporary Hindu and Buddhist temples. During India's classical Gupta period (*c.* 320–mid-5th century), stone carving reached an aesthetic high point, and although few ivories survive from this period, it is likely that sculptors worked both in stone and ivory, so ivory carving was presumably of the same high standard. By the 8th century, exquisitely carved ivory images of Buddhist deities were being produced in Kashmir in the northeast of India.

By the 13th century, a great tradition of ivory carving emerged in Orissa in Eastern India and flourished until the 19th century. In this region, which is home to two major Hindu temples, the Sun Temple at Konarak and the Jagannath Temple at Puri, many ivory carvings depict Hindu deities, such as the elephant-headed god Ganesha. The intricate treatment of the jewelry, head ornaments and tassels echo details of the magnificent stone sculptures at Konarak. Orissan ivory carvers also specialized in ivory furniture, including beds and thrones supported on legs ornately carved with lions, elephants and other powerful beasts. They also famously produced bed panels often embellished with openwork erotic designs of lovers in acrobatic positions. In contrast,

IVORY

RIGHT: *Madonna and Christ Child, Goa, 18th century. Indian Christian ivories are modelled after European prototypes. Often, the hair and flesh details are incised or stained darker tones.*

OPPOSITE ABOVE: *Powder primer flask, India, Mughal period, 17th century. Mughal ivories were often carved with animal heads and floral scrolls.*

OPPOSITE BELOW: *Portrait of Emperor Humayun (r. 1530–40; 1555–56), Mughal period, Delhi, c. 1875, opaque watercolours and gold. Ivory was also used in India as a surface for painting. Sections of ivory were flattened out and cut into rectangular sheets, and opaque watercolours and gold were mixed with an adhesive and applied to the ivory as if onto paper.*

Goa in southwestern India, emerged as a centre for Christian ivories after the port was colonized by the Portuguese in the 16th century. Generally modelled after European prototypes, most Goan ivory figures depict the Virgin Mary, the Christ Child or Christian saints.

Under the Islamic Mughal Dynasty (1526–1857), ivory was widely used for court objects such as handles for swords, daggers, fly whisks and fans. Weapon handles and archers' rings, worn on the thumb to help the archer draw the bow string, were often fashioned out of walrus ivory, since it was believed in the Islamic world that this material prevented hand cramps and healed wounds. Many personal items such as jewelry, combs and boxes were carved in relief and often affixed with gilt-metal mounts, hinges or handles or painted with flowers. Later, in the 18th and 19th centuries, ivory was also used in the Mughal court as a surface for paintings, including portraits of emperors.

Furniture for the Mughal Court was also decorated with ivory from court workshops in Delhi as well as at the ivory workshops in Orissa and in Madras, Mysore and Madurai in southern India. These centres and ivory workshops in Gujarat, Murshidabad (West

ABOVE: *Buddha Shakyamuni and attendants, ivory with pigments, Sri Lanka, 18th century. The fine carving of Sinhalese ivory workers is apparent in the details of the Buddha's face, the soft folds of his robes, and the elaborate clothing and jewelry of his attendants. Many Sri Lankan ivories were further embellished with black and red pigments, of which some traces still remain.*

Bengal) and Travancore (Kerala) produced elaborate furniture decorated with ivory veneers for both the domestic and export markets. The most notable perhaps was the large ivory-veneered throne that was presented by one of the Maharajas of Travancore to Queen Victoria in 1851. Some of the largest Indian ivory objects were the model ivory boats made at Murshidabad in the late 19th and early 20th centuries. These elaborate model boats, known as peacock barges, were often carved out of a whole tusk and embellished with pavilions and figures of the ruler of Bengal, his guests and entertainers.

Sri Lanka has also been a notable centre for ivory carving. The Sinhalese ivory carvers of Sri Lanka are renowned for their intricate detailing of human and animal figures as well as decorative scrolling foliage. In this region, both Hindu and Buddhist figures were carved from ivory as objects of devotion. Many significant Buddhist figures were produced during the Kandy period (1592–1815), in particular during the 18th century under the reign of the Buddhist king, Kirti Raja Simha (r. 1747–80). Besides religious ivories, many decorative objects such as combs and other personal items were carved from ivory. Many Sri Lankan ivories were further embellished with black and red pigments, of which some traces still remain.

IVORY WAS NOT readily available in the Himalayas, so countries such as Nepal and Tibet have not traditionally specialized in ivory carving. In Nepal, which has a celebrated wood carving tradition, some finely carved ivories do exist, including figures of Buddhist and Hindu deities and articles such as combs, game pieces and dagger handles. In Tibet, objects, particularly those made for Buddhist rituals, have traditionally been made from human and animal bone rather than ivory. However, ivory has occasionally been employed for ritual objects such as water vessels, prayer wheels and ceremonial daggers. Ivory images of Buddhist deities and gurus are less common.

OPPOSITE RIGHT: *Ritual dagger (phurpa) ivory, silver, carnelian, possibly Eastern Tibet, 17th century. Daggers are used in Tibetan Buddhist rituals to exorcize evil spirits, and often feature frightening imagery such as snakes, skulls and wrathful faces.*

TIBET AND NEPAL

LEFT: *Comb with Hindu god Vishnu, Nepal, ivory, c. 1725.*

CHINA

IVORY HAS BEEN carved artistically in China since at least 5,000 BC, when the Asian elephant inhabited northern China. Excavations of some of the oldest tombs of the Shang (1500–1027 BC) and Zhou dynasties (1050–221 BC) have unearthed ivory hair pins, beads, sword fittings, dagger hilts, jewelry and vessels with decoration similar to that of contemporary jades and bronzes.

By the time of the cosmopolitan Tang dynasty (618–906), ivory was considered desirable as a trade and tribute good and was supplied to China from Thailand, Burma and Malaysia. Chinese ivory carving and inlay are believed to have achieved a high level of sophistication, and it is recorded that imperial carriages were inlaid with ivory, jade and other precious materials. The Shosoin, Japan's 8th century Imperial Repository in Nara, houses musical instruments made using ivory and probably of Tang Chinese origin. Buddhist figures were also carved out of ivory using stone sculptures as models.

Very little material can be dated to the Song (960–1279) or Yuan (1279–1368) dynasties, although a government bureau was established under the Yuan for carvings of ivory and rhinoceros horn, so fine quality objects surely existed. In particular, ivory Buddhist statuary appears to have been significant. Ivory carving flourished during the Ming dynasty (1368–1644). Both African ivory, brought to China by Arab traders, and

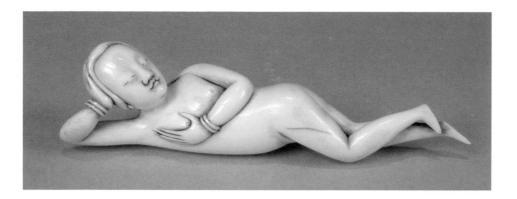

ABOVE: 'Medicine Lady', China, 19th century.
Early Western texts describe these figurines as
tools used by a Chinese lady when visiting the
doctor; she would point to the spot on the
figure's body where she felt pain. Most scholars
now believe that these figures were actually
modelled on ivory carvings of the Holy Child, as
they share identical poses and the Holy Child is
often depicted with long hair. Unlike their
Christian prototypes, however, these female
figures were likely used as erotic toys.

ABOVE: God of Longevity (Shoulao), late Ming
dynasty. One of the Daoist deities most often
represented in ivory, Shoulao is usually depicted
with a long head, to suggest his advanced age,
and a deer by his side.

Asian ivory from India and Southeast Asia were carved at Court and in workshops in
southern China, in particular the port of Zhangzhou in Fujian province. The more
functional Ming ivories were small cases, gaming pieces, incense boxes, jewelry and
toggles, as well as some items for the scholar's desk, chiefly brush pots, wrist rests and
seals. The end mounts on the dowels for scroll paintings were also often made of ivory.
Around the mid-16th century, Portuguese Christians and traders established a presence
in southern China. Because of the long tradition of Christian ivory carvings in Europe,
southern Chinese carvers soon began producing ivory Christian icons for the Portuguese
settlers and for export to the Spanish in the Philippines. These Christian images were
modelled on earlier European figures and similar carvings from the Portuguese colony
of Goa in India.

These Christian images may have influenced local non-Christian ivory figure carvings,
most notably of the Buddhist deity, Guanyin. Another female ivory figure that may relate to
Christian ivory carvings is the so-called 'doctor's model' or 'medicine lady', a naked or semi-
naked woman reclining on her right side with her head supported by her right arm. These
dolls were likely enjoyed by the Chinese as erotica, although this was not how they were
marketed to relatively prudish foreign visitors. As well as the Christian-inspired figures,

ABOVE and RIGHT: *Cricket cages made from gourds with pierced ivory lids, China. The designs of dragons and flowers on the lid are pierced to allow air into the container.*

ABOVE: *Brush pot with carved decoration, China, 19th century. Brush pots were often decorated with carved or incised scenes of scholars in a landscape.*

ivory images of Buddhist and Daoist deities, particularly Buddhist *luohan* (sages), and the Eight Daoist Immortals, were abundant in the Ming and Qing (1644–1911) dynasties.

In the Qing dynasty, the Chinese imported much ivory from Southeast Asia and from India via the Europeans. Imperial workshops in the capital and commercial workshops in southern China produced an extraordinary variety of ivory objects. For the scholar's desk, ivory brush pots, wrist rests, seals, table screens and boxes were particularly popular. The various paraphernalia associated with snuff, including boxes, bottles and trays, were also carved from ivory, as were cricket cages or the pierced lids for cages made of gourds.

Some of the most elaborate Qing ivories were made in response to the European taste for things both 'Oriental' and rococo in style. From the 18th century, ivory model pagodas, temples, boats and chess sets were exported to European aristocrats in large numbers. Pierced ivory baskets, devil's balls, pierced baskets and folding ivory fans were also widely sought after. In addition to the ivory objects, many Europeans purchased or commissioned furniture inlaid with ivory, including beds, chairs, tables and cabinets.

JAPAN DOES NOT HAVE an ancient tradition of ivory carving. The earliest ivories found in Japan are the ivory items, probably Chinese in origin, in the 8th-century Shosoin Repository in Nara. Over the centuries, small numbers of objects including personal seals, the ends of scroll rollers, lids for small tea caddies, plectrums (for plucking stringed instruments) and small Buddhist images were made from ivory.

Japan's most celebrated ivory carvings are the small toggles known as *netsuke* designed to be used with the *inro*, small containers worn suspended from the *kimono* sash during the Edo period (1600–1868). Most *netsuke* are made of wood or ivory and are small enough to clutch in the palm. Many are carved in the round, but a type known as *manju*, as their form resembles a flat, sweet bun of that name, feature designs in low and high relief. Typical motifs are animals, mythical beings, comical characters, folk deities and demons. At the peak of *netsuke* carving, in the 18th and 19th centuries, carvers, often descendants of carvers of Buddhist statues and theatrical masks, characters incised or carved their signatures into a corner of the toggle.

In the second half of the 19th century, Japan opened its doors to the West. During the Meiji period (1868–1912), ivory carvers were suffering from a decline in demand for *netsuke* from the Japanese, who were increasingly wearing Western clothing with pockets. They found a new market in the Westerners who were fascinated by Japanese culture, and began to carve figures of Japanese people engaged in traditional activities to sell to foreigners.

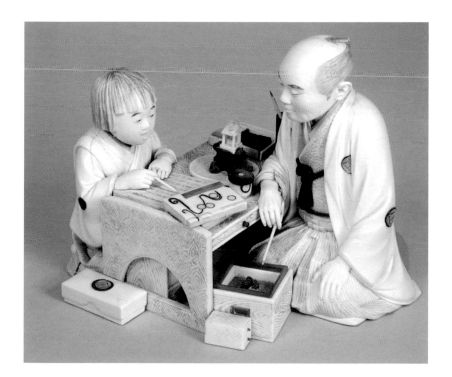

ABOVE: *Netsuke toggle of a monkey contemplating a persimmon with beetle, ivory, Japan, 19th century. Since the traditional Japanese* kimono *has no pockets, personal objects were suspended from the obi, or sash, using a braided silk cord that was passed under the obi and anchored at the top with a netsuke.*

LEFT: *Okimono (ornament) of teacher and student, Japan, late 19th century. An okimono was a decorative piece, often placed in a guest room in a house. Many okimono were sold to foreigners as souvenirs.*

ABOVE: *Virgin Mary, Philippines, 17th century. The most popular Christian ivories in the Philippines were painted with mineral pigments on the clothing and hair, although some are created naked and then dressed and decorated with jewels by worshippers.*

The Philippines

Although Spanish records note that the Filipinos crafted religious statuary, jewelry and weapons out of ivory, there is sparse evidence of a thriving ivory carving tradition in the Philippines before the arrival of the Spanish in the 16th century. The Spanish promoted Christianity to the local people and brought with them Christian images in wood and ivory from Spain. Southern Chinese ivory carvers from ports such as Zhangzhou began to settle in Manila and by the 1590s were carving Christian figurines, known as *santos*, for the Spanish. Their ivory carving skills were eventually passed on to the Filipinos, and in the 18th and 19th centuries, ivory carving was done entirely by Filipino artists. Like the Chinese Christian ivories, those made in the Philippines were modelled closely on examples from Europe and Goa.

Indonesia

Although ivory carving is not one of the major artistic traditions of Indonesia, it should be mentioned that in Java and Bali, many elaborate ivory handles were created for ceremonial swords known as *kerises*. These were often carved with magnificent designs of deities and mythical beings and embellished with inset precious and semi-precious gems.

Thailand

Elephants have inhabited Thailand for 15 million years, and they have been abundant in the region until recent decades. Despite the relative availability of ivory in Thailand, it appears that much of it was traditionally exported to countries such as China. At Ban Chiang in Udon Thani Province in northeastern Thailand, excavations have revealed ivory beads dating to 3600 BC. Ivory bracelets and combs have been excavated from sites dating up until AD 200, but following this period, very little evidence exists of ivory working before the 18th century, when ivory Buddhist imagery and furniture were made.

During the reign of King Rama V (1868–1910), many ivory objects were carved for the royal court, including weapon handles, musical instruments, game pieces and jewelry. Since that time, both the court and Buddhist temples have patronized ivory carvers, resulting in many elaborate carvings of Buddhist deities, mythical creatures and elephants, as well as furnishings and sword fittings.

Burma

In Burma, another country that was once home to many elephants, evidence of a continuous ivory carving tradition is also scarce. A small ivory Burmese Buddha has been dated to the 12th or 13th century, and the Shan people of Kachin State in the north are known to have worked ivory, but very little Burmese ivory predates the 18th century. Ivory carving only began on a large scale around the 1860s in the court of King Mindon (*r.* 1853–78), who

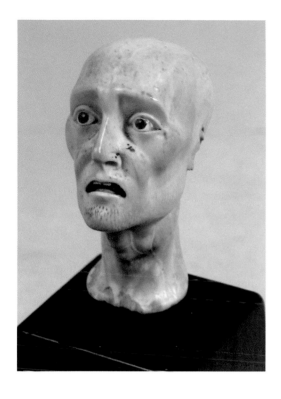

ABOVE: *Head of St Jerome, the Philippines, 19th century. Some of these Philippine santos figures had wooden torsos and heads and limbs of ivory, while others were carved entirely of ivory. Many of these images have realistically carved facial expressions, inlaid glass eyes and even inserted human hair, creating an aura of intense spirituality.*

BELOW RIGHT: *Keris (dagger) handle, Indonesia, 16th century.*

ABOVE: *Bejewelled elephant, with gemstones set in gilt silver, Thailand, 20th century.*

moved his capital to Mandalay. Many of the 19th century ivories carved there were sold to the British, who wanted card cases, cigarette holders, and paper knives, and to the Indians, who preferred ivory bangles and carvings of Hindu deities. Carvings of Buddhist deities were also created in the 19th and 20th centuries and found particular popularity under the Japanese occupiers in the 1940s. Despite the international ban on ivory, the ivories carved in Burma today are generally tourist souvenirs and include entire carved tusks, Buddhist and Daoist deities and erotic subjects.

OPPOSITE: *Detail of bamboo basket entitled Ripple by Kajiwara Koho, Japan, 1998.*

FAR LEFT: *Paper roll holder, Korea. See p. 147.*

LEFT: *Bamboo brush pot, China. See p. 144.*

BELOW: *Fan, Japan. See p. 151.*

BAMBOO

BAMBOO IS ONE of the most universally useful plants on the planet. It can be used to build homes, bridges, boats and furniture and can be made into fishing rods, weapons, containers, musical instruments, paper, clothing, eating utensils, and even food and medicine. What makes it unique among the materials featured in this book is that it is not only the material from which exquisite flower baskets, figurative carvings and other art objects are crafted, but it can also be made into a tool that is used to create art – the brush used for painting or calligraphy – and is even the very subject of the painting itself. The live plant is also an important element in garden design in many parts of Asia. This extraordinary grass probably derives its name from the Malay word for the explosive cracking sound it makes when it burns – 'bam-boo!' Often standing several metres tall, it grows vigorously in most of Asia, mainly China, Japan, India and Southeast Asia. In these regions, bamboo has traditionally been such an integral part of life there that is hard to imagine their cultures without the plant.

The Noble Character of Bamboo

Bamboo is both strong and flexible. In East Asia, it has long symbolized strength, flexibility and integrity of character. Bamboo is grouped with the plum, orchid and chrysanthemum as one of the Four Noble Plants, which represent the virtuous qualities for a scholar and gentleman. More famously, bamboo is one of the Three Friends of Winter – plum, bamboo and pine, which thrive at the most adverse time of the year. Plum blooms when there is still snow on the ground so represents resilience. Bamboo represents a patient, flexible nature, and pine is an evergreen, thus symbolizing long life. Together, these Three Friends also represent the three religious or spiritual traditions of China – Daoism, Buddhism and Confucianism – and their founders, Laozi, the Buddha, and Confucius, respectively. In the illustration below, the Three Friends grace the interior of a Chinese blue and white porcelain bowl from the Ming dynasty.

In some Asian cultures, because bamboo grows like a mother plant surrounded by offspring plants, it is assigned the virtues of a noble and selfless mother who provides nourishment for her children before herself. For this reason, village women in parts of India have traditionally painted bamboo groves on their walls as a prayer for a happy family life. In areas of East and Southeast Asia, a knife made of bamboo has traditionally been used to cut the umbilical cord of a newborn baby.

THERE ARE OVER 1,200 different species of bamboo in Asia. Its main characteristics are the structure of its stem, which grows in sections divided by nodes, its rapid growth, and its singular flowering habits. As a material, it is lightweight, flexible yet strong and can be split with ease in one direction and heated so as to retain a desired shape. In East Asia, as with jade, the physical qualities of the material – primarily its strength and flexibility – have made it a symbol of resilience in the human character.

RIGHT: *Bamboo grove, Hokokuji temple garden, Kamakura, Japan.*

FAR RIGHT TOP: *Bamboo shoot emerging from the ground.*

FAR RIGHT CENTRE: *Leaves growing from node of bamboo.*

FAR RIGHT BOTTOM: *Sympodial clumping bamboo, Bambusa beechiana. With clumping sympodial bamboo, which generally thrives in tropical regions such as Southeast Asia, the short, fat rhizome sends out a shoot (culm) that grows upwards and breaks the ground very close to the mother plant.*

Bamboo Growth

THE WAY BAMBOO GROWS and propagates itself is both unusual and fascinating. The bamboo plant has two main sections; the stem, or culm, which grows above ground and produces branches and leaves, and the rhizome and roots underground, with the rhizome producing new shoots. A bamboo shoot grows out from the rhizome and breaks the ground surface already measuring the diameter of a fully grown plant. It then grows extremely rapidly, sometimes up to 12 inches (30 cm) in a day, attaining its full height in a single growing season of roughly two months. The culm of the bamboo can grow to a few inches or several feet high depending on the species. It is divided into vertical sections by joints, or nodes; the culm is hollow, but the nodes are solid. From the nodes, branches grow outward and sprout leaves, which act like factories using the energy of the sun to break down nutrients and water brought up from the roots to produce food. After the culm has attained full height, it concentrates on reproduction, and plant growth continues underground. Nutrients and water are absorbed by the rhizomes under the ground. The rhizome generates buds which form shoots, and depending on the type of bamboo, these shoots will either grow up right next to the mother plant or at a distance. With clumping sympodial bamboo, which generally grows in tropical regions such as

BAMBOO

ABOVE: *Flower of the Bambusa beechiana. After bamboo flowers, the plant weakens or dies. In 1966, one of Japan's most important bamboo species, madake, bloomed and then died all over the country and in some locations overseas, dealing a considerable blow to the bamboo industry.*

BELOW: *Cut bamboo drying in the sun, Japan. Solid nodes divide the hollow sections.*

Southeast Asia, the short, fat rhizome sends out a shoot (culm) that travels upwards and breaks the ground close to the mother plant. With running monopodial bamboos, which grow prolifically in more temperate countries such as Japan, the long, narrow rhizome travels for several feet underground before sending up a shoot some way from the mother plant creating a complex network of rhizomes underground that strengthens the ground, prevents soil erosion and provides a safe haven during earthquakes.

Reproduction

One of the most unique aspects of the bamboo's growth is its method of reproduction. The type of growth described above involves asexual reproduction, without flowers that produce seeds. However, at one point in the bamboo grove's life cycle, it does produce flowers, but then dies or is greatly weakened. This happens sporadically and unpredictably, depending on the species of bamboo, with some flowering as often as every six or seven years. The flowering can continue for months or even years. What is most remarkable about the flowering is that every plant from a particular species flowers at roughly the same time, even those plants grown in another country from a cutting from the same mother stock, if growing conditions are similar. After a flowering, a grove may die or be greatly weakened from the energy required for the flowers to bloom. However, the flowers produce seeds which, along with any healthy rhizomes still remaining underground, can help to generate a new grove of bamboos.

Shape and Colour

BAMBOOS NATURALLY grow straight and round in cross section, and this basic shape makes cut bamboo infinitely useful for poles used in construction, flutes, brushes, arrows, cups, brush pots, and so on. A few species are slightly square in cross section; in Japan, some larger types are trained to grow square, while others are bound with rope to create distorted surfaces. Bamboos range in colour from golden yellow and green to mahogany and black; many species are striped. The surface of the skin, or outer layer, is generally smooth and light in colour and can be removed to reveal a darker wood underneath. In some bamboos, attractive cloudlike patterns occur naturally on their outer layer.

Harvesting

THE TIMING AND TECHNIQUES used in harvesting bamboo vary from place to place. In Japan, for example, bamboo is generally cut when it is between two and five years old, depending on the species. If it is cut too young, it will be pliant, and if cut too old, the wood will be hard and prone to insect damage. It is generally cut in the cooler months when its starch (and so sugar) content is lower and it is less attractive to insects. In order to remove the remaining moisture from the culm and prevent mould and infection, the bamboo must be left in the sun to dry, or season, for weeks or even months in the case of certain species. In addition, the oil is removed from the culm by heating, steaming, or submerging the bamboo in a chemical solution. This hardens the wood and reduces its starch level, making the material less hospitable to boring beetles and other insects.

ABOVE LEFT: *Carrying large bamboo poles on a bicycle, Vietnam. Larger, wider poles tend to be stronger and are used widely in traditional Asian architecture as walls, roofing, flooring, doors, fences and gates. Shorter, narrower poles are light, strong and pliant and may be used for brushes, arrows and musical instruments.*

ABOVE RIGHT: *Bamboo flower vase, Japan, Edo period (1600–1868). In simple vessels such as this example, the node of the bamboo serves as the base of the vessel.*

BAMBOO

Cutting, Splitting and Weaving

THE INITIAL CUTTING of the bamboo is horizontal or transverse, leaving a long pole that can be used variously depending on its size. Poles are divided into sections several inches long by nodes; inside each node, a diaphragm stretches across the width of the bamboo and seals the section off. To make bamboo pipes, water channels, or flutes, the diaphragm must be removed with a knife or gouge at each node to allow the water or air to pass freely through the bamboo tube. However, for small hollow vessels such as brush pots, flower vases or betel nut containers, the diaphragm is retained in order to serve as the base of the vessel. Nodes often serve a decorative function in architecture or fencing, when a number of poles are aligned with the nodes either at the same height for a formal scheme or at varying heights to create a playful, rhythmic pattern.

In many Asian cultures, bamboo is cut vertically, or split, to create thin strips that can be woven into baskets, mats, furniture, and numerous other items, or even glued or tied together and lacquered to create a wide variety of vessels, both functional and ceremonial. To split small poles, the artist first quarters the culm by cutting four breaches at one end of the bamboo. Once split into long, thin sections, bamboo can be woven into a multitude of objects. Most often it is used to make baskets for carrying and processing food, catching fish or even snakes, or for storing clothing and other personal items. Some of the most elaborate baskets are those made traditionally in China and Japan for floral arrangements. Basketmakers select their bamboo carefully, often travelling to the countryside to find the right bamboo for their basket. They clean it and then split it vertically into narrow, flat strips, often removing some of the flesh from the inside of the bamboo. When a darker colour is desired, basket makers may dye, stain or smoke the bamboo strips prior to weaving. They begin by weaving the base, usually round or square,

ABOVE: *Basket entitled* Galaxy *by Honda Shoryu, Beppu, Japan, 2001. Japanese bamboo basket makers in particular use such a wide variety of bamboos types and weaving techniques that their exquisite flower baskets are often closer to abstract sculpture than functional objects.*

LEFT: *Japanese bamboo basket maker Abe Motoshi starting a basket by weaving from the base outwards and upwards. A number of different weaving and twining techniques can be used to create horizontal, vertical or diagonal patterns in the basket surface, and weaving strips of varying widths may be employed to create designs.*

BAMBOO

ABOVE and RIGHT: *Miniature mountain with pavilions and figures, carved out of the bamboo rhizome, China, Ming dynasty (1368–1644). This Chinese mountain landscape is a masterpiece of bamboo carving. Bamboo carving is similar to wood carving and is executed with knives, chisels, gouges and sometimes small drills. Carvers must be careful to follow the grain of the bamboo; otherwise, surrounding areas may flake and chip off.*

and plaiting the bamboo strips outwards and upwards. For less traditional shapes that require sharp angles, the basketmaker may bend the bamboo strips by holding them over fire. The mortar holding the fibres of the bamboo together becomes flexible and allows bending. Once the strip has been bent, it retains its shape after cooling.

Incising and Carving

ONE OF THE SIMPLEST methods of decorating a bamboo object is to incise designs into the outer layer, or skin, of the bamboo. Pigments may be added to the incised lines to create polychrome designs. More complex carving is also possible on bamboo and requires similar tools and techniques to wood carving. In many Asian cultures, sections of the bamboo culm and the rhizome are carved into figurines or containers bearing designs carved in relief on the surface. In most bamboo carvings, the lighter outer layer of the bamboo is removed before carving, but in some cases, it is retained and incorporated into the design, leaving a lighter pattern contrasting with a darker background.

BAMBOO HAS FLOURISHED in China for thousands of years, and although it once grew abundantly in most regions of China, changes of weather and deforestation in the north gradually drove the plant further south, and it is now found mostly in Zhejiang, Jiangsu and other regions of southern China. A Neolithic Chinese spearhead dating to around 6000 BC is one of the earliest examples of worked bamboo in the world. The Chinese

CHINA

appear to have used bamboo for thousands of years to build homes, bridges and boats and to craft weapons, musical instruments and containers. Of great cultural significance was the early use of bamboo to create China's first books. These early books are made of strips of bamboo, each bearing a single column of characters and bound together side by side with string to form a mat-like roll. It is likely that such bamboo strips were used for writing as early as the Shang dynasty (1500–1027 BC) and account for the vertical direction of Chinese writing, which can be seen on bronze objects from that period.

Baskets, bows, brush handles and other utilitarian objects have been excavated from Chinese tombs dating to the first centuries BC and a number of lacquered bamboo containers, fans, hairpins, bowls and cups have been found in Han dynasty (206 BC–AD 220) tombs, both in China and Chinese colonies in modern North Korea. During the Tang dynasty (618–906), objects were both woven and carved out of bamboo. Tang Chinese musical instruments, brush handles and boxes made of bamboo have been preserved in the Shosoin Imperial Repository in Japan, and later histories tell of a Tang bamboo carver who engraved intricate military scenes on a brush handle.

BAMBOO

LEFT: *Carved bamboo figure of Daoist Immortal with attendants, China, Qing dynasty (1644–1911).*

Bamboo carving, arguably China's greatest bamboo art tradition, blossomed in the Song dynasty (AD 960–1279), though very little material remains from this period. It was at this time that bamboo, with its associations with scholarly ideals such as integrity, simplicity and flexibility, grew popular with Chinese scholars and artists. From the Song well into the Ming dynasty (1368–1644), bamboo was crafted into brushes, brush pots, wrist rests and other items used in traditional painting, calligraphy and poetry composition, three of China's most respected artistic pursuits. In fact, this simple material was generally considered to be more appropriate for scholarly items than more precious materials such as ivory, horn or lacquered wood. Scholars even took to carving bamboo themselves, equating the working of bamboo with a knife with the application of brush and ink to paper. In the Ming dynasty, outstanding bamboo carvings were created at various centres in southern China, many for use by scholarly gentlemen. Bamboo carvers in Zhejiang province pioneered a technique known as 'leaving the skin in relief', in which the lighter coloured outer layer of the bamboo is left standing proud of the darker tone of the carved areas.

During the Qing dynasty (1644–1911), bamboo carving became particularly elaborate and was elevated to a court art, attaining particular sophistication during the reigns of the Qianlong (1736–96) and Jiaqing (1796–1821) emperors. Traditional items such as brush pots, wrist rests and incense burners were decorated with elaborate engraved and carved designs, and figurines of Daoist immortals, Buddhist deities and holy men (Chinese: *luohan*) were produced in large numbers. A fashion for archaism in the 18th century led artists to imitate ancient bronze vessel forms in porcelain, jade, ceramic and even bamboo. Woven flower baskets, made for flower arrangements in the Ming and Qing dynasties, were created to imitate bronze vessel forms, with their dark colouring and tightly woven shapes. Though Chinese furniture has traditionally been made from rosewood, sandalwood and camphor-wood, bamboo has also been used to make household furnishings and was particularly popular in the studios of scholarly gentlemen. By the 18th century, fine bamboo furnishings made from spotted and other rarer bamboos were employed in the homes of the nobility.

BAMBOO HAS BEEN used in Korea from an early date, and has traditionally been grown and worked in the warmer southern part of the Korean peninsula, in particular the southwestern region of Cholla-do. The oldest extant objects are the Chinese lacquered bamboo boxes, bowls and cups found in the tomb of a minor official of the Chinese colony of Lelang (Korean: Nang Nang) near Pyongyang in modern North Korea. Over the centuries, as in the rest of Asia, bamboo has been woven into baskets, mats, hats and other articles and has also been used to make furniture, but very little material predates the late Joseon dynasty (1392–1910).

BAMBOO

KOREA

OPPOSITE: *Bamboo archaic wine vessel (hu), China, 18th century. Throughout Chinese history, ancient bronze ritual vessels have been imitated in porcelain, jade, lacquered wood, glass, and even bamboo. This bamboo example features the monster mask, or taotie, that served a protective function on ancient ritual burial vessels.*

LEFT: *Holder for paper rolls, Korea, 18th to 19th century. Unlike Chinese brush pots and paper holders, Korean examples traditionally combine two, three or more bamboo culms on a wooden base. This example is made from several curved sections of the bamboo culm that have been joined together and mounted on a wooden base. These containers often feature painted, carved and lacquered designs, usually of auspicious creatures, such as cranes and deer representing long life.*

Although bamboo has been a predominant motif in Korean painting and ceramics, it has not occupied a major role as a material in the arts of Korea. However, as in China, bamboo has also been a popular material for articles for the Korean scholar's desk, and in the Joseon dynasty, many brush pots, brush handles, writing boxes and paper holders were crafted from bamboo. On some Korean bamboo items, decorative motifs were burnt or branded onto the bamboo surface with a hot iron in a traditional type of pyrography.

Another traditional Korean use of bamboo is as a veneer for furniture. In the 18th and 19th centuries, mosaic patterns created with sections of bamboo, sometimes of contrasting colours, embellished desks, shelves, wardrobes and tables.

JAPAN

JAPAN HAS VALUED its bamboo arts perhaps more than any other culture. Bamboo grows profusely in Japan and has been used in all aspects of Japanese life for hundreds of years. The earliest bamboo items were woven objects, such as utilitarian baskets for fishing and farming, or objects cut from lengths of bamboo such as brushes, musical instruments, including the *shakuhachi* flute, and bows and arrows; these have changed little and are still used today. The oldest surviving bamboo objects in Japan are the 8th century musical instruments, brush handles; boxes made of bamboo have been preserved in the Shosoin Imperial Repository, but these are most likely Chinese in manufacture.

As in many cultures, bamboo was originally regarded in Japan as a functional but not precious material and so, other than the few Imperial items in the Shosoin, bamboo items

Bamboo and the Japanese Tea Ceremony

Tea masters like Sen Rikyu (1522–92) emphasized simplicity, austerity and humility in the serving of tea. One of the most important aesthetic terms associated with the tea ceremony is wabi, *a term that refers to a cultivated sense of poverty and austerity. Bamboo, a plant that was available for use by even the poorest of farmers, was an ideal material to express the sense of* wabi *in the tea house. Rikyu and other tea masters designed tea rooms with bamboo roofs, doors, window frames and alcove pillars, tea gardens with bamboo fences and gates, and water ladles for cleansing the hands, a feature borrowed from Shinto shrines. Often, these items were created by the most celebrated craftsmen of the day, but they had the appearance of simplicity and humility.*

Some of the most important utensils used in the tea ceremony have been crafted from bamboo, often by the tea masters themselves: simple bamboo spoons for scooping the powdered tea, bamboo ladles for pouring the hot water (above) and delicately split bamboo tea whisks for whisking up the powdered tea in the bowl (right). Tea masters also fashion simple flower vases out of a length of bamboo and decorate the room with a single flower arrangement. Some of these humble bamboo objects, because of their embodiment of tea ceremony principles and their association with particular tea masters or historical figures, are now among the country's national treasures.

were not initially preserved as treasures. However, with the emergence of the tea ceremony as an important cultural and artistic phenomenon in the 15th and 16th centuries, items such as bamboo tea spoons, water ladles, and flower vases were elevated to a high cultural status and many have been treasured and preserved for centuries.

As well as the tea ceremony, flower arrangement, or *ikebana*, also greatly influenced bamboo art in Japan. The art of flower arranging had its beginnings in the offerings of

TOP: *Bamboo water ladle, Japan, 19th–20th century. This ladle is used for pouring hot water in the traditional tea ceremony.*

ABOVE: *Japanese bamboo tea whisk, Japan, 19th–20th century. The finely split bamboo whisk stirs up the powdered tea leaves.*

RIGHT: *Flower basket by Wada Waichisai III, Japan, 20th century. The handle of this basket is made from a single thin bamboo culm that has been shaped with the help of heat. It serves as a reminder of the natural material from which the basket was woven.*

BELOW: *Basket entitled* Afternoon Nap, *by Living National Treasure Iizuka Shokansai, 1979. Iizuka Shokansai was the second bamboo basket maker to be awarded the title of Living National Treasure by the Japanese government in 1982. Of his art, Iizuka says, 'Bamboo is most beautiful when in nature. To split it, to strip it, to shape it, to express its beauty in the world of craft art is hard work but very rewarding. It has taught me a lot.' (from* Contemporary Japanese Bamboo Arts *by Rob Coffland, 1999)*

flowers to Buddhist deities in temples, but became secularized in part due to the spread of the tea ceremony, which encouraged the use of simple flower arrangements in a domestic setting. In the Edo period (1600–1868), woven bamboo became a favourite material for flower arrangement vases and baskets, both in temples and homes. Some of the earlier bamboo flower vases imitated formal Chinese flower baskets, but increasingly Japanese bamboo artists worked in a looser native style to produce vases and baskets that celebrated the natural qualities of bamboo. Although the makers of these flower baskets have traditionally shared many of the same techniques and materials as the makers of domestic and agricultural baskets, these specialized basket makers have been

BAMBOO

regarded more as artists than craftsmen. In the last fifty years, the Japanese government has awarded three of them the title of Living National Treasure.

Japan has produced many other bamboo art works, including brush pots, wrist rests and brush handles in the Chinese tradition, and more traditionally Japanese items such as folding fans and umbrellas, made of paper with a bamboo frame. Various items have been beautifully carved out of bamboo, such as *inro* (small carrying cases), pipes, portable calligraphy sets, all of which were suspended from the *kimono* sash by means of a cord and decorative toggle or *netsuke*, which was also often carved or woven out of bamboo. These items may be coated with lacquer, or left natural to show off the grain of the bamboo.

SOUTHEAST ASIA

Bamboo also thrives in Southeast Asia, and it is the clumping, or sympodial, varieties that are found here due to the tropical climate of many parts of this region. In most cultures in both continental and insular Southeast Asia, bamboo has been indispensable over the centuries in the manufacture of the walls, roofs and furnishings of homes. In fact, entire houses can be constructed out of bamboo in some regions. Throughout Southeast Asia, bamboo has been used along with rattan and pandanus leaves to weave mats for the floors and walls of homes as well as for clothing and containers.

Baskets, in particular, play a significant role in daily and religious life in many regions. Probably the most celebrated bamboo wares of Southeast Asia are the beautiful yet highly functional baskets made in the Cordillera Central of the island of Luzon in the Philippines. Made by a number of cultural groups known collectively as the Igorot peoples, these baskets have been made for centuries for use in agriculture, fishing and daily life. Baskets are the main craft of the indigenous peoples of this region and play a central role in both the daily and ritual aspects of their lives. Woven by both men and women depending on the particular culture, these baskets are used for winnowing rice, carrying crops, catching fish and eels. They are worn as hats and coats as protection from the sun and rain and as back packs for carrying various goods and personal items. They are used to carry new born infants, to hold the remains of the dead and as important containers for rice and meat at weddings.

ABOVE: *Bamboo carrying basket (gimata), Bontoc, the Philippines. Bontoc men attach these carrying baskets to a pole which they lay across their shoulders; they use the baskets to carry sweet potatoes and rice.*

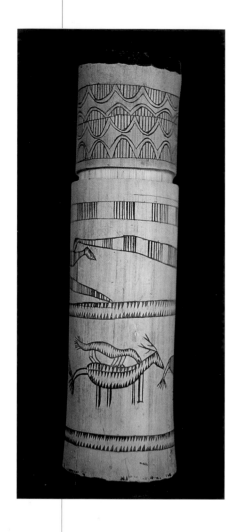

ABOVE: *Betel nut container with incised designs, the Philippines. Betel nut containers, generally referred to as lokub (a Maranao word from the island of Mindanao in the Philippines), usually feature incised designs of animals, birds or geometrical patterns.*

ABOVE RIGHT: *Bamboo strips being made into containers, Chiangmai, Thailand.*

In Thailand, Burma, and Vietnam, strips of bamboo may also be tied or glued together and built up into round, square or even multi-sided vessels, in a technique that is commonly referred to as 'spun bamboo'. After these vessels are constructed, they are coated with lacquer of various colours and used to hold and serve food in homes and in temples as ritual offerings. The strips of bamboo form a pattern that is visible through the lacquer (see p. 111).

In many areas of Southeast Asia, small sections of the bamboo culm have long been fashioned into cylindrical arrow cases, document holders and containers for chewing tobacco and betel nut. The custom of betel chewing is widespread in Southeast Asia. In Indonesia and the Philippines in particular, the betel nut cases of the lower classes have traditionally been made from bamboo and incised with lively designs. Patterns may also be burnt into the outer layer of the bamboo. In the Philippines colourful patterns are created on the surface of the bamboo by pasting coloured paper cuts around the tube and applying water to the paper with a sponge to transfer the dye onto the bamboo.

Throughout Southeast Asia, many musical instruments such as flutes, pipes and percussion instruments are also crafted out of bamboo. The covers of palm leaf Buddhist books are often cut from bamboo and decorated with religious symbols. Significantly, throughout the region, it has been traditional to cut the umbilical cord of a new born baby with a knife made from bamboo. These knives may be decorated with incised or burnt patterns. In addition, household furnishings, made from large and small bamboo poles, are made throughout Southeast Asia. Chairs, tables, beds, lamps, screens and blinds are currently crafted out of bamboo to meet the growing demand for bamboo furnishings in the West.

Bamboo in Traditional East Asian Gardens

Many types of bamboo are an important element of garden design. In particular, smaller, narrow bamboos and a short, shrub-like bamboo variety known in Japan as sasa, are selected for their colour, the shape of their leaves and their growth patterns. Japanese gardens, for example, are traditionally tranquil environments, and the soft rustling sound of bamboo leaves in the breeze enhances the sense of calm. In a traditional Chinese scholar's garden, bamboo might be used more symbolically, often alongside plum and pine to remind the scholar of the qualities he should cultivate in himself (see 'The Noble Character of Bamboo', p. 136). Bamboo may also be planted along a white wall so that the shadows of the plant play on the wall and evoke a sense of mist.

Cut bamboo has also been a key element in garden design in many parts of Asia. Fences, gates, path and border markers and armatures are often made of bamboo poles tied together with wire and decorative rope to create a patterned structure. At the edge of the garden or property, these fences are typically solid to ensure privacy, but on the inside, they are usually transparent, allowing views across the garden through the patterned bamboo framework. In Japan, bamboo fences are an art form, and particular aristocratic residences and Buddhist temples have their own unique fencing styles and patterns.

ABOVE: *Detail of garden fence, Japan. The patterned forms of bamboo fences are considered important components in the garden's design.*

LEFT: *Bamboo in a traditional Japanese garden, Shirnbudo, Kyoto. The rustling of leaves and the gentle swaying motion of the bamboo in the breeze enhance the tranquillity of the traditional Japanese garden.*

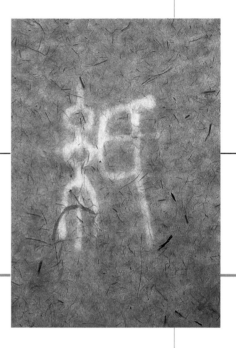

PAPER

PAPER IS MADE from plant fibres that are mashed into a pulp and then felted together into a sheet using a sieve-like screen. Although not as inherently precious as some of the other materials featured in this book, paper is one of the most important materials ever created in Asia, not only in terms of the creation of art, but for the progress of human civilization. Its invention in China over 2,000 years ago led to the creation of lightweight, inexpensive books that have been the most effective method of storing and disseminating thoughts and information until our current electronic age. The softness and absorbency of paper also led to the development of printing, which allows multiple editions of the same text to be produced quickly and inexpensively, another boon to education and civilization.

OPPOSITE: *Detail of Japanese paper with spiral pattern, 20th century. See p. 162.*

ABOVE LEFT: *Detail of paper umbrella, Japan, 20th century.*

ABOVE CENTRE: *Detail of four-panel screen, Korea. See p. 167.*

ABOVE RIGHT: *Detail of traditional Japanese paper embossed with character kami for paper, Japan, 20th century.*

LEFT: *Painting in ink on paper of a plum blossom, China, 18th century. This painting on paper was mounted on a vertical hanging scroll and hung on a wall of a home or scholar's studio, to be viewed by all who entered the room.*

ABOVE: *Travelling to the Southern Sacred Peak, hand scroll, ink and colour on paper, China, Middle Qing dynasty, about 1700–1800. Landscapes became a popular subject for scholar-artists in China during the Song dynasty. Paintings were often mounted as hand scrolls, made of a number of sheets glued together to form a horizontal roll. Hand scrolls are viewed by a small number of people at once and are unrolled from right to left, with about an arm's length of the image visible at one time.*

IN ASIAN ART, paper has worked harmoniously with brush and ink for about 2,000 years in the creation of painting and calligraphy, two of the most respected art forms of the region. It has also been one of the principal materials used in the woodblock printed texts and images produced widely in East Asia. Furthermore, paper has served to cover functional yet beautiful items such as fans and umbrellas, lamps, windows and screen doors. Decorative papers have been used for letter writing, wrapping and presenting gifts have, and items made of folded or cut paper have been significant in religious rituals and as decoration for the home. Paper is also used widely in play, with many cultures producing toys, kites and masks out of colourfully dyed and painted paper and in papier maché. Perhaps more than any other material, paper has allowed for the creation of art works for all levels of society and for all areas of life.

THE MATERIAL

MUCH OF THE PAPER we use today is made from wood pulp. In Asia, paper is traditionally made from plant fibres that are softened into a pulp and felted together on a mat or screen. Because the fibres are not broken down, but retain their length and become interwoven with each other during the papermaking process, traditional Asian papers tend to be strong as well as textured. Over the centuries, different regions in Asia have

Cai Lun and the Invention of Paper

Paper was invented in China during the Han dynasty (206 BC–AD 220). Since around the 2nd century BC, the Chinese had made a paper-like material from soaking and pounding plant fibres and rags, but it was not light enough to provide a good writing surface. The official invention of paper is generally credited to a Chinese government official and eunuch called Cai Lun (c. AD 50–121), who pioneered paper made from the pulp of mulberry bark (see illustration below right). According to tradition, the Han Emperor Hedi (AD 79–106) sought a writing surface that was both portable and inexpensive and instructed Cai Lun to perfect paper. Cai Lun was from Hunan province in southern China, where locals made cloth by soaking and beating mulberry bark fibres. He likely adapted this practice by making pulp from the bark fibres and mixing the pulp in a water suspension, which he then poured onto a bamboo screen to form paper sheets. In 105, the Emperor officially announced the invention of paper, and Cai Lun was handsomely rewarded. Since then, he has been the patron saint of papermakers in China.

After paper technology was perfected in China, it soon spread to neighbouring countries, reaching Vietnam and Korea around the 3rd century and Japan in the 7th. It also reached India in the 7th century, Western Asia in the 8th century and Africa in the 10th century. It was first made in Europe in the 12th century – 1,000 years after its invention in China – the Americas in the 16th century and Australia in the 19th century. It is now produced throughout the world from a variety of fibres.

ABOVE: *Cai Lun, the Chinese government official credited with the invention of paper in the 2nd century AD; woodblock printed image.*

BELOW: *Bundles of paper mulberry fibres showing white inner bark, Japan.*

made paper from different fibres. In China in the early years of papermaking, hemp, paper mulberry (*Brousonetia papyrifera*) and rattan were commonly used; later, paper mulberry and bamboo were the most widely used fibres. In Japan, paper mulberry has been the predominant fibre, although *gampi*, a type of daphne, and *mitsumata* have also been significant. In India, paper has mostly been made using hemp, jute and linen, but paper mulberry, bamboo, cotton, recycled rags have also been important. In Southeast Asia, depending on the region, paper mulberry, daphne, bamboo and rice straw have traditionally been employed.

There is a popular misconception that rice paper is used for Asian art works such as Chinese paintings and Japanese woodblock prints. It should be noted that Asian paper is rarely made from rice, as this type of paper is very brittle. Occasionally, rice straw and husks have been used to make low grade paper. Papermakers have been known to add rice powder to paper pulp to increase its whiteness, but since this powder can attract insects, it is generally avoided.

RIGHT: *Woodblock print depicting a papermaking village, Japan, 20th century.*

FAR RIGHT: *Steaming the fibres in a wooden vat, Japan, 20th century.*

OPPOSITE: *Detail of a 19th century Japanese printed book illustrating the papermaking process. A seated man beats the fibre pulp; women dip screens into a vat containing the water and pulp mixture; the prepared sheets are piled together on a table; another woman lays a sheet of paper out on a board to dry. Behind her are bundles of paper packed up ready for despatch. Two men (on the right) prepare to carry away bound packages of paper to be sold.*

TECHNIQUES

Preparing the Fibres

METHODS VARY IN all Asian cultures, but they share some common techniques – the macerating of the fibres, the creation of pulp, and the draining of the pulp through a screen to create sheets. Japanese papermakers have used the same techniques for centuries, and their methods are well documented and widely imitated. The following is the traditional method for making paper from the paper mulberry plant, *kozo*, in Japan.

The plant is harvested and the bark removed, tied into bundles and steamed in wooden barrels to soften and loosen the fibres. The three layers of bark are separated: first, the outer black layer is removed; then the green layer is scraped away with a knife. The more green bark is removed, the whiter the finished paper will be. The remaining white bark is dried in a cool, shaded area, then soaked and bleached, traditionally in the sunlight. The fibres are then cooked for about two hours in a solution of water and an alkaline substance extracted from wood ash (pot ash) – slaked lime, soda ash, caustic soda, or lye are generally used nowadays. The alkaline solution breaks down the fibres into long strands and eliminates lignin, which cause the fibre to turn yellow over time. A stronger alkali dissolves non-cellulose materials in the fibres, resulting in a soft paper, while using a weaker alkali results in a paper with more body. Any remaining impurities are removed, and the fibres are bleached, traditionally by the sun, but more recently using chemical bleach. The fibres are then beaten on a stone with a wooden mallet.

160

機篁家玄紙

敷古まて玄を光て不る不多い上剥・妻妻蕃
かいまな
分り・妻妻蕃・剥・鼠・大廣・れか廣・和あき
つやあ・雲班・天長・大鼻・中たり・小引
あれも紙の杜ろ～つやさてつう・凡日かう
ちぶ紙のくやさてつう・凡日かう紙るわく出る中よ
なおまを多濠ぶと～實玄の和内額村をつ兜ふす紙を上割し

Forming Sheets of Paper

THE FIBRE PULP is mixed into a vat of water creating a water suspension. To form sheets of paper, the papermaker uses a wooden frame and sieve-like bamboo screen that fits into the frame. Typically, the entire frame is dipped into the water suspension and drawn up, catching some of the pulp on the surface of the screen, while the water drains away. This can be done in two different ways. The older 'accumulation method' was originally developed in China: the pulp is mixed into a water suspension and the frame is lowered into the mixture, picking up enough pulp on the screen to make a single sheet of paper.

The second method, *nagashizuki*, or the 'discharge method', was developed in Japan around the 8th century. First, *neri*, a slimy substance made from the root of the *tororo-aoi* plant, a member of the hibiscus family, is added to the pulp and water mixture. This coats the fibres and prevents them from adhering to each other. It also thickens the

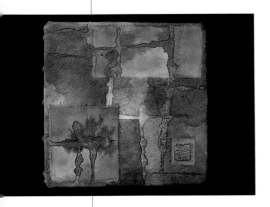

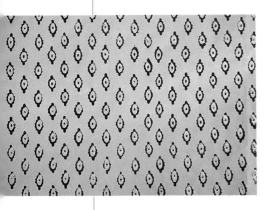

LEFT: *(from top to bottom) Japanese paper with bark fibre pattern; lamp with hand-dyed paper, Japan; woodblock printed paper, Pakistan; Japanese decorative papers, Kyoto. All 20th century. See 'Decorating Paper', below.*

mixture and slows down the draining process. When the papermaker picks up the pulpy mixture with the screen, instead of simply letting the mixture accumulate, he sloshes the mixture rapidly back and forth across the screen to form the sheet. This allows the fibres to become interwoven, thus strengthening the paper. The fibre settles and the step is repeated until the desired thickness is achieved. Any excess pulp is cast away.

Once a sheet of paper is formed on the screen, it is removed and placed onto a pile of new papers to drain naturally overnight. Then the sheets are pressed for several hours to

Decorating Paper

Most paper is white or close to white in colour, since it is made to be used as a surface for written or printed texts and images. However, handmade Asian papers are often exquisitely decorated and are used for gift wrapping, paper folding or for special decorations. One of the most subtle and natural types of paper decoration is the use of fibre or vegetable matter within the paper itself. In traditional Japanese paper, for example, long strands of the bark fibre are introduced into the pulp mixture on the screen and arranged to create a pattern on the paper surface (see left, top, and p. 156). Leaves, dried flowers and gold leaf or powder are also laid or sprinkled into the pulp mixture to create decorative details.

Paper may also be dyed using natural or chemical pigments, sometimes by dipping the paper into these pigments, or by applying the pigments to the paper surface with a brush, as can be seen in this lamp, made with handmade and handpainted Japanese paper (see left, second from top). Many decorative papers feature printed patterns, traditionally applied using wood blocks, such as this wrapping paper from Pakistan (see left, third from top). Some of the most intricate printed designs are on the colourful Japanese papers made for gift wrapping or origami making; the designs often relate closely to patterns on textiles (see left, bottom). On a larger scale, the Chinese produced wallpaper with elaborate handpainted and printed designs.

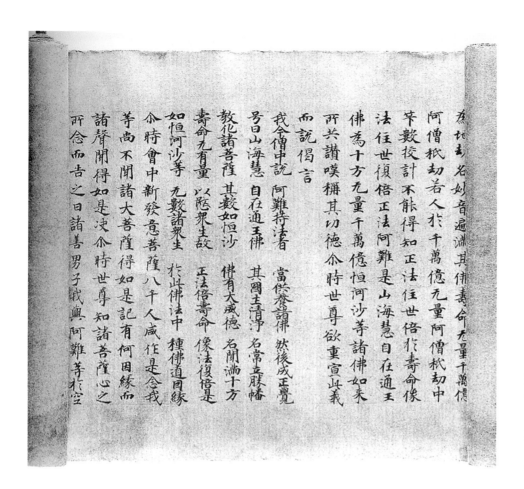

PAPER

LEFT: *Lotus Sutra from Dunhuang, Tang dynasty, 7th century. One of the most important repositories of early Chinese paper items was the Buddhist cave temple complex of Dunhuang in Western China on the old Silk Road. Excavated by Europeans in the early 20th century, the cave revealed over 30,000 paper books and documents made from hemp and mulberry fibres. They were primarily Buddhist, Daoist and Confucian texts and paintings dating from the 4th century to the 10th century* AD.

remove additional moisture. Because the sheets are individually strong and are not generally sticky, they do not adhere to each other. Finally, the sheets are separated and placed one by one on drying boards and left outside to be dried and bleached by the sun.

CHINA

THE EARLIEST SURVIVING paper fragments were found in northern China and date to the 2nd century BC; true paper is believed to have been invented in AD 105 (see p. 159). Over the centuries, paper replaced silk, bamboo and the early paper-like materials as the principal writing surface. Early paper was made primarily of hemp and mulberry bark, although rattan was also used widely in southern China. Paper was used for writing, painting and ink rubbings of stone inscriptions, and in many colours, with some dyes protecting against insects. It was also crafted into umbrellas, fans, kites and lamps.

During the Tang dynasty (618–906), China experienced a period of political stability and economic prosperity. The government officially promoted scholarship, causing an increased demand for paper. To meet this demand, the government required that several regions, particularly in southern China, pay tribute to the Imperial Court in

眼觸為緣所生諸受善非善增語及耳鼻舌
身意觸為緣所生諸受善非善增語此增語
既非有如何可言即眼觸為緣所生諸受若
善若非善增語是菩薩摩訶薩即耳鼻舌身
意觸為緣所生諸受若善若非善增語是菩
薩摩訶薩善現汝復觀何義言即眼觸為緣

ABOVE: *Greater Sutra of the Perfection of Wisdom, woodblock print, ink on paper, China, Song dynasty. By the 11th and 12th centuries, many Chinese Buddhist texts were printed onto paper using woodblocks, enabling the widespread dissemination of Buddhist teachings.*

ABOVE RIGHT: *Rubbing of Spring Purification Festival at the Orchid Pavilion, China, 17th-century rubbing of a 16th-century stone engraving, based on an 11th-century painting. Rubbings are taken by applying damp paper to the stone surface. The paper is squeezed into the lines, so that when inked, the sunken areas remain white against a black ground.*

paper. Around the late 7th century, woodblock printing was invented, resulting in the publication of large numbers of official texts by the government and of religious texts by Buddhist and Daoist temples. Printing also led to the invention of paper currency around the 8th or 9th century. Paper replicas of money and worldly goods were made for use in funerals and sacrificial ceremonies, where they were burnt as offerings to the spirits.

In the Song dynasty, paper remained a desirable commodity, and the Imperial Court continued to demand yearly tributes in paper. By this time, supplies of rattan were exhausted in southern China, so papermakers turned to bamboo as a raw material. Under the encouragement of the Imperial Court, the arts of paper – painting, calligraphy and printing – flourished. Paper was named as one of the Four Treasures of the Scholar's Studio, along with the brush, ink and ink stone, and was favoured by scholar-artists as a material over silk, while artists of the Court still preferred luxurious silk. Paintings of landscapes, birds and flowers were executed on paper and silk by both types of artists and mounted on hanging scrolls, hand scrolls, fans and in albums. Large numbers of religious and secular books were printed for wide distribution. Poems written in elegant

calligraphy, and rubbings taken on paper of ancient texts carved into stone, were also admired and collected.

During the Ming dynasty (1368–1644), the paper mills of southern China remained the principal producers of paper from bamboo, while mulberry bark was the main ingredient in other regions. Artists continued to create paintings and calligraphy on paper, while a large quantity of paper was used to print civil service examinations – records claim almost 17,000 sheets a year. An increasingly literate population created a demand for printed books. In the late Ming dynasty, some books were printed in colour, the world's first examples of colour printing. Handmade paper continued to be used widely in the Qing dynasty (1644–1911) for painting and calligraphy, official documents and religious texts. Some of the finest was the stiff yellow paper used for official announcements. Many of these papers were decorated with the imperial dragon and scented with sandalwood and other fragrances. In the 18th and 19th centuries, painted and printed wallpaper was admired by visiting Europeans. In the mid-19th century, the same Europeans brought paper made by machine from wood pulp. This paper was much less expensive and led to the demise of many Chinese paper mills.

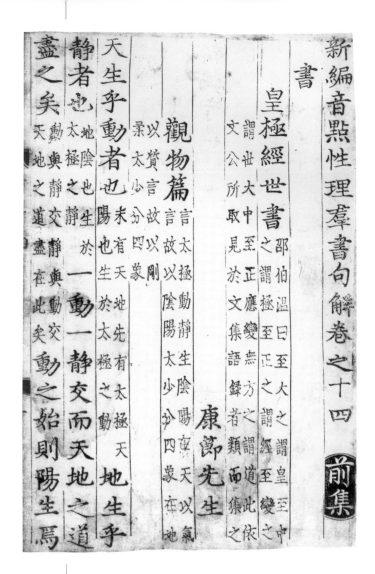

KOREA

PAPER WAS PROBABLY INTRODUCED to Korea from China by the 3rd century AD and was certainly being made in Korea by the 6th century AD, since a Korean monk is said to have introduced papermaking to Japan in AD 610. The Koreans made paper using the same techniques as the Chinese and many of the same materials, including hemp, rattan, bamboo, and especially paper mulberry. The earliest surviving example of Korean paper was discovered in North Korea and dates to the Goguryeo period (37 BC–AD 668); it is a glossy white paper made from hemp fibres. Later, by the 7th and 8th centuries, Korean paper was of such fine quality that it was sent as a tribute item by the Koreans to the Tang Court and was highly praised by Chinese artists and scholars.

For centuries, paper has been used in Korea for painting, calligraphy, and books. Early in their history, the Koreans excelled at printing on paper, and the earliest datable example of woodblock printed text has been found in Korea. The Buddhist text was found inside a

pagoda dating to around AD 750 but may be of Chinese origin. A complete set of 81,258 woodblocks dating to the 13th century was used to print the entire Buddhist *Tripitaka* and is still preserved at the Haein-sa temple in South Korea. A century later, movable-type printing was invented in Korea, first using wood characters in the 14th century and then metal characters by the early 15th century.

Like the Chinese, Korean artists have painted on both silk and paper. Korean calligraphers have also excelled in the writing of beautiful Chinese inscriptions or texts in their own native alphabet, *hangul*, which was invented in the 15th century. Some of the finest Korean paintings on paper are landscapes and bird and flower images reminiscent of Chinese examples, but with a native Korean style. Some of the most outstanding works on paper by Korean artists are the screen paintings of books and objects associated with the scholar.

ABOVE: *Scholar's books and objects (Ch'aekkori), pair of four-panel screens, ink and colour on paper, Korea, end of the Joseon period, about 1800–1910. In these screen paintings, which graced the studios of upper class scholars, paper is not only the medium for the painting, but, in the form of scholarly books, the subject of the painting itself.*

PAPER

JAPAN

ACCORDING TO EARLY Japanese historical texts, Chinese papermaking techniques were introduced to Japan in 610 by a Korean Buddhist monk and doctor known in Japanese as Doncho. Japanese rulers soon encouraged the cultivation of hemp for the production of paper. Bark from *gampi*, a type of daphne that grows in the wild, was also used. By the 8th century, two innovations in papermaking led to the emergence of true Japanese paper, or *washi*. The first was the addition of wood ash to the boiling bark fibres, and the second was the discharge, or *nagashizuki*, technique (see pp. 161–62). Soon, almost 200 different kinds of paper, including papers of different colours, were being made in Japan.

In Japan's native Shinto religion, priests associated pure white paper with sacred places and objects inhabited by higher beings. Coincidentally, the Japanese word for paper, *kami*, has the same pronunciation as the word for higher being, *kami*, and this undoubtedly led to an emotional connection between the two. Shinto priests still mark off sacred spaces believed to be inhabited by *kami* using folded strips of white paper.

However, it was in the context of Buddhism that paper gained great importance. By the 8th century, Buddhism was sponsored by the State as the national religion. Monks and lay practitioners copied out *sutras* (sacred texts) on paper and offered them to temples to attain merit. The introduction of woodblock printing from China facilitated the spread of Buddhist texts and images throughout the nation.

Developments in papermaking and use were associated increasingly with the Imperial Court. In the Heian period (794–1185), the Court moved to Kyoto and established Imperial paper mills that produced high quality paper primarily out of mulberry bark. This paper was used not only for government documents but by aristocrats for poetry composition, calligraphy and love letters. Some papers of this period were dyed in a wide range of colours, while others featured painted or stencilled designs or with flecks of gold and silver. Some contained flowers and fabrics and even perfume. These papers were often combined to form a patchwork of different colours and textures arranged to complement a calligraphic inscription. Paintings mounted as vertical hanging scrolls or horizontal hand scrolls were also enjoyed by the Court, and paper was incorporated into architecture in the form of translucent white *shoji* screens, opaque *fusuma* sliding doors that often featured paintings, and folding *byobu* screens.

PAPER

RIGHT: *A scene of young lovers by Suzuki Harunobu (1724–70), full colour woodblock print on paper, Japan, c. 1765. Credited with the development of full-colour woodblock printing in Japan, Harunobu depicted many scenes of the pleasure quarters in his prints. A young couple is shown parting after a night of pleasure. All around them are articles made of paper – shoji screen doors, a paper lamp and a paper fan.*

BELOW: South Wind at Clear Dawn, *from the series* The Thirty-Six Views of Mount Fuji *by Katsushika Hokusai (1769–1840), full colour woodblock print on paper, c. 1830. Unlike the paintings on paper and silk produced by renowned artists for sale to the wealthy, these mass-produced prints were not considered valuable art works in Japan. Western interest in the prints from the late 19th onwards transformed them into great treasures.*

During the Edo period (1600–1868), papermaking centres increased throughout Japan, making paper more generally available. In the late 16th century, the *mitsumata* fibre became very important in Japanese papermaking as it produces fine quality paper. As Japan's population grew more literate, woodblock printed guidebooks, literary, and historical texts were produced in the thousands. Woodblock prints depicting pictures of the Pleasure Quarters, or Floating World (Japanese: *ukiyo-e*), were particularly popular during the 17th and 18th centuries. Later, a wide interest in the landscape of Japan led to the production of landscape prints designed by some of Japan's most famous artists.

With the increased availability of paper, great numbers of items were made of paper, from architectural elements such as screen doors and windows to practical items such as fans and containers. Paper was often coated in lacquer to render it waterproof, so could be made into objects used outdoors, such as the lanterns and lamps that illuminated Japanese streets and homes, and the paper umbrellas that protected people from sun and rain (see p. 157). Even waterproof clothing was occasionally made out of paper, and paper stencils reinforced with persimmon juice were used to apply patterns onto *kimono* (see pp. 59–61). Toys, kites, masks and dolls were crafted from paper or papier maché.

BEFORE THE ADVENT of paper to India, writing surfaces included clay, stone, metal, tree bark, leaves, wood, leather, bones and cloth. Early books were made from the palm leaf, which was a rectangular shape and inscribed with a stylus; the leaves were then pierced, a cord was passed through and used to bind the whole together. Paper may have been known in India by the second half of the 7th century, having been transmitted via Tibet, where paper had been used since AD 650. However, the first recorded use of paper in India dates to the 11th century, when Jewish and probably Muslim merchants exported paper from Egypt and Arabia to their colleagues in Gujarat in Western India.

Very little early paper from the Indian subcontinent has survived. The earliest known paper mills were established in Kashmir in the 15th century. The fibres used for papermaking varied with each region, but fibres such as hemp, sunn-hemp (a local hemp),

SOUTH ASIA, HIMALAYAS

BELOW: *'Three Monks' folio from the Kalpasutra (Book of Sacred Precepts), opaque watercolour and gold on paper, India, c. 1475. Some of the earliest paper books in India were made in the same shape and size as earlier long, rectangular palm leaf manuscripts.*

ABOVE: Babur Marches from Kabul to Hindustan in 1507 (1589–90), from a Baburnama (Story of Babur) manuscript, illustrates an episode from the life of the first Mughal emperor Babur (r. 1526–30).

ABOVE RIGHT: Mughal prince, ink and opaque watercolours on paper, Indian, Mughal period, 17th cenutry. This painting of a prince is a fine example of the minute brushwork used by the master painters of the Mughal court.

jute and flax were widely used, as were cotton and bamboo in some regions. Papermakers in India have traditionally recycled old rags, rope bags and fishing nets, breaking them down into a pulp and forming paper sheets from them. The quality of traditional paper has varied from rough, thick sheets to extremely thin, fine papers that are polished to create a smooth surface.

It was during the Mughal dynasty (1526–1857) that papermaking truly flourished in the Indian subcontinent, as the Muslim Mughal emperors highly valued the arts of the book and illustrations on paper and commissioned and collected large numbers of beautiful manuscripts and albums (see p. 173). Illustrated religious and poetic manuscripts had been produced for centuries in workshops for Jain and Hindu patrons of all classes. In addition, brightly coloured paper has long been used in India to make

Mughal Miniature Painting and the Muslim Papermakers of India

The Mughal emperors of India were great patrons of the arts of the book and sponsored some of Asia's most exquisite works of art on paper. In the tradition of contemporary Islamic rulers, such as Ottoman Turks and the Safavid Persians, the Mughals commissioned copies of the Koran written in exquisite Arabic calligraphy, as well as famous Persian poetic and literary texts and dynastic histories. Babur Marches from Kabul to Hindustan in 1507 (opposite left) from a Baburnama (Story of Babur) manuscript, painted in 1589–90, illustrates an episode from the life of the first Mughal emperor Babur (ruled 1526–30). Mughal paintings were often not much larger than the size of a modern postcard and painted with ink, opaque watercolours and gold using brushes made of fine animal hairs. These beautiful paintings contain remarkable detail in a compact space. The painting of a prince (opposite right) is a fine example of the minute brushwork used by the master painters of the Mughal court. In this 17th century miniature painting, even the pattern of the turban fabric and the stones on his ring can be distinguished and the borders around the image were delicately painted with flowers and animals.

To meet the demand for paper by the Mughals and other regional courts, papermaking centres emerged throughout India. Most papermakers were Muslim and employed techniques used by Chinese and Central Asian craftsmen. These included the preparation of the page for calligraphy and painting by burnishing the surface with a smooth stone such as agate. In the northwest were centres in Kashmir and the Punjab, well situated near sources of cool, clear water and important trade routes. In the northeast were Zafarabad, near Varanasi, and a number of towns in the east in Bihar and Bengal. In the west, Ahmedabad in Gujarat was known for its fine white papers, which were prized so highly that they were exported as far west as Iran and Turkey.

ABOVE: *Mask of a Hindu deity made of painted papier maché, Kashmir, 20th century.*

kites, fireworks, head-dresses, garlands of paper flowers and wallpaper. Paper has traditionally been an important ingredient in the production of papier maché in various centres of the subcontinent. In Kashmir in particular, Muslim papermakers have long produced papier maché objects with predominantly floral designs in rich colours and gold. In other regions, papier maché has been used to produce colourful masks and figures of deities to be used in traditional Hindu religious rituals and celebrations.

Paper was introduced to the Himalayas in the 7th century and was probably made there shortly afterwards. The fibre from which most Himalayan papers are made is the inner bark of various species of the daphne plant, which grows abundantly in mountainous regions. In Nepal, papermakers are primarily Hindu, while in Tibet and Bhutan, they have been predominantly Buddhist. Some of the earliest surviving texts on

PAPER

ABOVE: *Recitation of Noble Names of Manjushri, ink and colours on paper, Tibet, 16th century.*

paper are Tibetan Buddhist *sutras*, often accompanied by illustrations. Tibetan medical books and divination manuals have also traditionally been made of paper. Larger Tibetan Buddhist paintings used for worship, known as *thangkas*, are usually made of cloth and can be easily rolled and unrolled for portability, display and storage.

SOUTHEAST ASIA

BECAUSE NORTHERN VIETNAM was under Chinese control from the late 2nd century BC to 10th century, Vietnam acquired Chinese writing and Chinese papermaking techniques and began making paper as early as the 3rd century AD. Records mention rolls of paper made from tree barks, fern and seaweed being sent to China as tributes at that time from areas that are now in northern Vietnam. Even after northern Vietnam's independence from China in the 10th century, paper fans from Vietnam were sent in the thousands to the Chinese Court. Vietnamese paper has traditionally been made following Chinese methods, and the Vietnamese have employed materials such as bamboo, rice straw, seaweed and the bark of the daphne tree, which is native to the area. The Vietnamese have used paper for similar art forms as the Chinese, namely painting, calligraphy and printing.

Other regions of Southeast Asia did not know or use paper for many more centuries. Some regions such as Burma, Thailand and Indonesia, which were strongly influenced by Indian culture and religions, primarily used palm leaf and birch bark for writing sacred texts. In Cambodia, a parchment made of deer and sheep skin was apparently used. In Indonesia and Malaysia, a bark cloth called *tapa* was made by pounding bark fibres and

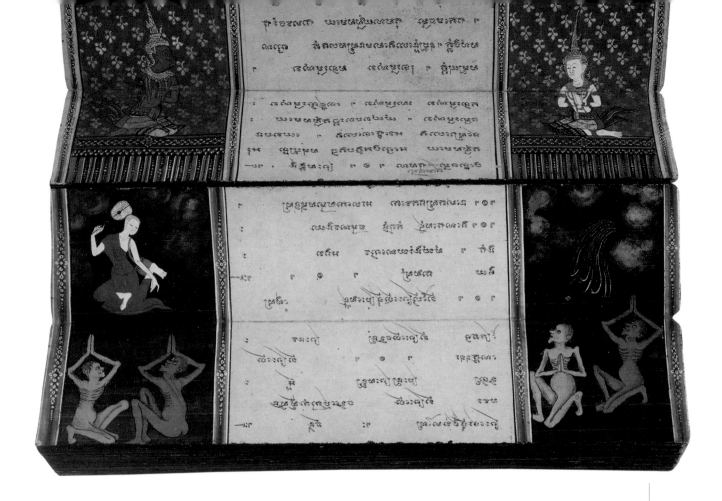

felting them together. In the Philippines, bamboo, leaves, bark and *tapa* cloth were used. It is not clear exactly when paper was introduced and when papermaking began in the various regions of Southeast Asia.

It seems likely that paper was first made in Thailand around the 13th or 14th century, primarily for writing Buddhist texts. This early Thai paper was made from the inner bark of a tree known as the *khoi*, or *Streblus asper*. Later Thai paintings of both religious subjects and secular genre scenes were made on paper, cloth and wood. By the early 20th century, the *khoi* tree was becoming rare, and Thai papermakers, under the influence of the Japanese in the mid-20th century, began to use paper mulberry for papermaking.

In the Philippines, paper was first used significantly after printing was introduced to the Philippines by Jesuit missionaries in the 16th century in order to spread the Christian faith. Paper was not actually made in the Philippines until the 20th century, when paper mills were established to produce paper from bamboo. Although there is not a long tradition of painting on paper in the Philippines, there have been very vibrant traditions of decorating coloured papers for celebrations.

ABOVE: *Phra Malai folding manuscript, ink and colours on paper, Thailand, 1866. This Buddhist manuscript tells and illustrates the legend of the monk Phra Malai, who is able to visit Heaven and Hell to preach the Buddha's teachings.*

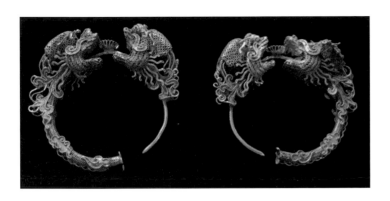

GOLD

GOLD IS THE most universally valuable material featured in this book. Though not necessarily the most precious material in every Asian culture – for example, jade holds greater importance in China – it has been highly prized throughout the continent for its colour, luminescence, rarity and durability. Gold has long been regarded as a symbol of wealth and power and has been crafted into jewelry, ornaments and ceremonial vessels for the royal and powerful. It has also been closely associated with divinity (see 'Gold and Divinity', p. 180) and so has been employed extensively in religious imagery and ritual objects. In some Asian cultures, because of its value and durability, gold has also been minted into coins or ingots and employed as currency.

OPPOSITE: *Gold plaque, Thailand. See p. 191.*

ABOVE: *Cloisonné vase, China, 18th century.*

ABOVE LEFT: *Gold earrings, China, Ming dynasty.*

BELOW: *Gold dinar, India. See p. 184.*

GOLD

IN ASIA, gold has not only been crafted into jewelry, ornaments and precious and religious objects, but it has also been applied to art works made of other materials to enhance their beauty and value. In fact, all of the other materials in this book – jade, silk, porcelain, lacquer, ivory, bamboo, paper, wood and stone – have been embellished with gold in one or more Asian cultures in a number of techniques unique to Asia.

THE MATERIAL

GOLD IS A shiny metallic chemical element with the atomic number 79 and the symbol Au. It is one of the heaviest substances known; it is also very durable and resistant to climatic forces or corrosion since it generally does not oxidize or dissolve in water. In its pure form (100 per cent gold equals 24 carats or karats, usually represented by 'K'), it is too soft and malleable to be worked effectively, so it usually hardened by mixing it with another metal, usually copper or silver, typically reducing its purity to 22K, 18K or 14K. If gold objects tarnish, it is most likely because the other metals (alloys) mixed with it have oxidized and blackened, and not the gold itself. However, ongoing research on the subject of gold oxidation has shown that under very specific conditions, very high karat gold has shown oxidation and tarnishing, leaving an oxidized film over the surface of the object, often referred to as a 'patina'.

Gold is found either embedded in rocks or as grains or flakes scattered in the alluvial deposits of river beds or buried under rocks. Gold found in veins in quartz rock usually

contains some other trace elements that have to be removed. This gold is traditionally accessed using picks and other mining equipment employed to detach the ore and bring it to the surface, where it is then pulverized and purified. Alluvial gold is generally more easily accessed.

Forming the Object: Casting and Hammering

IN ASIA, as in many other parts of the world, one of the most common techniques employed to create elaborate forms in gold is casting. The basic technique of casting involves running liquid gold into a mould. There are two major types of casting: piece-mould casting and lost-wax casting. Both have been used widely in Asia. In piece-mould gold casting, a mould is made out of ceramic or plaster and molten gold is poured into it. After the gold has cooled and hardened, the mould is broken off to reveal the object. In lost-wax casting, a model of the desired object is first made out of wax and then enclosed in a ceramic or plaster mould. The wax cavity is melted away through a hole and molten gold is run into the cavity. In the making of hollow objects, a core of clay is made, and the wax occupies the space between the core and the outer mould.

In contrast, the *repoussé* method of forming gold does not involve molten gold, but instead begins with a thin sheet of the metal. With *repoussé*, sometimes referred to as embossing, gold is beaten into a thin sheet and then the sheet is hammered from the back into a relief design.

TECHNIQUES

ABOVE: *Miniature funerary mask (front and back, showing hammering marks on the back), repoussé gold, China, Liao dynasty (907–1125). Burial items of the Liao dynasty included openwork crowns, belts, jewelry, boots and masks of gold made using the repoussé technique. The gold is generally laid face down onto a softer surface such as pitch, wood or lead, while the back is hammered. Details are finished on the front using chasing tools. This technique has been used widely in Asia and is often used for plaques and decorative panels for boxes and book covers.*

ABOVE LEFT: *Standing Shakyamuni, gilt copper, Nepal or Tibet, 12th century.*

ABOVE RIGHT: *Emperor Jahangir, opaque water colours and gold on paper, 18th century, India, Mughal period.*

Gold and Divinity

Throughout the world, because of its intrinsic value and rarity, gold has long symbolized wealth and power. Its colour has led to its association with the sun and, by extension, with divine power. As elsewhere, the artists of Asia have embellished representations of deities with gold to suggest their divine nature and power. In particular, images of the Buddha are often gilded to symbolize his enlightened state. The Buddha is believed to have been born with golden skin, a sign that he would either become a great king or spiritual leader. The golden skin is apparent here in this 12th century gilt-copper figure of Shakyamuni Buddha from Tibet or Nepal (left). Another motivation for the widespread gilding of Buddha images is the desire for religious merit. Many Buddhist devotees commission golden Buddha images to donate to temples believing that the more valuable their offerings, the more merit they will accrue.

In many Asian paintings of divine beings, the deity is surrounded by a halo or aureole of gold to suggest the divine light and power that he or she emanates. Many rulers in Asia have commissioned portraits of themselves emanating a similar divine light, again represented by a golden aureole. In this 18th century Mughal portrait in opaque watercolours and gold on paper of Emperor Jahangir (above), the gold halo around the Emperor's head illustrates his belief in the divine sanction of his rule.

GOLD

Adding Fine Details

A NUMBER OF DIFFERENT techniques have been used in Asia to decorate the surface of a gold object. Details have traditionally been applied using methods such as engraving and chasing, in which a sharp point is used to inscribe a linear design into the surface of the metal. A similar technique, tracing, is done with a pointed tool that is hit with a hammer, displacing material to both sides of a groove, without removing any of the metal. To create small circular patterns, known as ringmatting, or fish roe, a tracing tool with a ring outline is hammered straight down to leave a ring on the surface of the gold. In filigree work, usually used in jewelry and smaller objects, fine gold wires and balls are soldered to each other and to the surface of the object using tiny copper wires. Borders resembling a chain of beads or pearls can be created using a technique known as granulation, in which small gold beads are soldered onto the surface of a gold object, using fine copper wires.

Gilding other Materials

IN MANY AREAS OF ASIA, objects cast out of other materials such as bronze, copper, silver and wood are coated with a layer of gold, or gilded. The process varies widely. One of the most ancient methods used in Asia is the fire gilding method, also known as mercury amalgam gilding. In this technique, which was used in China as early as the Warring States period (475–221 BC), milled gold is mixed with mercury to form a paste that is spread over the surface of a metal object and then heated until the gold fuses with the surface and the mercury burns off. In the case of parcel gilt, gold is only applied to certain elements of an object made of silver to create a contrasting design. Although this

Gold Leaf

Gold leaf is used prolifically in Asian art to cover almost every kind of material. Traditionally, ultra-thin sheets of gold are made by heating a stick or brick of gold and then beating it for hours with a hammer until it becomes a sheet. The sheet is then cut into small squares, which are piled up, separated by waxed paper and then beaten for several more hours into thinner sheets. This process is then repeated until the resulting sheets are as fine as 1/200,000th of an inch in thickness. Gold leaf is usually sold in sheets that measure about 3 or 4 inches (8–10 cm) square.

Gold leaf may be applied in large pieces to a surface, for example, when gilding larger wood or bronze sculptures. In some parts of Asia, such as Thailand, gold leaf is applied by devotees to already-gilded images of the Buddha as an act of reverence (below). It may also be applied in sheets to paper as a painting surface, as in the case of Japanese screens. Gold leaf may also be applied to create patterns on surfaces such as lacquer and silk cloth. In Japanese surihaku textile design, adhesive is first applied to the silk using a stencil (left, top). Then the gold leaf is applied to the surface of the cloth (left, centre) and sticks to the adhesive, creating patterns (left, bottom). In Thailand, gold leaf is also applied to a black lacquered wood surface using the lai rot nam or 'washing with water' technique, discussed in Chapter 4, 'Lacquer' (p. 107).

LEFT: *Japanese surihaku textile design. Adhesive is first applied to the silk using a stencil (top). Then the gold leaf is applied to the surface of the cloth (centre) and sticks to the adhesive, creating patterns (bottom).*

RIGHT: *Buddha, Thailand. In some parts of Asia, such as Thailand, gold leaf is applied by devotees to already gilded images of the Buddha as an act of reverence.*

LEFT: *Detail of Korean celadon oil pot with Japanese gold lacquer repair, 13th century. For centuries, the Japanese have used a mixture of gold and lacquer to repair broken ceramics. The gold repair often adds to their beauty.*

RIGHT: *Handle for a peacock-feather fly whisk, light green nephrite jade inlaid with rubies set in gold, India, Mughal period, late 18th century. First grooves were abraded into the jade and filled with a mixture of lacquer and pure gold. Then the gems were set into the gold lacquer.*

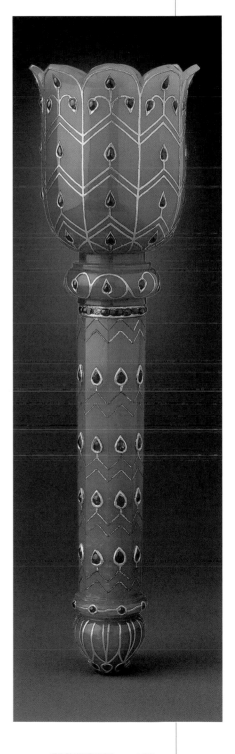

technique produces a durable gold surface, it is both difficult, especially in the case of large bronze statues, and dangerous because of the toxicity of the mercury. Gilding is also important in *cloisonné* enamelling, in which enamels of different colours are applied to a copper or bronze vessel and enclosed by gilded copper wires that form sections, or *cloisons*.

The gilding of many materials, including wood and bronze, is also done throughout Asia using thin sheets of gold leaf (see 'Gold Leaf', p. 182). Gold leaf is a less labour-intensive and dangerous alternative to fire gilding. It is also a favoured method for gilding extremely large statuary and architectural elements and is applied to paper, silk and other fine materials.

Applied Gold Detailing

There are many ways in which gold can be applied to create decorative details. In Japanese *maki-e*, powdered gold is sprinkled onto coloured lacquer (see pp. 96, 102–3). In many Asian cultures, gold is inlaid into linear patterns engraved in the surface of lacquer or metals such as silver and bronze. In a technique known as *kundan*, Indian craftsmen use a combination of lacquer and gold to set gems into jewelry. A piece of jewelry is made with a thin layer of gold over a core of lac, a natural resin. Then details are chased or engraved, and holes are made for the gems. Lac is inserted into the back so it is visible through the hole. The lac is then coated with highly refined gold leaf, or *kundan*, and the gem is pushed into the *kundan*. Mughal craftsmen used this technique to decorate hard stones such as jade with inlaid precious gems. Gold can also be used as a painting pigment on jade, porcelain, ivory, paper, cloth, wood and other surfaces. Gold is even used as a means of repairing damaged objects.

GOLD

INDIA AND THE HIMALAYAS

BELOW: *Gold dinar of Chandragupta II, India, c. 376–414). Gupta period coins usually featured images of the king accompanied by Hindu or Buddhist deities, symbolizing divine support for the ruler.*

GOLD HAS BEEN USED and valued highly in South Asia for much of the region's history. Although India has long had an insatiable appetite for this material, local deposits of gold have been rare, most of its gold being mined in the state of Karnataka in southern India. India has generally imported much of its gold from regions such as modern Nepal, which has been blessed with plentiful gold deposits.

Jewelry has been an important part of personal adornment and identity in South Asia for millennia. Gold was used for jewelry as early as the Indus Valley Civilization (3000–1700 BC) of northwestern India and Pakistan. By the first centuries BC, gold working techniques had reached an advanced level, as can be seen in the fine gold jewelry from Southern India crafted from sheets of gold and *repoussé* and featuring filigree work and inlaid precious gems. Fine gold jewelry and other items were also being made at that time in the ancient region of Gandhara, now in modern Afghanistan, Pakistan and northwestern India. Gold work continued in this region over the following centuries and included Buddhist reliquaries, amulets and other sacred items cast and hammered out of gold, as well as gold coins. Under the Gupta dynasty, which ruled northern India from the early 4th to mid 6th centuries, some of India's finest gold coins were minted. Few objects made of gold have survived in this region from the next thousand years or so, so it is difficult to determine how much gold was actually used in jewelry and art. Most religious imagery created in the Indian subcontinent was carved out of stone or cast in bronze or copper, and sometimes gilded.

GOLD

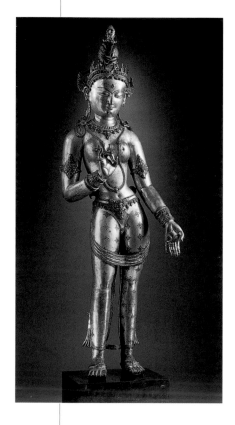

ABOVE and RIGHT: *Tara, gilt copper with polychrome and semi-precious stones, Nepal, c. 1300. Many Himalayan Buddhist figures are cast in copper or bronze and then gilded and embellished with semi-precious stones.*

From the 1st millennium AD in the Himalayan region, Buddhist and Hindu figures have been cast in bronze, copper and brass and gilded. In particular, the Newari metalworkers of the Kathmandu Valley in Nepal excelled in the bronze figures of deities and ritual objects, which were gilded and often embellished with semi-precious stones. Gold has also been used widely to embellish religious paintings and manuscripts; it was used in the text and illustrations of these sacred books, and to gild the carved wooden book covers.

The Indian Mughal emperors (1526–1857) were great lovers of gold and gems. They commissioned spectacular gold jewelry, typically inset with precious and semi-precious stones. The Mughals and other rulers also commissioned exquisite books featuring paintings with gold details as well as calligraphic texts masterfully penned in gold.

ABOVE LEFT: *Vajra, gilded copper, Tibet, c. 1500. The vajra, a type of Buddhist ritual sceptre, is used by monks in Buddhist rituals and symbolizes the power of the Buddha's teachings to cut through ignorance and evil.*

LEFT: *Mughal bracelet inset with turquoise using the kundan technique, India, 18th century. The gems were set into lac covered with gold leaf.*

ABOVE: *Page of calligraphy by Abul Baqa al-Musavi (c. 1625–1700), ink, opaque watercolour and gold on paper, Hyderabad, Andra Pradesh, India, 1675–1700.*

GOLD

SOUTHEAST ASIA

IN SOUTHEAST ASIA, gold has been found at sites in mainland regions as well as on a number of the islands. It has been a major part of the artistic heritage of many of the cultures, and has also been an important commodity in international trade. Significant gold deposits are found in Burma, Laos, Thailand and Vietnam on the mainland and on the islands of Java and Sumatra and Borneo in Indonesia, as well as in Malaysia and the Philippines. In most of these cultures, gold has featured primarily in the royal and sacred arts.

INDONESIA

INDONESIA HAS HAD a long history of gold working, no doubt because of its abundant deposits on Java, Sumatra and in Kalimantan on Borneo. Some of the earliest gold artifacts found in the archipelago were gold beads unearthed from Bronze Age burial sites dating to the 1st millennium BC. After this period, the most abundant findings of gold artifacts, both religious and secular, date to the 8th and 9th centuries. Particularly remarkable was a cache discovered in Central Java containing nearly 16 kg (35 lb) of gold objects, including finely cast bowls bearing elaborate relief designs of scenes from

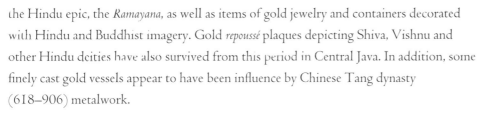

the Hindu epic, the *Ramayana*, as well as items of gold jewelry and containers decorated with Hindu and Buddhist imagery. Gold *repoussé* plaques depicting Shiva, Vishnu and other Hindu deities have also survived from this period in Central Java. In addition, some finely cast gold vessels appear to have been influence by Chinese Tang dynasty (618–906) metalwork.

In later Indonesian metalwork, gold features prominently in Hindu and Buddhist ritual objects. Many wood sculptures and architectural elements from Java, Bali and other regions have also been coated with gold leaf and sometimes inset with stones and glass. Some of the most spectacular and important objects worked in gold in this region are the ceremonial *kerises*, or daggers, that have ornate handles cast in gold and often decorated with elaborate moulded designs or inset gems.

Gold has been an important status symbol in this region. Gold has also been used widely in the textiles worn by the royalty of many parts of Southeast Asia. Gold jewelry has also been significant in many of the cultures. Some of the most spectacular gold jewelry has been worked in Malaysia and in the Philippines.

GOLD

THAILAND

ABOVE LEFT: *Gilded guardian figures and gilded architectural decoration, Wat Prakaeo, Grand Palace, Bangkok, Thailand.*

ABOVE RIGHT: *Scene of revival of Maddi, from the Vessantara Jataka, opaque watercolour and gold on cloth, Bangkok, Thailand, c. 1700–50.*

OPPOSITE: *Vishnu and attendant, gold repoussé plaque, Thailand. Si-Thep (?), Mon-Dvaravati period, c. 700. Plaques like this one may have been used in temple dedications. In the secular realm, fine gold jewelry dating to the Dvaravati period (6th–10th century) has also survived, providing evidence of early Thai gold casting technology.*

ALTHOUGH GOLD HAS NOT historically been found in abundance in Thailand, it has played an important role in the arts of Thailand for many centuries. Much Thai gold was likely acquired through trade with neighbouring countries and as spoils of war. No gold has been found among the artifacts of the Ban Chiang culture (3600 BC–2nd century AD), and little gold material exists from the 1st millennium AD. A number of early Hindu and Buddhist stone and bronze statues were covered with gold leaf, and gold *repoussé* plaques feature designs of Hindu and Buddhist deities.

Throughout much of Thailand's history, the material has been reserved for use by the royal court and religious institutions. From the 11th century through the Sukhothai period (1238–1368), the gilding of bronze and stone sculpture continued, and during the latter period, gold was also used as a finish on lacquered wood and bronze Buddhist figures. A wealth of gold religious and secular items have been discovered in the temple ruins of the Ayutthaya period (1350–1767), including large gold figures of the Buddha. In addition, finely crafted gold ornaments, vessels, swords, crowns and other royal goods have been discovered, many featuring filigree, granulation, enamelling and inset gems.

Over the following centuries, much Thai Buddhist art has been embellished with gold, from the roofs and walls of temples buildings to lacquered wood book cabinets with gold leaf designs on a black lacquer ground. Many sacred Buddhist books have also been decorated with details in gold.

GOLD

RIGHT: *Buddha as Cosmic Monarch (Jambhupati), wood with lacquer and gilding, Burma, 19th century. Many later Burmese Buddhist figures are very elaborate. The Jambhupati images of the Buddha as a Cosmic Monarch wearing full regalia and coated with gold leaf became popular in Burma in the 17th century.*

BURMA

ABOVE RIGHT: *The Buddha receiving alms, detail from a Burmese manuscript, 19th century. Most Burmese Buddhist manuscripts have pages made of palm-leaf or paper and are long and rectangular in format with covers of wood. In specially commissioned manuscripts made for donation to monasteries, the pages were often lavishly decorated with gold detailing and protected between covers of lacquered and gilded wood. In this image of the Buddha receiving food from a devotee, the robes of the Buddha are painted in gold, indicating his central role in this scene.*

BURMA, LIKE THAILAND, has been blessed with plentiful supplies of the material. Not much early Burmese gold has survived, but some examples exist of gilt bronze Buddhist figures dating to the 8th and 9th century, when the Upper region of Burma was ruled by the Pyu people. During the following Pagan period (1044–1287), the northern and southern regions of Burma were unified under the Pagan kings with their capital at Pagan in central Burma. Theravada, or monastic, Buddhism became the dominant religion of Burma, and in Pagan, many temples, pagodas and stupas were built out of brick and completely covered in gold. Bronze, brass and silver Buddha images were also coated with gold leaf. In the late 18th and 19th centuries, many Buddhist figures were made of wood and stone and were lacquered and gilded. Gold has also played a significant role in the painting tradition of Burma and in particular in the art of the Buddhist manuscript.

Because of the abundance of gold in the region, the material has also been used widely to decorate wood carving and furniture. Many lacquered objects have long been decorated with gold leaf (see pp. 95–96, 107–11). Gold jewelry has also played an important role in Burmese culture, and gold necklaces, bracelets, rings, earrings, have also been donated to monasteries by the wealthy in hope of attaining enlightenment. The finest surviving Burmese gold jewelry, mostly dating to the Konbaung period (1752–1824), features inlaid precious gems such as rubies, emeralds and sapphires, and exquisite filigree work.

FAR LEFT: *Cosmetic or medicine box in the form of a clamshell with phoenix, hammered silver with gilding, China, Middle Tang dynasty, c. 700–800. In the Tang dynasty, many vessels were made of cast or beaten gold and silver and decorated using chasing, tracing, granulation and filigree, which entered China from Western and Central Asia. This box features a chased design of a phoenix among scrolling leaves. The main area of the design has been gilded; the background has been covered with ringmatting, or 'fish roe'.*

LEFT: *Bear, gilded bronze, China, Han dynasty.*

BELOW: *Bodhisattva Guanyin with many arms, gilt bronze, China, Ming dynasty.*

CHINA

THE CHINESE HAVE mined gold for centuries in Shandong, Yunnan, Kansu and Szechuan provinces and used gold as early as the Shang dynasty (1500–1027 BC). However, gold has not traditionally enjoyed the high status of jade, bronze and lacquer in ceremonial life, and during the first two millennia BC, gold and silver were used primarily to decorate ritual bronze vessels rather than as independent media. By around the 6th century BC, bronzes were decorated with ornate gold and silver inlay and surface patterns made of hammered gold foil. In the Han dynasty (206 BC–AD 220), with the decline in bronze manufacture, the use of precious metals increased, and gold was cast and hammered and decorated with granulation, and used to gild many bronze items. In the Han dynasty, many decorative items, such as belt hooks and dress ornaments were either made of gold or gilded bronze.

During the Tang dynasty (618–906), gold and silver working reached a new level of sophistication and popularity. Many drinking and eating vessels, lidded boxes, mirrors and vases were inspired by Middle Eastern metalwork in form and decoration. The northern Liao dynasty (907–1125) also produced remarkable ceremonial and luxury items in gold and silver, many of which have been found in their royal tombs (see p. 179).

Gold has been predominant in Chinese Buddhist imagery. Buddhism entered China from the Central Asian region, where it was traditional to embellish religious images with gold and store relics in silver and gold containers. From the 4th century, Chinese Buddhist figures have been cast in bronze and gilded, a practice that has continued until

LEFT: *Gold filigree lion, China, Qing dynasty, Kangxi period (1662–1722). This extraordinary lion-shaped vessel is overlaid entirely with gold filigree and granulated decoration. It is believed to have been made for use by the Kangxi Emperor at the Summer Palace and was later obtained from the Forbidden City in Beijing by Count Otto von Bismarck during the Boxer Rebellion in 1900. Copyright 2005 The Kelton Foundation.*

BELOW LEFT: *Gold filigree hair ornament and earrings, China, Ming dynasty. Many items of jewelry were made in the form of auspicious creatures such dragons, phoenixes and bats, which symbolize happiness.*

the present day. Over the centuries, many of the interiors of Buddhist and Daoist temples and the objects used in rituals have also been gilded.

In the secular context, gold embellished architectural elements, vessels and personal items made of lacquer, jade, porcelain and silk. In the Tang and the Song (960–1279) dynasties, aristocrats wore gold jewelry and ornaments, including hairpins, combs, rings and bangles, and used gold eating and drinking vessels, all decorated with openwork details created using granulation and filigree. In the Ming (1368–1644) and Qing (1644–1911) dynasties, jewelry and ornaments were often fashioned from gold using elaborate filigree work. Some of the most remarkable Chinese filigree work was used for the decoration of Imperial vessels and containers. The spectacular *cloisonné* enamel work of the Ming and Qing dynasties also featured gilded details (see p. 177).

FAR LEFT: *Gold earrings, Silla Kingdom, Korea, 6th century. Some of the most exquisite Korean gold burial objects are the earrings worn by both men and women of the Court. They typically feature gold loops, a central section and flat leaf-like pendants of cut and hammered gold.*

LEFT: *Seated Buddha, gilt bronze, Joseon dynasty (1392–1910), Korea.*

THE EARLIEST SURVIVING Korean objects made from or decorated with gold date to the 6th century AD, and most of them have been recovered from royal tombs of the southern kingdoms of Silla and Baekje. Silla, in particular, had gold mines, which produced gold for the use of its own aristocracy and for export to Tang China. Among the gold objects that have been excavated from the tombs are crowns and headdress ornaments cut from sheets of gold and decorated with hammered and chased details and dangling leaf-shaped pendants attached with gold wires. Also found were gold hairpins, gold necklaces and earrings embellished with intricate filigree and granulation work.

From the 6th century, gold was used in Korea to gild Buddhist bronze statues. This tradition continued for some 800 years on Buddhist figures, ritual vessels and reliquaries. It was also used in Buddhist paintings, applied primarily to the robes of the deities. In

KOREA

195

GOLD

clothing, gold leaf was applied in patterns onto silk and wrapped around threads to create gold threads that were woven into or couched onto the fabric. After the Joseon dynasty took power in 1392, Buddhism was replaced by the more austere Confucianism as the country's main philosophy, and the use of gold declined in art and ritual.

JAPAN

GOLD HAS BEEN in use in Japan for roughly 2000 years. The oldest examples of gold working in Japan are the gilt bronze swords and fittings found in Imperial tombs of the 6th and 7th centuries AD. Around the same time, following the arrival of Buddhism, the Japanese began gilding bronze figures of Buddhist deities. By the mid-8th century, Japanese gilders had mastered this technique well enough to gild the colossal Buddha image in the Todaiji temple in Nara. The statue, commissioned by the devout Buddhist Emperor Shomu (*r.* 724–749), was cast in bronze and measured about 16 metres (53 feet) high. Gold deposits were first discovered in Japan in 749, in time to cover the entire figure in gold leaf.

Gold was not abundant in Japan for much of its history, so has been used sparingly, mostly in Buddhist temples and the Imperial Court. Over the centuries, many Japanese Buddhist statues were carved out of wood and gilded. Many Buddhist ritual objects were

also gilded, as were the architectural details of Buddhist temples and small shrines containing the objects of worship. In addition, gold leaf has been used in Buddhist paintings from around the 11th or 12th century to depict the golden skin of the Buddha and the patterns on the robes of deities. For the upper classes, gold was a decorative element on various fine objects including lacquerware, paper and silk robes. Japanese lacquer artists, in particular, excelled in the use of *maki-e* (sprinkled gold) to create designs on lacquer items (see pp. 96–97, 102–3).

In 1542, the Sado Mine on Sado Island in the Japan Sea, the largest gold and silver producer in Japan, was discovered and has been in production intermittently ever since. This discovery led to the increased use of gold in Japanese art, most impressively on traditional screen doors and folding screens. From the late 16th century onwards, many Japanese textiles, including Noh actors' robes and the *obi* sash that secures the *kimono*, have featured gold-wrapped threads, and many lacquer items have been produced with elaborate gold decoration (see p. 182). There has never been a tradition of gold jewelry in Japan. Small personal items, such as mirrors and cosmetic boxes used by women, were sometimes decorated with gold. However, gold has been used to decorate sword fittings used by men.

ABOVE LEFT: *Two-panel screen with cranes, ink and colours on gold leaf on paper, Japan, Kano school, 17th century. Japanese interiors are traditionally very dark and are only lit at night using oil lamps. The gold background on screens served to reflect the lamp light and brighten the interiors of Japanese temples, castles, and aristocratic residences.*

ABOVE RIGHT: *Pair of* menuki *depicting Shoki the Demon Killer chasing a demon, gold, Japan, c. 1800. Some of the most exquisite examples of Japanese gold working are the tiny sword fittings called* menuki *that are fitted into the sword hilt to improve the grip of the hand.*

OPPOSITE: *Detail of headpiece, India.* *See p. 207.*

FAR LEFT: Bodhisattva *and consort in loving embrace, wood with polychrome and gold decoration, China, early 15th century.*

LEFT: *Pillow, zelkova, teak and other woods, China, 18th–19th century.*

BELOW: *Detail of* torgam *cabinet, Tibet.* *See p. 209.*

WOOD

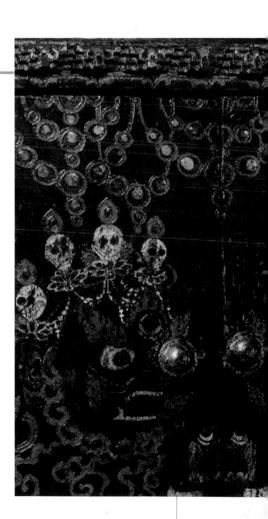

WOOD IS ONE of the most widely used materials in Asian art. Wood has been used all over Asia to build religious and secular structures, to decorate their interiors and exteriors and to furnish them. It has also been carved into the sacred imagery and ritual objects of all of the religious traditions of the region. In the realm of education and entertainment, wood has been carved into woodblocks for printing texts and images, and into masks for theatre and religious rituals and toys for children. It has also been used to fashion numerous functional objects such as tools, weapons and containers. In addition, wood soot is also used to make the ink used in traditional calligraphy and painting in many parts of Asia.

THE
MATERIAL

IT IS PERHAPS WITH WOOD, more than any other material, that the line between a
functional object and a work of art is hardest to draw. The wooden statues of Asia's
religious traditions, for example, were not created as works of art, but as sacred images to
be revered. Yet wooden images of deities have become important treasures in our art
museums. Wooden furniture, though often beautiful, was primarily meant to be used in
daily living. Functional wooden items, such as tools, containers and woodblocks, have
often attained the status of works of art because of the great skill used to create them.

IN MANY PARTS of Asia, different types of wood have traditionally been available in
abundance, most notably camphor, cedar, cherry, cypress, ebony, mahogany, rosewood,
sandalwood and teak. Most beautiful and durable woods have generally been reserved for the
ruling elite and religious institutions. In particular, slow-growing hardwoods, which have
historically been both rare and durable, and woods featuring an attractive grain, such as *zelkova*
and camphorwood, have been among the most admired. In China, the highest ranking woods
are the rare hardwoods such as rosewoods and *huanghuali* (see 'The Fine Woods of Chinese
Furniture', opposite) that have long been made into furniture for the royal and wealthy.

The Fine Woods of Chinese Furniture

Many fine native and imported woods were used in classical Chinese furniture during the Ming (1368–1644) and Qing (1644–1911) dynasties. These woods are generally known by poetic names and are not always identifiable in the West. Probably the most well known of these is a hardwood known in Chinese as huanghuali, meaning 'yellow flowering pear'. Huanghuali is generally identified as padauk, one of several woods of genus Pterocarpus. Grown primarily in Southeast Asia and on Hainan Island off the coast of southern China, huanghuali is prized for its strength, warm tone and fine grain. It has long been a favourite material of the upper classes for tables, such as this Ming dynasty altar table (right), chairs and cabinets.

Zitan, 'purple sandalwood', is a very tightly grained, dense hardwood of the Pterocarpus genus of rosewoods. Ranging from purplish-black to blackish-red in colour, this wood is found in southern China, Hainan Island and Southeast Asia. It is the most valuable of all hardwoods used in Chinese furniture. It was extremely popular with the aristocracy during the Qing dynasty for its strength and beauty, particularly for tables, chairs, and incense stands (opposite top right). A third important wood, jichimu, or 'chicken wing wood', is prized for its grain resembling chicken feathers. This decorative hardwood, of the genus Ormosia, is also from Hainan Island, and is usually employed on cabinet fronts and other large, flat surfaces where the grain is clearly visible.

In some cultures, certain trees are considered sacred, so any item carved from the wood of that tree possesses some of its divine power. In India, Japan and several other cultures, certain ancient and strangely formed trees have been revered as spiritual conduits, and the wood from these sacred trees has been crafted into sacred statuary and objects. According to Buddhist tradition, the Buddha attained enlightenment under a large pipal tree (*Ficus religiosa*) at Bodh Gaya, in modern Nepal. The wood from this *bodhi*, or enlightenment, tree has been used to make prayer beads and other devotional items.

ABOVE: *Altar table made of* huanghuali *wood, China, Ming dynasty (1368–1644).*

LEFT: *Table with carved decoration, Tibet, 15th century.*

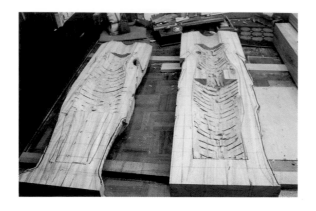

ABOVE: *Long sections of camphorwood for the body of a bodhisattva figure after hollowing out, by sculptor Yamataka Ryoun, Japan, 20th century. Sculptors hollow out the heartwood of several blocks of wood and then assemble them to create a large, more lightweight sculpture that is unlikely to crack. The multiple-block technique also allows the creation of figures of varying sizes and forms.*

RIGHT: *Rough carving of the head of a bodhisattva, by Yamataka Ryoun, Japan, 20th century. Here, Japanese sculptor Yamataka Ryoun is carving the basic form of the head of the bodhisattva Avalokiteshvara (Japanese: Kannon).*

BELOW: *The finished bodhisattva head, by Yamataka Ryoun, Japan, 20th century.*

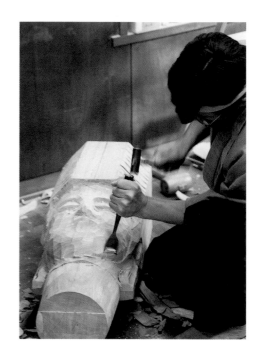

TECHNIQUES

Carving

TO CARVE FIGURAL sculptures in the round, sculptors in Asia, as in most other cultures, use tools such as chisels, hammers, saws, awls, and knives. Figural wood carving generally begins with a log of a tree, which is either left whole for large carvings or split into sections using saws. Before it is carved, the wood is generally dried or 'seasoned' so that any shrinkage or distortion in form occurs prior to carving.

Smaller figures may then be carved out of the single log. However, in the case of larger sculptures, a more complex technique is often necessary. A single log consists of the heartwood at the core and the sapwood that surrounds it. The heartwood is much denser and less prone to shrinkage than the sapwood, and the tension between the two parts can cause the wood to crack and split. To avoid cracking, sculptors in many parts of Asia construct a figure out of several smaller blocks of wood.

Once the sections of wood are ready, the sculptor begins carving the rough form using large chisels to cut away the unnecessary wood, including the heartwood. The sculptor then uses smaller tools for more detailed work. Once the separate sections of the figure have all been carved, they are assembled using wooden tenons and a little wood glue, and final touches are added to the carved details of the face and robes of the figure.

LEFT: *Tibetan carpenter creating openwork carving using a fret saw, Kathmandu, Nepal, 2004. Openwork carving is relatively weak in structure but allows both light and air to pass through the carving. It is often reserved for windows, transom pieces and other functional architectural elements.*

RIGHT: *Detail of relief carving in a pair of wood doors, Indonesia, 20th century. This pair of doors, carved with low relief scenes from the Indian epic the* Ramayana, *was made for export to the West.*

Relief and Openwork Carving

SOME OF THE FINEST Asian woodcarving is done on flat surfaces. Scenes depicting deities, people, animals and birds can be found on the walls, doors, doorframes, windows and roof gables of religious and secular buildings and furniture. Carving may be executed in low relief, embellishing a surface without compromising its strength and integrity.

To produce designs in higher relief, a sculptor forces his chisels deeper into the wood, removing more of the background of the image and creating a more dynamic design, enlivened by the play of light and shadow. High relief carvings are often found on wall panels, the brackets supporting roofs and on decorative roof gables. One step beyond high relief carving is openwork carving, in which the carver completely cuts away the background of the design using chisels and saws.

Joinery in Furniture

MOST CULTURES IN Asia construct furniture from local and imported wood. Typically, furniture makers are not only responsible for the building of the item but also any carved decoration. (Painted and lacquered decoration is generally applied by other artists.) Some of the most remarkable items of furniture in technical terms are those constructed using

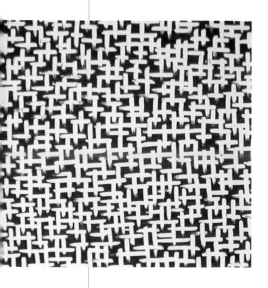

sophisticated joinery involving minimum use of nails or glue. The furniture makers of China and Japan are particularly renowned for their skilful, and often decorative, use of mortise-and-tenon joinery, in which one piece of wood has a protrusion, or tenon, that fits neatly into the opening, or mortise, in another piece. This system allows for the expansion and contraction of the wood during temperature changes, preventing warping and cracking. On many fine pieces of Chinese furniture, the mortise-and-tenon joinery is incorporated into the furniture design.

Inlay and Marquetry

IN CERTAIN CULTURES, other materials are used as inlays in wood, most often in the case of furniture and decorative boxes. Striking patterns have often been created by inlaying materials such as ivory and bone into dark woods such as ebony. A similar technique is marquetry, in which thin slivers of woods of different colours as well as ivory and other materials, are cut into triangles, squares and circles and pasted onto a wooden background to create geometrical patterns.

Painting, Gilding and Lacquering

MANY ASIAN CARVED wood figural and decorative relief sculptures are embellished with colour or gold. To create polychrome decoration, artists applies mineral (and

ABOVE: *Detail of marquetry pattern on Japanese box, 20th century. Marquetry, a type of wood mosaic, has been employed for centuries in certain parts of Asia in the decoration of boxes.*

ABOVE: *Detail of carved and gilded wooden temple architecture, Bangkok, Thailand.*

occasionally, vegetable) pigments to the wood, sometimes over a layer of gesso in between. Gold is also applied in the form of thin sheets or strips of gold leaf (see pp. 182–83) that are affixed to the wood with an adhesive such as lacquer. Wood items are often lacquered for protection and decoration (see pp. 92, 97).

INDIA

NUMEROUS WOODS are used in architecture, furnishings and sculpture in this region. Teak (*Tectona grandis*), a large deciduous hardwood, is native to India and Southeast Asia. Its hard, durable wood is mostly used for furniture and shipbuilding. Ebony, a very dark hardwood, is also used in furniture and as a contrasting inlay in objects made of lighter woods. Another popular wood is sandalwood, the scented wood from trees of the genus *Santalum*. A number of rosewoods, scented woods from the genus *Dalbergia*, are also employed particularly for furniture making because of their close grain and strength.

Because of the hot and humid climate of much of South Asia, very few early examples of Indian woodworking have survived. However, it is likely that the art of wood carving has a long history in the region. Some of the most spectacular work is found in southern India, from the Deccan plateau to the states of Karnataka, Kerala, Andra Pradesh and Tamil Nadu. For centuries, southern woodworkers have constructed and decorated temples, homes and the huge wheeled chariots, or *rathas*, that contain images of the gods.

WOOD

The wooden bases of these chariots, which are pulled along streets during Hindu festivals, are boldly carved with a profusion of deities, narrative scenes, fantastic and real animals and protective creatures. Similar dynamic carving is found on the wooden headdresses worn by dancers in these festivals.

The northern states of India, including Gujarat, Rajasthan, Kashmir, Bengal and Assam, have also been home to vibrant wood carving traditions, manifested both on architectural elements and on religious statuary.

In South Asia, much furniture has been produced in wood, with different regions specializing in different styles of furniture. For example, certain woodworking centres in Gujarat specialize in marquetry, and inlay has long been used by furniture makers in

Uttar Pradesh and Karnataka. During the Mughal period (1526–1857), many items of furniture and objects such as writing boxes were decorated with intricate inlay work for use by the Mughal Court.

In the Himalayas, wood is an extremely important artistic material. Buildings, furniture (see 'The Wooden Furniture of Tibet', p. 209) and religious carvings have traditionally been made from woods such as spruce, fir, pine and native deodar cedar. These woods are readily available in this mountainous region and are durable. Deodar, in particular, is resistant to insects. Much of the finest wood carving in the Himalayas has been done in the service of Buddhism, from carved figures of Buddhist deities to sculptures in temples and monasteries and covers for sacred Buddhist texts.

The Wooden Furniture of Tibet

For centuries, Tibetan woodworkers have constructed wooden cabinets, tables, boxes and trunks for use in temples, monasteries and homes. Although they are embellished with painted and carved decoration of Buddhist motifs and other local and foreign designs, these objects have been primarily functional. After the destruction of many Buddhist temples and monasteries during the Chinese takeover in 1950 and the Cultural Revolution (1966–76), many pieces found their way out of Tibet and into Western art museums and private collections.

Tables of all sizes are used in temples and homes. Middle-sized tables, or thri ma chog, such as this example dating to the 15th or 16th century (below), are traditionally placed in front of the lamas' thrones in their private apartments and in the homes of noblemen. Many feature extremely fine relief carving. Here, Buddhist auspicious symbols are carved along the upper panel, and the legs of the table seem to issue forth from the mouths of mythical beasts. Decorated wooden cabinets are also used widely in traditional Tibetan temples and homes. This cabinet from the 17th or 18th century (right) is a torgam made to hold the torga, or ritual offering cake, that is presented to deities during ceremonies. Torgam generally feature painted decoration. This cabinet was made for offerings to Mahakala, the wrathful, black-faced deity depicted on the cabinet doors.

WOOD

ABOVE: *A ritual offering cabinet, or torgam, wood with painted decoration, Tibet, 17th – 18th century.*

LEFT: *Table with carved and painted designs, Tibet, 15th–16th century.*

WOOD

RIGHT: *Detail of temple architecture, Bangkok, Thailand.*

SOUTHEAST ASIA

HISTORICALLY, SOUTHEAST ASIA has been blessed with an abundance of tropical hardwoods, so wood is the principal building material of the region. Wood carvings are ubiquitous, as decorative architectural details such as roof gables, doors and extended floor beams. Teak is the most common hardwood employed in the region for building, furniture and wood carvings. It is both relatively easy to carve and is resistant to termites and other wood-eating creatures. Mahogany, a reddish-brown tropical hardwood, is also used widely in furniture, especially the wood from *Swietenia mahagonia*. Southeast Asian hardwoods have been exported to China and other regions for centuries. Recent international demand for these hardwoods has led to large-scale logging in the region, and these woods are rapidly becoming scarce.

THAILAND, BURMA AND VIETNAM

WOOD HAS BEEN one of the most common materials in Thai architecture and sculpture. Wood carving is one of the country's most celebrated art forms; it has long been employed in the decoration of temples and shrines, and to embellish royal buildings, thrones, palanquins and barges. These carvings, usually of teak wood, have often been lavishly coated with gold leaf. Some of the earliest existing wood carvings date to the Ayutthaya period (1350–1767), a high point in Thai decorative arts. During this period, the roofs, gables, doors and walls of temples and palaces were carved in both high and low relief with depictions of mythical creatures such as *naga* serpent deities and *kinnari* figures (female creatures, half-human, half-bird), as well as gods and scenes of Hindu

LEFT: *Dragon, gilded wood and glass inlay, Wat Haripunchai, Lamphun, Chiangmai province, Thailand.*

RIGHT: *A crowned Buddha, wood with traces of gilding, lacquer and pigments, Burma, Pagan, 13th century. This figure, with its slender body, simple but elegant ornamentation and gentle facial features, displays the typical grace of Pagan period wood carved Buddhist imagery.*

origin, all surrounded with swirling foliage tapering into a flame-like flourish. These carvings and many from subsequent periods are not only gilded but painted or inset with coloured glass mosaics that sparkle like gems.

Wood has also played a long-standing role in the arts of Burma, with hardwoods such as teak featuring prominently in its architecture and sculpture. As in Thailand, Burma's religious and secular architecture have traditionally been constructed of wood, and carved and gilded details have embellished the roofs, gables, doors, doorways, and ceilings. Burma has had a long tradition of Buddhist statuary, the oldest examples being of stone and bronze. Some of the earliest surviving Burmese wood figures date to the Pagan period (11th–13th century) and were often coated with lacquer, pigments and gold. During the Pagan period, many royal Buddhist temples were constructed, some housing gigantic carved wood Buddha images; others were home to elaborate relief carvings of Buddhist legends. The large wooden doors of these temples, some of which have survived intact, were also carved with designs of birds, animals and protective mythical creatures.

Most surviving Burmese wood and lacquered Buddhist figures date to the Konbaung period (1752–1824). Many of these later figures are more elaborate, a typical example being images of the Buddha as a Cosmic Monarch wearing full regalia (see p. 192). Later Buddha figures are generally lacquered and partially or fully gilded. As well as these figures, Burma's wood workers also carved relief sculpture to decorate the interiors and exteriors of temple buildings. Book covers, ritual vessels and containers were also made of wood and finished with lacquer and gilding.

WOOD

Wood has been an important material in the arts and culture of Vietnam, featuring primarily in the country's architectural and religious arts. Very rare wooden Buddha figures have survived from the 6th century, attesting to an early tradition of wood sculpture in the region. Most Buddhist sculptures in wood date to the 16th century onwards, and include images of seated Buddhas, bodhisattvas and Buddhist holy men, carved in wood and then coated with lacquer and often gilded. Carved wood details have also been important in the decoration of Buddhist and Daoist temples.

INDONESIA, MALAYSIA AND THE PHILIPPINES

INDONESIA AND MALAYSIA have been rich in fine hardwoods and have used them in their architecture and shipbuilding, sculpture and furniture for many centuries. Much of the region's wood working relates to the Buddhist and Hindu beliefs transmitted from India in the 1st millennium. Wood carvings depicting Hindu deities can be found widely in Bali and Java, often as devotional sculpture or as decorative elements in religious buildings. Islam also reached these regions and had a profound impact on both countries, though this is not widely reflected in the wood carving traditions, since figural

LEFT: *Indra on elephant, wood with polychrome, Bali, Indonesia, 19th century. The finely detailed carvings of Hindu deities are often coated with pigments and gilding.*

RIGHT: *Asmat Shield, W. Papua, Indonesia, wood with pigments, early 20th century. Shields from the Asmat culture are often made of a flat section of mangrove wood, carved with protective motifs and coated with pigments such as lime and ochre. They are believed to be containers for spirits of the ancestors returning to the material world.*

BELOW: *Container (lakub), wood, Mindanao, the Philippines, 20th century. Traditional containers, made to hold betel nut, tobacco and other materials, are often embellished with exuberant scrolling designs by the Maranao wood carvers of Mindanao.*

representation of deities is not traditional in this faith. In some areas of Indonesia, such as West Papua, which shares an island with Papua New Guinea, wood working reflects more indigenous beliefs and artistic styles.

The Philippines have also experienced degrees of foreign influence, including Christianity and Islam, both of which have strongly affected local culture and artistic expression. Wood carving is an ancient tradition in the Philippines and has been employed for architecture, furniture, and religious statuary and ritual objects. Some of the most spectacular examples are the wood carvings of the Moronao people on the island of Mindanao in the southern Philippines. Many architectural details and wooden objects are carved with ornate openwork scrolling leaf and vine patterns. Even items used by the Muslims of the region, such as book stands for the Koran, the holy book of Islam, are carved with similar scrolling motifs. Following the advent of Christianity in the 16th century, local wood carvers used traditional wood carving techniques to create sacred Christian statuary and church furnishings such as pulpits, confessionals, altar tables and altar furnishings. Many of these carvings are heavily influenced by European Christian figures and furnishings, although they were gradually infused with local styles and details.

CHINA

ABOVE: *Folding chair,* huanghuali *wood, metal and twine, China, Qing dynasty.*

OPPOSITE: *Seated figure of Guanyin, wood and pigments, China, Jin dynasty. This majestic figure of Guanyin seated in the Royal Ease position was made up of multiple blocks of a type of paulownia wood and then carved and painted with mineral and vegetable pigments.*

IN CHINA, a number of different woods have traditionally been used for architecture, sculpture and furniture making. Of the softwoods, elm has been used historically in northern China, while cedar has been available in China south of the Yangzi River, on Hainan Island. Both cedar and camphorwood, used widely throughout East Asia, have a fragrance that is pleasant to humans but is repellant to insects, so they are ideal for storage chests. Fine Chinese furniture is generally made from imported hardwoods such as *huanghuali* and *zitan* (see 'The Fine Woods of Chinese Furniture', p. 201).

Chinese wood sculptures is known to date back to at least as early as the Eastern Zhou period (770–256 BC), since carved wooden figures of humans and animals have been excavated from tombs from the 5th and 6th centuries BC. These figures, which were buried in tombs as substitutes for live human sacrifices, often feature carved and painted details representing clothing. Over the next few centuries, such figures continued to be made of wood (and increasingly of clay). Lacquered wood coffins and vessels, including ritual food dishes and lidded boxes, were also buried in tombs.

There is little evidence of wooden Buddhist sculpture or ritual items prior to the Tang dynasty (AD 618–906). However, a number of large carvings of the *bodhisattva* Avalokiteshvara (Chinese: Guanyin) have survived from the 10th through the 13th century, when northern China was ruled by the Khitan or Liao dynasty (907–1125) and then the Jurchen or Jin dynasty (1115–1234). Demand continued for carved wooden Buddhist and Daoist figures for temples and for personal worship at home until recent years. Similarly, the woodblock printing of texts and images, a technique invented in China in the late 7th century, continued to be important in both the religious and secular realms in China until recent decades.

Relief and openwork wood carving has also flourished in the decoration of cabinets, screens and other home furnishings. Much of this wood carving was gilded or lacquered. However, in the Ming (1368–1644) and Qing (1644–1911) dynasties, many tables, cabinets, chairs, stools and stands made of the finest hardwoods such as *huanghuali* and *zitan*, were made in relatively simple and elegant forms with no lacquer or gilding. In addition to fine furniture, Chinese woodworkers also excelled in smaller carved items for palaces and scholars' studios, including brush pots, brush rests, incense stands, and even wooden head rests and pillows.

KOREA

IN KOREA, the most commonly used wood in architecture, sculpture and furniture has been pine, a wood that grows abundantly on the peninsula. Korea also has a long history of using wood for religious, decorative and functional purposes. Very little early material has survived in Korea; a small number of lacquered wood burial items have been excavated from tombs dating to the 5th and 6th centuries. From the Goryeo period

(918–1392), lacquered boxes with inlaid mother-of-pearl designs became popular, and some of these early examples have survived from temple and palace sites. Very little wooden Buddhist sculpture has survived in Korea, although some finely carved wooden sculptures of Buddhist figures do exist from the Joseon period (1392–1911), often painted with mineral pigments. Many carved wooden figures from Korea's indigenous shamanistic tradition have survived from the Joseon period, including the tall wooden *changsung* posts with carved or painted faces, which serve as symbols of fertility as well as guardians of villages and temples. Some of the most imaginative wood carvings are the wooden masks used in traditional Korean dance-drama and festivals, often associated with ancient shamanistic beliefs and rituals.

Much Korean architecture has traditionally been built from wood, though stone is also widely used. Typically, the wooden brackets supporting roofs and the wooden panels on the sides of temples and other buildings were painted with auspicious motifs in vivid colours. Inside Korean temples, palaces and homes, only a small amount of furniture was used, and this was made of wood, typically *zelkova*, a type of elm with a beautiful grain and considerable strength, and *paulownia*, which has a fine grain and is resistant to warping and cracking in Korea's very dry winters. Many Korean wood furnishings are lacquered and decorated with mother-of-pearl inlay (see p. 102).

OPPOSITE: *Seated Arhat (Korean: Nahan), or Buddhist sage, probably Bhadra (Palt'ara) with a tiger, carved wood with pigments, Korea, 19th century.*

ABOVE: *Mask, carved wood with string. Korea, end of the Joseon period, 1800–1910. Masks such as this example represent people, deities and real and imaginary animals and were used during the Joseon period (1392–1910) in the village dance dramas performed by ordinary people as a way of making fun of the upper classes.*

WOOD

RIGHT: Netsuke *of God of Long Life (Jurojin) and his deer, ebony and gilded bronze, Japan, 19th century. Netsuke were used to secure carrying cases that were suspended from the kimono sash and feature very intricate carving.*

BELOW: *Noh mask of a woman, carved and painted wood, Japan, Edo period. Noh masks were carved so skilfully that the expression on the face appeared to change with the subtle movements of the actor's head.*

JAPAN

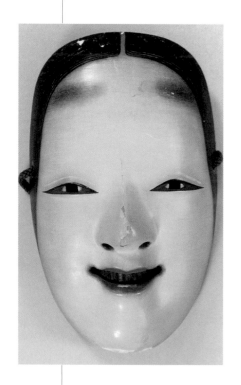

THE ISLANDS OF JAPAN have historically been densely forested with a wide array of fine woods. Since very little workable stone has been available, wood has been the principal material used in architecture and sculpture. Cypress has been the preferred wood for sculpture, with its smooth texture, light colour, attractive grain and fragrance. Cedar and camphorwood have a fine grain and are used extensively in architecture and sculpture. Cherrywood has been the principal wood used in the carving of wood blocks (see 'Woodblock Printing', p. 204). Camphorwood and *paulownia*, both of which have insect-repelling properties, have been important woods used in Japanese furniture and storage boxes. *Zelkova serrata* (Japanese grey bark elm) has also been used for Japanese furniture.

Japan boasts the world's oldest wooden buildings, belonging to the Horyuji Buddhist temple near Nara. Established in the 7th century, this temple attests to the sophistication of early Japanese carpentry, joinery and wood carving. Some of the finest Japanese wood figural sculptures date to the 11th through 13th centuries, when large figures of the Buddha and other deities were typically constructed using multiple blocks of wood that were hollowed out, reunited and then carved (see p. 202). Many were fitted with eyes of rock crystal and decorated with gold leaf and polychrome. Smaller devotional figures, made for worship in homes, were also finely carved and gilded.

Though Japanese sculptors have continued to carve religious imagery out of wood until the present, many of the finest carved wooden sculptures produced in more recent centuries have been the masks that were made for use in traditional theatre, dance and

festivals. In the 18th and 19th centuries, descendants of earlier mask makers carved tiny *netsuke* toggles out of both ivory and various precious woods.

Some of Japan's finest woodworking is found in its architecture, from the often lavishly decorated brackets that support the heavy roofs of temples and palaces to the carved elements inside traditional Japanese buildings. Particularly noteworthy are the *ranma*, or transom pieces, that fill the space between the top of the sliding screen doors and the ceiling of a traditional Japanese room. Often intricately carved with openwork designs, such as auspicious symbols, floral motifs and landscapes, these decorative features also allow ventilation and light into the interior of a house. A traditional Japanese interior contained little furniture, so there is very little old Japanese wooden furniture. Storage chests, stands, small tables and other small furnishings were often made of wood and decorated with lacquer. Some of the most celebrated unlacquered wood furnishings are the large wooden chests and cabinets called *tansu*, which provided storage space in the traditional Japanese home.

One of the greatest achievements of the Japanese wood carver has been woodblock printing (see 'Woodblock Printing', p. 204). First employed in Japan in the 8th century in Buddhist temples to print Buddhist texts and images, woodblock printing had entered the secular realm of entertainment by the 17th century. Block carvers were hired to carve out images of *kabuki* actors, beautiful courtesans and dramatic landscapes, often with hair-thin outlines and minute detailing. Although it is the designers of the original drawings, such as Harunobu and Hokusai (see p. 170), who are celebrated for their work, the extraordinary skill of the block carvers should also be remembered.

STONE

THE CONTINENT OF ASIA is vast and varied, and its geology has provided a rich variety of stone types, from the extremely hard granite to soft sandstone. In the continental cultures of India, China and Cambodia, it has been a primary material for building and carving, while in island cultures, wood has generally been dominant.

OPPOSITE: *Relief carving in stone of a female celestial deity, the Bayon, Angkor, Cambodia, 12th century.*

ABOVE LEFT: *Detail of dharmachakra, 7th–8th century, Thailand. See p. 235.*

ABOVE: *Hindu deities Shiva and Parvati, marble, Gujarat or Western Rajasthan, India, 12th century.*

LEFT: *Detail of architectural element depicting iris plants, marble, India, 17th century. See p. 233.*

STONE

ABOVE: *Elaborate carved decoration around stone staircase, Polonnaruwa, Sri Lanka.*

ABOVE RIGHT: *Relief carving of celestial beings, or apsaras, sandstone, the Bayon, Angkor, Cambodia, 12th century.*

FOR BOTH WOOD AND STONE, sculpture and architecture are closely linked art forms, since much sculpture is created to embellish buildings. In this chapter, the primary focus will be the stone sculptural traditions of Asia, most of which are religious. Unlike the stone carvings of Egypt, Greece, Rome and Central America, the stone carvings of Asia have rarely depicted portraits of historical kings and queens, although stone sculptures of deities occasionally have the facial features of a ruler. Most of the carved stone images discussed in this chapter are figures of gods, goddesses, perfected beings and guardians, hewn from stone with their longevity and immortality in mind.

THE MATERIAL

STONE COVERS the whole of our planet and is created by a variety of natural processes, so stones can have many different physical properties that dictate their use in building and sculpture. Ideally, stone used in sculpture should be soft enough to cut, but hard enough to retain the carving. The relative hardness of a particular stone is indicated by a number on the Mohs' scale, a scale of 1 to 10, with soft talc measuring 1 and extremely hard diamond measuring 10. Stones ranking 0 to 2.5 on this scale can be scratched with a fingernail. In addition, stone may be chosen for its colour and ability to take a polish.

ABOVE: *Detail of seated Buddha, Sri Lanka, granite, 12th century.*

There are three main types of stone or rock: igneous, sedimentary and metamorphic. Igneous rocks (from the Latin word *ignis*, fire) are created by fiery action of volcanoes or magma beneath the earth's crust and constitute the majority of the earth's known crust. Because they contain crystals that are fused together like glass at high temperatures, these rocks are some of the hardest of all. There are two types of igneous rocks: plutonic rocks, such as granite, which are formed by the slow crystallization of magma beneath the earth's crust; and volcanic rocks, such as basalt and andesite, which crystallize more quickly above the earth's surface after a volcanic eruption (see 'Igneous Rocks', above).

Sedimentary rocks are formed from the accumulation of sediment such as sand, mud and silt. Over time, wind, rain and the alternate heating and cooling from the sun erode rocks, and the particles are washed or blown down from mountainous areas to lower ground, where they are deposited in layers. Remains of plants and animals often drift into the sediment and become fossilized. Over millions of years, the overlaying layers compact the sediment, and minerals in the water crystallize to cement the sediment together. These rocks can feature a grain, or 'bedding,' created by the layering of sediment when it is deposited. These rocks can be split relatively easily along the bedding surfaces (see 'Sedimentary Rocks', p. 224 overleaf).

STONE

Sedimentary Rocks

Sandstone is a relatively hard, durable stone (Mohs' scale 6–7) and is composed mainly of quartz grains cemented by silica, calcium carbonate or iron oxide. Sandstone is found in a range of colours and may display bedding. Sandstone is used widely in the sculpture and architecture of northern India, Thailand and Cambodia, and has been the medium for many fine low relief sculptures, such as this 12th century carving of phoenixes at Angkor in Cambodia (below left).

Limestone is composed mainly of the mineral calcite, or calcium carbonate. It may form on the sea bed from lime sediment and the shells of primitive sea creatures and sometimes contains fossils of these creatures. Typically, it can be black, grey, white, yellow or brown. Denser varieties can be polished, though the polish does not survive well outdoors. Limestone can have a smooth granular surface and varies in hardness (Mohs' scale 2.5–3), so it is relatively easy to carve and can take small detail work, as can be seen in this Chinese carving of flying apsaras from the early 6th century (below). It breaks fairly predictably along the bedding surfaces. Limestone is found in areas of northern China.

ABOVE: *Low relief carving of phoenix roundels on sandstone temple walls, Angkor, Cambodia, 12th century.*

RIGHT: *Flying apsaras (Feitien) carrying an incense burner, limestone, China, Six Dynasties period, Northern Wei dynasty, 500–534.*

Metamorphic rocks have gone through a transformation as a result of heat or pressure. These forces cause the constituents of the rock to crystallize to varying degrees, possibly forming new mineral components. Metamorphic rocks can be relatively soft and easy to carve, such as soapstone and alabaster, or harder, as in the case of marble (see 'Metamorphic Rocks', below).

Metamorphic Rocks

Marble is metamorphosized limestone. It is a moderately hard stone to carve (Mohs' scale 2.5–5) and holds detail well once it is carved. Marble is found in a wide variety of colours and has a high crystalline content so sparkles when polished. Because of its durability and attractive surface, marble has been the favourite stone in many sculptural traditions, in particular in Rajasthan in India. It has been used in China, Korea and Burma. An example of fine relief carving of a lotus can be seen on the base of a Chinese marble lion (right).

Soapstone (often referred to as steatite from the Latin and Greek for tallow, the fat used for making candles and soap), is one of the softest stones (Mohs' scale 1–2.5) carved by Asian sculptors. This rock is rich in talc, a crystalline form of magnesium silicate that occurs in soft, flat plates. It has a slippery texture like soap, hence its name. This stone comes in a variety of colours.

Schist is a foliated metamorphic rock formed of layers of different minerals – mica, chlorite, talc, and hematite – and splits into irregular plates. It has a medium to coarse grain and is generally grey to black in colour. Grey schist, or phyllite, was used for the early Gandharan Buddhist sculptures of northwestern India, northern Pakistan and Afghanistan, such as this high relief frieze dating to the 2nd or 3rd century AD (above). It was most likely quarried locally in the lower Swat River Valley. Another type of schist, black chlorite schist, is also used in northeastern Indian sculpture.

ABOVE LEFT: *Buddhist scene depicted in high relief, Gandhara (probably modern Afghanistan), schist, 2nd or 3rd century* AD.

ABOVE: *Carving of scrolling lotuses on base of a marble stone lion, China, 18th century.*

STONE

Semi-Precious Stones

Smaller carvings and luxury items are also made from a number of semi-precious stones, which are highly valued variously for their colour, grain and lustre. Although they will not be discussed at length here, it is worth noting those semi-precious stones that figure prominently in Asian jewelry and sculpture. The most notable is jade (see Chapter 1). Lapis lazuli, or lazurite (Mohs' scale 5–6), is a dark blue stone, formed in limestone. Found primarily in northeastern Afghanistan, lapis has been used in Asia for thousands of years for sculptures, inlay and jewelry, particularly in South Asia and the Himalayas. Turquoise (Mohs' scale 5–6), an opaque phosphate of aluminium, which derives its colour from traces of copper, has also been used for millennia in jewelry, inlay and occasionally sculpture in South Asia, the Himalayas and China. Agate (Mohs' scale 6.5–7) is a type of chalcedony, with a banded or irregular, variegated appearance.

TECHNIQUES

ABOVE: *Snuff bottle with fish, crab and lotus, agate, China, middle to late Qing dynasty, 1700–1800. Agate is a microcrystalline form of silica with a waxy, smooth surface and is usually translucent with grain-like patterns. It is a very hard stone, but has been worked into luxury items such as Chinese snuff bottles.*

SINCE ANCIENT TIMES, stone has been carved with tools made from harder stones or metal. Knives and chisels can cut into softer stone, such as soapstone, allowing curving lines and more precise detailing. With harder stones such as granite, the stone is chipped away, usually resulting in more angular carving and less delineation of detail. The tools used by a stone carver are fairly similar all around the world. The principal tools are saws, hammers, chisels, rasps and polishing materials such as sandpaper or powdered stones.

The sculptor generally first chooses the stone, sometimes based on the shape, colour and pattern of the stone, and then determines the direction of the bedding, or grain, of the stone. The stone will split easily along the bedding surface and less easily across the bedding, so the sculptor generally opts to have the grain running along the length of the design. The sculptor then draws the design onto all sides of the stone and prepares for carving.

The first cuts are usually made with a pitching tool, a type of large chisel that is hit hard with a hammer to knock away the corners of the stone block. In some regions, a saw is used to make the basic form of the carving. It takes many hours of sawing to cut through this relatively hard stone, but stone carvers of this region have used this technique for centuries for sculpture and architecture. A point chisel is then used to carve out the rough form of the sculpture. Usually this chisel is used to create parallel grooves in the stone; these are then cross-hatched and each small section is chipped away. Because the resulting surface is rough, the sculptor uses a tooth chisel, with grooves along its edge, to render the surface more even. Then a flat chisel is used to smooth down the ridges left by the tooth chisel. If the surface is to be decorated with linear designs, a tracing tool with a sharp edge is hammered into the stone to incise the grooves. Finally, the surface is smoothed further with rasps and then polished with sandpaper or a similar abrasive.

STONE SCULPTURE is arguably the most admired artistic medium of South Asia and has a long and illustrious history, particularly in the arts of Hinduism and Buddhism. From as early as the Indus Valley Civilization (3500–1700 BC) in northwestern India and Pakistan, figural forms were sculpted in limestone and steatite. Much later, under the Mauryan King Ashoka (r. *c.* 273–232 BC), sculptures and edicts were carved into sandstone on a large scale with the aim of promulgating peace and unification under the rubric of divine law, or *dharma*. Powerful lions carved from sandstone were placed on top of tall pillars to roar out the law. The best preserved capital is the famous lion sculpture from Sarnath, the site of the Buddha's first sermon, where he first taught his *dharma*, and a major site of Buddhist pilgrimage since the 3rd century BC. This superbly carved figure was adopted as the emblem of the modern republic of India.

INDIA, PAKISTAN AND THE HIMALAYAS

STONE

LEFT: *Standing bodhisattva, grey schist, Gandhara (Afghanistan), 2nd–3rd century* AD. *Gandharan Buddhist figures carved out of grey schist display many Greco-Roman characteristics, such as European facial features, wavy hair and toga-like robes.*

RIGHT: *Head of a Buddha, sandstone, India, c. 475. This Buddha head displays the grace and serenity of Gupta period imagery. The eyelids are carved to appear heavy, creating a sense of the Buddha's inward gaze.*

OPPOSITE: *Two addorsed tree dryads, from Stupa I at Sanchi, sandstone, India, Madhya Pradesh, 50* BC–AD *25. These tree spirits represent a move in Indian stone sculpture towards dynamic figural imagery.*

As Buddhism grew in popularity, monasteries, worship halls and *stupas* (reliquary mounds) were built throughout the region. Begun in the 3rd century BC, the Great Stupa at Sanchi, Madhya Pradesh, was augmented by sandstone gates in the 1st century BC. The gates were embellished with elaborate carvings of plants, animals and nature spirits. The first iconic stone images of the Buddha were created in the 1st century AD in Mathura, 137 km (85 miles) south of Delhi, and in Gandhara, in modern day Afghanistan, Pakistan and northwestern India. Mathuran images were carved from the local reddish sandstone and feature a native style, descended from early figures of nature divinities and holy ascetic teachers. In contrast, sculptors in Gandhara, situated along trade routes linking the Eastern and Western worlds, followed the Greco-Roman sculptural tradition.

The Gupta period (4th–5th century AD) is often considered the 'Classical' period of Indian art. Sculptors produced sandstone Buddhist figures characterized by a refined simplicity and grace that became the standard for Buddhist images elsewhere. The Gupta period was also an important time for Hindu and Jain sculpture, and much imagery from all three traditions was carved into temple and shrine walls. These carved stone temples were the inspiration for similar structures throughout Asia over the following centuries.

Sandstone continued to be the preferred material for sculpture in central and southern India. In northeastern India, Hindu and Buddhist statuary, often carved by the

STONE

RIGHT: *Shiva's family, sandstone, Haryana or Uttar Pradesh, c. mid-10th century. Here, the god Shiva is shown with his family, his consort Parvati and their two sons, Ganesha, the elephant-headed god, and the five-headed Skanda. They are accompanied by Shiva's bull Nandi.*

same studios of artists, was created out of dark-coloured schist under the Pala kings, who reigned in the area that is now modern Bihar and Bengal from *c.* 750 to *c.* 1200. Among the masterfully carved Buddhist and Hindu imagery are both figural and symbolic representations of deities. Schist features prominently in the sculpture of southern India created under the Hoysala kings (late 900s–early 1300s). Most of the sculpture of this region is Hindu, and many of the exuberantly carved figural sculptures originally adorned temples.

In northwestern India, especially Rajasthan, many buildings and sculptures have been created from marble. Marble carving was also prevalent within the context of the Jain

OPPOSITE LEFT: *Sarasvati, marble, 1153, India, Jagadeva, Gujarat. This fine high relief marble sculpture depicts Sarasvati, goddess of culture, music and the arts, standing in the typically Indian* tribhanga *(triple bend) pose. She is deeply carved, almost in the round, with extraordinary undercutting behind the hands and earrings.*

OPPOSITE RIGHT: *Jina Ajitanatha and his Divine Assembly, marble, India, Gujarat, dated 1062. This elegant figure of a jina, or perfected being, is typical of Jain figural sculptures, since jina are often depicted standing with their arms hanging at their sides and with a marking on their chests.*

ABOVE: *Architectural element depicting iris plants, marble, India, 17th century. Some of India's finest marble carving was the detailing on Mughal architecture, both the pietra dura coloured stone inlay and the deep relief carving of natural motifs, such as plants and animals.*

religion, which emerged around the same time as Buddhism. Many Jain temples were decorated with elaborate marble sculpture, most notably the Vimala Shah Temple on Mount Abu in Rajasthan. Jain perfected beings, or *jinas*, were also carved from marble.

Marble has also been used in South Asia in secular architecture and decorative arts, particularly during the reign of the Mughal emperors (1526–1857). The world's most celebrated example of marble architecture is the Taj Mahal, a mausoleum completed in 1653 by the Emperor Shah Jahan (*r.* 1628–58) for his wife, Mumtaz Mahal. The building is completely faceted in marble with decoration in stone inlay. Mughal marble architecture featured fine relief carving. The Mughal Court also commissioned decorative objects made from stones including jade (see Chapter 1), rock crystal and agate. Precious gems, such as rubies, emeralds and diamonds, were inlaid into stones and metalwork.

Stone has been used widely in Sri Lanka for religious statuary. Much of Sri Lanka's stone sculpture depicts figures of the Buddha himself either teaching his law or reclining just before his passing. Some of Sri Lanka's most spectacular stone Buddhist imagery dates to the 12th century, after Buddhism's demise on the mainland. The colossal Buddha and Ananda figures at Polonnaruwa are among the world's most impressive stone sculptures. These huge figures (the reclining Buddha is 46 feet long and Ananda is 23

STONE

BURMA

feet high) are carved out of solid granite. The facial features are finely carved, and the undulating grain of the rock lends the image a particular grace, despite its immense scale.

In the Himalayan region, most religious imagery has been traditionally made from wood, or more often metals such as copper and bronze, with gilding. Good stone for carving was difficult to transport into the region, so its use has been limited. However, precious stones such as rock crystal have been used for Buddhist ritual objects such as ceremonial daggers and axes, and lapis lazuli and turquoise have been used widely in jewelry and decorative inlay.

VERY LITTLE EARLY Burmese stone material survives. Excavations of temples, *stupas* and other early sites have shown that early inhabitants, the Pyu in upper Burma and the Mon in lower Burma, created Buddhist and Hindu figures out of stone, bronze and terracotta. A number of sandstone steles dating to around the 4th or 5th century AD have been found featuring relief carvings of warrior kings and Buddhist deities. Sculptures in the round of seated Buddhas and other figures have also been excavated from Pyu pagodas and show the influence of Indian Gupta period sculpture in their slender forms and diaphanous robes. Many sandstone images of Vishnu were created during this period. The Mon in the southern region produced stone sculptures, primarily of Hindu deities.

During the Pagan period (1044–1287), the Classical period of Burmese culture, northern and southern Burma were unified under the Pagan kings with their capital at Pagan. Theravada, or monastic, Buddhism prevailed, and images were carved from sandstone and phyllite, a schist similar to that used in northeastern India. Most surviving work dates to the Konbaung period (1752–1824), particularly the 19th century.

STONE HAS BEEN WORKED in Thailand for thousands of years. Early stone bangles date from the Ban Chiang period (3600 BC–2nd century AD). The earliest surviving stone sculpture in Thailand dates to the Mon-Dvaravati period (6th–11th century AD). The Dvaravati people were mainly Mon, probably related to the Mon of Burma. The predominant religion at this time was Buddhism, but Hinduism also had a presence. Most extant sculptures of this period are Buddhist images influenced by Indian styles. Some of the most elaborate sculptures of the early period are the carved stone Buddhist wheels that were probably placed on top of stone columns. Other regional styles of sculpture also existed in Thailand, including the Srivijaya style in peninsular Thailand, ruled by Indonesian kingdoms to the south; these sculptures feature the elegant, swaying forms of Indian Gupta figures and the elaborate ornamentation of Pala sculptures.

From around the 6th century, the Khmer entered areas of Thailand and Cambodia. They increased their power, and from the 10th to the 13th centuries they ruled areas of

THAILAND AND CAMBODIA

ABOVE: *The Buddha Shakyamuni, sandstone, Thailand, Mon-Dvaravati period, Si Thep, 9th century.*

LEFT: *Dharmachakra, stone, Mon-Dvaravati, 7th–8th century, Thailand. Wheels represent the constant motion of the Buddha's teachings.*

LEFT: *Vishnu, sandstone, Cambodia, Angkor period, c. 950. This figure of the Hindu god Vishnu features many characteristics of Khmer figural sculpture, including a sinewy yet powerful physique, a broad face and nose, sensuous lips with a slight smile. The simple rendering of the body also contrasts with the elaborate detail of the crown and the folds of his garment.*

northeastern Thailand. Much Thai sculpture from the region under Khmer control strongly resembled Khmer sculpture. After the 13th century or so, stone declined in favour of bronze for smaller images and stuccoed brick for monumental sculpture.

Early in the first millennium, Cambodia comprised a number of small states which had contact with both India and China and practised Hinduism and Buddhism. The region's most artistically sophisticated and varied sculpture was created under the reign of the Khmer, who ruled in Cambodia from 802 to 1432. Mostly carved from sandstone, Khmer figural carving, both Hindu and Buddhist, possess grace and solidity.

The stonework of the Khmer reached its zenith in the Angkor period (10th–13th century). Angkor, the Khmer capital in western Cambodia, was the site of many Buddhist and Hindu temples, most famously the Hindu temple Angkor Wat. Khmer buildings were made of sandstone quarried near Angkor, and embellished with high- and low-relief carvings of Hindu and Buddhist deities, scenes showing the exploits of Khmer monarchs, and exquisite patterning using natural motifs (see 'Stone Carving at Angkor', p. 237).

Stone Carving at Angkor

The ancient Khmer capital of Angkor is home to some of Asia's most spectacular sculpture. Among the most celebrated stone carvings are the low reliefs carved along the gallery walls at Angkor Wat depicting scenes from Hindu epics and mythology and historical battle scenes of Khmer armies defeating their enemies (below). This detail depicts warriors marching to battle at the climax of the epic, the Mahabharata; it shows remarkable attention to their faces and ornamentation and a powerful rhythm in their synchronized stride. Also depicted along the gallery walls is the Hindu creation myth in which the gods and demons churned up the ocean in a cosmic tug-of-war, thus creating the whole universe. Sculptures of gods and demons engaged pulling in this tug-of-war are also found along the road leading into the ancient fortified city of Angkor Thom.

Probably the most powerful carvings at Angkor are the large faces carved in high relief on the towers of the Bayon, a mountain-like Buddhist temple within Angkor Thom (right). The faces, perhaps modelled on the face of Khmer ruler Jayavarman VII (r. 1181–1219) or possibly representing either the bodhisattva Avalokiteshvara or the Hindu god Vishnu, gaze out compassionately and protectively in all directions.

ABOVE RIGHT. *Head of bodhisattva or deity carved on towers of the Bayon, a mountain-like Buddhist temple within Angkor Thom, Cambodia.*

BELOW: *Low reliefs at Angkor Wat, Cambodia. This detail depicts warriors marching to battle at the climax of the Indian epic, the Mahabharata.*

LEFT: *Stone stele supported by turtle, 15th century, Hanoi. A total of 82 stone steles supported by turtles have survived at the Temple of Literature in Hanoi, a temple which was originally dedicated to Confucius in 1070 and became Vietnam's first university. The steles are inscribed with the names and home towns of doctoral students.*

VIETNAM

VIETNAM'S EARLIEST surviving stone sculpture dates to the Champa period (AD 192–15th century), when the Cham people occupied two thirds of today's Vietnam. The Cham battled intermittently with the Annamese and the Chinese to the north and with the Khmer to the west, and by the 17th century had been conquered by the northern Annamese. Like much of Southeast Asia, the Champa kingdom was heavily influenced by Indian culture in the first millennium, so much of this region's early stone sculpture features Hindu and Buddhist deities.

Following the defeat of the Cham, Vietnam was dominated by the culture of the Annamese, who were heavily influenced by China to the north. Over the next few centuries, religious sculpture was cast in bronze or carved from wood and lacquered; very little statuary was made in stone. Much of the stone statuary of the last few centuries has been Chinese in inspiration. Carved architectural elements and stone steles resting on animal bases have been some of Vietnam's most expressive stone carvings.

OPPOSITE: *Mythical animal and celestial female, sandstone, Vietnam, Ancient Champa, 11th–12th century. Like much of the Champa period stone carving from Vietnam, this figural carving depicts mythological imagery from Hinduism, a female deity emerging from the mouth of a makara, or sea creature.*

INDONESIA

MOST OF THE STONE SCULPTURE from Indonesia has been created on the islands of Java and Bali from rough, dark volcanic stone known as andesite. One of the most significant periods in the development of Indonesian stone sculpture was the Shailendra dynasty (AD 730–930) of central Java, which commissioned large Buddhist monuments, such as Borobodur. Built around 800, the pyramid-like structure has been described as a funerary monument, a *stupa* and a three-dimensional mandala, or model of the universe. Along the walls of its lower terraces are elaborate relief carvings depicting scenes from

ABOVE: *Vishnu riding Garuda, andesite, Java, Indonesia, 13th century. This image of the god Vishnu riding his vehicle Garuda is typical of the columnar composition of the stone statuary of the period.*

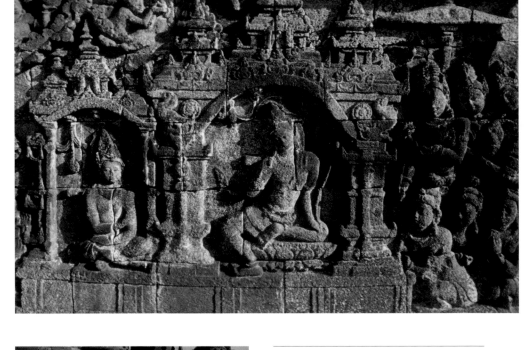

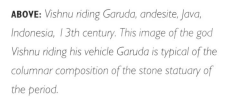

ABOVE: *Relief carvings on terrace walls, andesite, Borobodur, Java, Indonesia, c. 800. These carvings cover the walls on the lowest levels of Borobodur, and are believed to show the earthly realm of passion and desire.*

LEFT: *Seated Buddha, andesite, Borobodur, c. 800. The beautifully carved seated Buddhas are in the middle section of the structure, which represents the celestial realm of the universe. Above these are stupas, both empty and containing Buddha images, representing the realm of formlessness and ultimate enlightenment.*

this world and past lives of the Buddha. On the middle terraces are 108 seated Buddhas carved in the round with finely proportioned bodies and gentle facial expressions. On the upper levels are 72 *stupas*, each containing a seated Buddha.

Much of the later stone imagery of Java depicts Hindu deities, especially Shiva and Vishnu. Some of the most outstanding stone sculptures are the depictions of local rulers in the form of Hindu deities, in particular the god Vishnu, dating to the 13th and 14th centuries.

RIGHT: *Daoist Immortal Liu Hai, soapstone/steatite, China, 18th–19th century. This figure of a Daoist immortal is carved from soapstone and features the fine detailing that is possible in softer stones. As with many images of Daoist Immortals, it is also carved with great humour and warmth.*

BELOW: *Seated* bodhisattva *and attendants, stone, China, dated 1206, Jin dynasty. Many stone Buddhist images, such as this elegant figure of a* bodhisattva, *were commissioned as prayers for the salvation of a family member and donated to temples.*

CHINA

ALTHOUGH JADE was an important material in ancient Chinese burial practices (see Chapter 1), and turquoise was used as a decorative inlay as early as 3000 years ago, stone was not significant as a material for sculpture until the Han dynasty (206 BC–AD 220), when pictorial carvings in shallow relief of battles, daily life, and wise sages and poets decorated the stone walls of royal tombs. China's first large-scale stone sculptures of guardians and animals were also produced to protect the tomb contents and flanked the Spirit Roads leading up to royal tombs. Later, high-relief stone carvings decorated the terraces surrounding imperial tombs, most notably the realistically carved horses from the stables of the Tang Emperor Taizong (d. AD 649).

The introduction of Buddhism to China around the 4th century AD led to the creation of stone Buddhist statuary. Some of the most remarkable carvings are the colossal images of Buddhas and *bodhisattvas* carved into the limestone rock face at Yungang in northeastern China and further south at Luoyang and Longmen in the late 5th century. During the Tang dynasty (618–906), rulers such as the renowned 7th century Empress Wu continued the tradition of carving colossal stone Buddha images into the face of rocks as a demonstration of their power. The Empress also commissioned stone Buddhist pagodas decorated with relief carved panels. Smaller stone images of Buddhist and Daoist deities were also produced, although they were outnumbered by figures cast in bronze and clay. During later periods, Buddhist and Daoist stone carvings were relatively rare, though some extremely fine examples do exist.

Although much Chinese religious statuary from later periods was made of bronze and wood, in the Ming (1368–1644) and Qing (1644–1911) dynasties, many Buddhist,

STONE

Daoist and decorative secular sculptures were made of soapstone. Many small-scale figural carvings and snuff bottles were made from precious stones such as jade, agate, lapis lazuli, turquoise and rock crystal.

Some of the finest stone carving of the later period of Chinese history has been the sculptural detail on buildings, which have long been carved with auspicious designs of dragons, phoenixes, bats and floral motifs. The stone Buddha, or *Fo*, lions that flank the entrances to grand buildings are some of the most impressive large-scale carvings. In Chinese gardens, decorative *taihu* rocks from Lake Tai near Shanghai have been popular from as early as the Han dynasty. Formed from limestone at the bottom of this prehistoric lake, these rocks are porous and whimsical in form. However, some *taihu* rocks were carved into natural-looking shapes and then left in the lake to acquire the patina of age. Smaller rocks have also been collected as decorative objects since the Song dynasty (960–1279), particularly by scholars, who displayed them in their studios on carved wooden stands.

KOREA

IN KOREA, stone has long been used to build Buddhist temples, pagodas and statuary. One of the earliest surviving stone carvings is a 6th century AD soapstone figure of a seated Buddha from Baekche in the southwest of the peninsula. The soft stone allowed for fine carving in the face and the folds of the figure's robes. However, most stone Buddhist sculptures and buildings have been made from granite, which is abundant in the region. Many early stone carvings were relatively simplistic in detail because of the hardness of the stone. However, by the Unified Silla period (668–935), exceptional carving in granite was possible, as can be seen at the Sokkuram Buddhist cave temple near the ancient capital of Kyongju. Built between 751 and 774, the Sokkuram temple is modelled on Indian stone cave temples and features a large seated Buddha carved in the round, and 41 deities elegantly carved in relief on the walls around him.

The tradition of stone Buddhist statuary continued into the Goryeo period (918–1392), with stone being reserved for larger sculptures. Some figures carved in marble have remained from the early Goryeo period and exhibit extremely fine carving, particularly in the facial features and ornamentation. During the Joseon period (1392–1910), Buddhism fell out of official favour, and very few stone Buddha images appear to have been created. The stone figures that have survived from this period are the stone sculptures that flank the Spirit Roads leading up to the royal tombs and symbolically guard the contents of the tombs.

LEFT: *Guardian figure, granite, Korea, 15th century. Carved out of granite, many guardian figures are modelled after Court officials.*

LEFT: Bodhisattva *Kshitigarbha (Japanese: Jizo)*, granite, Japan, dated 1644. The bodhisattva *Jizo* is the protector of children and travellers, and stone figures of him can be seen all over Japan in temple grounds, along the side of roads and in the countryside.

JAPAN

STONE HAS NOT BEEN a preferred material in Japan, primarily because of the abundance of wood. In architecture, stone has been reserved for platforms or ramparts. For sculpture, wood and bronze have been more extensively employed, although some impressive Buddhist sculptures have survived from the Heian period (794–1185) in the Kunisaki peninsula. Carvings of compassionate *bodhisattvas* are often found in the grounds of temples and in the countryside, while stone lanterns light the way for visitors to Japan's Buddhist temples and Shinto shrines. In some Zen Buddhist temples, gardens are created as microcosmic representations of an idealized natural world. The gravel and rocks are arranged symbolically to represent the sea and mountains or islands, and stones are carefully selected by the garden designer to create a perfectly balanced composition. These stones are never carved or embellished, as the natural state of the stone is deeply admired for its tones and textures and revered for its timelessness. In Japan, perhaps more than in any other culture, the stone itself is a focus of spiritual attention.

ABOVE: *Stone and gravel garden, Ryoanji, Kyoto, Japan. Stone gardens are a feature of some of Japan's Zen Buddhist temples. Stones and gravel are arranged symbolically to represent islands and the sea, respectively. The most famous of these is the garden at the Ryoanji temple in Kyoto, shown here in spring.*

ILLUSTRATION CREDITS

ABBREVIATIONS

a: above; b: below; c: centre; l: left; r: right

PAM – Pacific Asia Museum, all photographs by Julian Bermudez;

LACMA – Los Angeles County Museum of Art;

PDF – Percival David Foundation of Chinese Art, School of Oriental and African Studies, London

1 (half-title) PAM, Museum purchase with funds provided by the Bressler Foundation; 2 (opposite title page) LACMA, Gift of the Friends of Far Eastern Art; 3 (title page) Private collection; 8 Interior design by Barefoot Elegance, Los Angeles, Photo by Douglas Hill; 9l PAM, Gift of Concettina and Allyn Arnold in memory of Milton Orth; 9c PAM, Gift of the International Netsuke Foundation; 9r Victoria & Albert Museum, London. Photo Eileen Tweedy; 10l Private collection; 10r Victoria & Albert Museum, London; 11l LACMA, Gift of Varya and Hans Cohn; 11ar LACMA, Gift of Miss Bella Mabury; 11br PAM, Gift of Ruth and Stan Allen; 12 Courtesy of Jon and Cari Markel, Silk Roads Design Gallery, Los Angeles; 13l Interior design by Georgia Johnstone, architecture by Steven Ball Architects, Photo by Christopher Covey; 13r Private Collection, Photo by Alan McArthur; 14al author; 14bl Jewelry design by David Humphrey, Photo by the author; 14r LACMA, Purchased with funds provided by Alice and Nahum Lainer, Carla and Fred Sands, Lenore and Richard Wayne, Jane and Marc B. Nathanson in honor of Lynda and Stewart Resnick, Kathy and Frank Baxter, Irene Christopher, and Marti and Tony Oppenheimer through the 2004 Collectors Committee; 15l LACMA, Raymond and Frances Bushell Collection; 15r PAM, Gift of David L. Kamansky; 16–17 Paper sculpture design and interior design by Shoichi and Colleen Sakurai, Photo by Arthur Sawamura; 18al PAM, Gift of Mr. David L. Kamansky in honor of Dick and Judith Bressler; 18bl Kim 3 International Furnishings, California; 18r PAM, Gift of Michiko Yoda; 19 Warisan, Bali, Indonesia, Los Angeles, USA, Dublin, Ireland; 20a Interior design by Beverly Messenger, Photo by Gale Beth Goldberg, Courtesy of Gibbs Smith, Publisher; 20bl,br Collection of Diane and Arthur Abbey, photo courtesy of Tai Gallery, Santa Fe; 21a Kim 3 International Furnishings, California; 21b author; 22a LACMA, Gift of the Far Eastern Art Council; 22b Collection of David Humphrey; 23a Victoria & Albert Museum, London; 23b Copyright The Kelton Foundation 2005, Photo Scott McClaine; 24 LACMA, Gift of Carl Holmes; 25l PAM, Gift of Mr. and Mrs. Barry H. Taper; 25c PAM, Gift of Mrs. Elizabeth S. Burton; 25r PAM, Gift of Mrs. Maria Lim McClay and her husband Mr. Booker McClay, in loving memory of her parents, Mr. and Mrs. T. P. Lim; 26 PAM, Gift of Mr. and Mrs. Barry H. Taper; 27l PAM, Gift of Mr. William T. Lim and Mrs. Catherine M. Lim, in loving memory of their parents, Mr. and Mrs. T. P. Lim; 27r PAM, Gift of Mrs. Harold Witherbee; 28 Photos by Richard W. Hughes / www.ruby-sapphire.com; 29 The British Library, London; 30al,r PAM, Gift of Dorothy C. Wagner in memory of Grace Rowley; 30b Photo by Richard W. Hughes / www.ruby-sapphire.com; 31 LACMA, From the Nasli and Alice Heeramaneck Collection, Museum Associates Purchase; 32 author; 33 LACMA, Gift of Carl Holmes; 34a PAM, Gift of Mr. and Mrs. Barry H. Taper; 34b,35l PAM, Gift of Robert Chasin; 35r PAM, Gift of Mr. and Mrs. H. A. Meselson in memory of Mr. Barney Dagan; 36 LACMA, Gift of the Marcia Israel Collection; 37 PAM, Gift of Mr. and Mrs. Barry H. Taper; 38 LACMA, Gift of Mr. and Mrs. Paul E. Manheim; 39l PAM, Gift of Mr. and Mrs. Barry H. Taper; 39r PAM, Gift of Mr. Joseph B. Fischer; 40al PAM, Gift of Mrs. Emma Dagan in honor of David Kamansky's 50th Birthday; 40bl PAM, Gift of David M. Goodman; 40r PAM, Gift of Mrs. Elizabeth S. Burton; 42,43 LACMA, From the Nasli and Alice Heeramaneck Collection, Museum Associates Purchase; 44 Courtesy of Dale Gluckman; 45l PAM, Gift of Mr. Harvey W. House; 45c PAM, Gift of Mrs. Russell Dod; 45r PAM, Gift of Dr. and Mrs. Milton Rubini; 46 Photo by Alan McArthur; 47 author; 48a Photo by Alan McArthur; 48b author; 49 Photos by Alan McArthur; 50,51 all drawings by Melanie Lum; 50a author; 50ca,cb,b Courtesy of Dale Gluckman; 51a PAM, Gift of Bea Brunt; 51ca Courtesy of Dale Gluckman; 51cb PAM, Museum Purchase; 51b PAM, Gift of Bea Brunt; 52a author; 52b Photo by Dale Gluckman; 53a author; 53bl,br Courtesy of Dale Gluckman; 54l author; 54r PAM, Gift of the Grilli Collection; 55r PAM, Gift of Mrs. Florence R. Pigman; 55l PAM, Gift of Mr. and Mrs. Henry Foster; 56a PAM, Museum Purchase with funds from the Collectors' Circle; 56b PAM, Gift of Mr. and Mrs. Frederick Hake; 57 PAM, Gift of Dr. and Mrs. Milton Rubini; 58l Courtesy of the National Folk Museum of Korea; 58r PAM, Gift of Mr. Harvey W. House; 59 PAM, Gift of Mr. and Mrs. Gerald Kamansky; 60 PAM, Gift of Mrs. Cora Jeanne Martin; 61a author; 61b Courtesy of Dale Gluckman; 62 The Norton Simon Museum, Gift of Ramesh and Urmil Kapoor; 63l,r Courtesy of Dale Gluckman; 64 author; 65l Photo by Alan McArthur; 65r Photo by Dale Gluckman; 66 LACMA, Ernest Larson Blank Memorial Fund; 67l PDF; 67c PAM, Gift of Lily Laub; 67r LACMA, Purchased with funds provided by the Art Museum Council; 68l PAM, Gift of Mr. and Mrs. Barry H. Taper; 68r PAM, Gift of Mr. and Mrs. Robert M. Snukal; 69,70 author; 71a Photo by Tsunemitsu Yajima, Monya Art Co. Ltd.; 71b author; 72 PAM, Gift of Chan Siu Kin; 73l,r PAM, Gift of Mr. And Mrs. Robert Snukal; 74 Copyright 2005 The Kelton Foundation; 75,76 PDF; 77 PAM, Museum Purchase; 78l PAM, Gift of David Kamansky; 78r PAM, Gift of Dr. And Mrs. Wilmont Gordon; 79l PAM, Gift of Lily Laub; 79r PAM, Gift of Dr. Lennox Tierney; 80 PAM, Gift of Mr. and Mrs. Robert Snukal; 81l LACMA, Purchased with Museum Funds; 81r Courtesy of Rae Terk; 82 Brooklyn Museum of Art, Gift of the Asian Art Council; 83 LACMA, Purchased with Museum Funds; 84 PAM, Museum Purchase; 85l PAM, Gift of the Hon. and Mrs. Jack Lydman; 85r LACMA, Ernest Larson Blank Memorial Fund; 86l author; 86r LACMA, Purchased with funds provided by the Art Museum Council; 87 LACMA, Purchased with funds provided by Max Palevsky, Camilla Chandler Frost, Mrs. Harry Lenart in memory of Daisy Belin, and Virginia and Raymond Atchley; 88 LACMA, Gift of the Kurtzman Family; 89l,r PAM, Gift of the Hon. and Mrs. Jack Lydman; 90 Courtesy of David Marsh; 91al PAM, Museum purchase with funds provided by the Bressler Foundation; 91ar PAM, Gift of Elly Nordskog; 91b Courtesy of Jon and Cari Markel, Silk Roads Design Gallery, Los Angeles; 92 author; 93 Photos by Alan McArthur; 94 Courtesy of Jon and Cari Markel, Silk Roads Design Gallery, Los Angeles; 95l author; 95c,r Photo by Hollis Goodall; 96 author; 97l Courtesy of Jon and Cari Markel, Silk Roads Design Gallery, Los Angeles; 97ar Photo by Alan McArthur; 97br Photo by Hollis Goodall; 98 LACMA, Gift of Dale and Nicole Lum; 99 LACMA, Far Eastern Art Council Acquisition Fund; 100l,r Courtesy of Donal and Althea Bassett; 101 LACMA, Purchased with Museum Funds; 102a Courtesy of John and Tammy Park; 102b author; 103l PAM, Gift of Elly Nordskog; 103r Courtesy of Michael and Janet Kadin; 104 Courtesy of David Kamanksy; 105l PAM, Museum Purchase with Funds from Raymond and Virginia Atchley, Elly Nordskog and David Kamansky; 105r Courtesy of Elly Nordskog; 106 LACMA, Gift of Dr. and Mrs. J. Stuart Cumming; 107 PAM, Gift of Margot and Hans Ries; 108 PAM, Gift of Mrs. Ruth Ann Yonglove; 109l,r Courtesy of Jon and Cari Markel, Silk Roads Design Gallery, Los Angeles; 110 PAM Gift of Mr. and Mrs. Andrew J. Bergensen; 111al author; 111ar PAM, Museum purchase with funds provided by the Bressler Foundation; 111b LACMA, Gift of Terence McInerney; 112 The

Metropolitan Museum of Art, Gift of Mr. and Mrs. J. J. Klejman, 1964. (64.102) Photography ©1999 The Metropolitan Museum of Art; 113l PAM, Gift of Mrs. Mahlom Arnett, in honor of Mr. Mahlom Edward Arnett; 113c LACMA, Gift of Corinne and Don Whitaker; 113r, 114l PAM, Leo Strassburg Memorial Collection donated in loving memory by his wife Lorraine Strassburg; 114r PAM, Gift of Mr. and Mrs. Barry H. Taper; 115 Photos by Daniel Stiles; 116l,r Courtesy of Kenneth Lapatin; 117 PAM, Leo Strassburg Memorial Collection donated in loving memory by his wife Lorraine Strassburg; 118al,ar Photo by Daniel Stiles; 118b Courtesy of Bryant University, Smithfield, Rhode Island; 119l Photo by Daniel Stiles; 119c PAM, Gift of David Kamansky; 119r Courtesy of David Kamansky; 120 Copyright The Kelton Foundation 2005. Photo by Scott McClaine; 121 The Norton Simon Foundation, Gift of Mr. Norton Simon; 122 Courtesy of David Kamansky; 123 LACMA, Gift of Corinne and Don Whitaker; 124 LACMA, Gift of Dr. and Mrs. Pratapaditya Pal; 125a LACMA, Gift of Corinne and Don Whitaker; 125b LACMA, Gift of Lillian Apodaca Weiner; 126l Purchased with funds provided by Christian Humann; 126r LACMA, Gift of Mrs. J. Leroy Davidson in memory of Dr. J. Leroy Davidson; 127 LACMA, Gift of Corinne and Don Whitaker; 128l Courtesy of David Kamansky; 128r Courtesy of David Kamansky; 129l PAM, Museum Purchase in memonry of Athanasius Boukidis; 129r LACMA, Far Eastern Art Council Fund; 130l,c PAM, Gift of Ruth Lewis; 130r PAM, Gift of Mr. and Mrs. Barry H. Taper; 131l PAM, Gift of Blanche Pope; 131r PAM, Gift of Elinor D. Herrick; 132, 133l Courtesy of David Kamansky; 133ar LACMA, Gift of the Helen Dorsey Trust; 133br LACMA, Gift of Jerome L. Joss; 134 Courtesy of Tai Gallery, Santa Fe, Photo by Pat Pollard; 135l Lutz Collection, Photo by Anthony D. Secker; 135c Lutz Collection, Photo by Shin Hada; 135r author; 136l PAM, Gift of Dr. George W. Housner; 136c Photo courtesy of Dana Levy; 136r PAM, Gift of Mr. and Mrs. Robert M. Snukal; 137, 138al Photos by the author, Courtesy of the Huntington Library, Art Collections and Botanical Gardens; 138bl,r Photos by Dana Levy; 139l Photo by Alan McArthur; 139r Lutz Collection, Photo by Eric Kvalsvik; 140 Photo courtesy of Dana Levy; 141a Courtesy of Tai Gallery, Santa Fe, Photo by Lois Ellen Frank; 141b Photo by Art Streiber; 142,143,144l Lutz Collection, Photos by Shin Hada; 144r Lutz Collection, Photo by Anthony D. Secker; 145 PAM, Gift of Mr. and Mrs. Robert Snukal; 146 Lutz Collection, Photo by Eric Kvalsvik; 147 Lutz Collection, Photo by Anthony D. Secker; 148l Denver Art Museum Collection, Gift of the Lutz Bamboo Collection, Photo by the Denver Art Museum; 148–49 Lutz Collection, Photo by Anthony D. Secker; 149r author; 150a Courtesy of the Lloyd Cotsen Collection, Photo by Pat Pollard; 150b Courtesy of Tai Gallery, Santa Fe, Photo by Pat Pollard; 151a author; 151c Lutz Collection, Photo by Eric Kvalsvik; 151r PAM, Gift of Raymond and Virginia Atchley; 152–53, 153r UCLA Fowler Museum of Cultural History, Photo by Don Cole; 154l Courtesy of PAM Store; 154r Photo by Alan McArthur; 155 Photos by Dana Levy; 156, 157l,r author; 157c, 158a LACMA, Far Eastern Art Council Fund; 158b PAM, Gift of the Grilli Collection; 159b Hiromi Paper International; 159a, 160l author; 160r Hiromi Paper International; 161 Courtesy of the Ruth Chandler Williamson Gallery, Scripps College, Claremont; 162 author; 163, 164l,r, 165l,r, 166l Sam Fogg, London; 166r author; 167 LACMA, Far Eastern Art Council Fund; 168l,r Sam Fogg, London; 168b author; 169 PAM, Gift of Mary Brumder; 170a PAM, Museum Purchase with funds from Frank and Toshi Mosher; 170b PAM, Gift of Mr. and Mrs. Everett A. Palmer Jr.; 171 LACMA, Gift of Dr. and Mrs. Pratapaditya Pal; 172l LACMA, Gift of the Walter Foundation; 172r PAM, Gift of the Nancy King Collection; 173 PAM Store; 174, 175 Sam Fogg, London; 176 The Norton Simon Foundation,; 177al Courtesy of David Humphrey; 177ar PAM, Gift of Mr. and Mrs. Robert Snukal; 177b LACMA, Gift of Anna Bing Arnold and Justin Dart; 178 Photo by Alan McArthur; 179al Photo by Richard W. Hughes / www.ruby-sapphire.com; 179ar,br Courtesy of David Humphrey; 180l The Norton Simon Foundation; 180r PAM, Gift of the Nancy King Collection; 181 Copyright The Kelton Foundation 2005, Photo by Scott McClaine; 182al,cl,bl Photos by Sharon Takeda; 182br author; 183l PAM, Gift of Mrs. Cynthia L. Mazo; 183r LACMA, Gift of Phyllis and Sidney Krystal; 184a PAM, Gift of David Kamansky in honor of Dr. Chaibai and Mrs. Mehria Mustamandy; 184b LACMA, Gift of Anna Bing Arnold and Justin Dart; 185 LACMA, Gift of Mr. and Mrs. J. J. Klejman of New York; 186l,r The Norton Simon Foundation; 187al PAM, Gift of David Kamansky in honor of Zelma Long; 187bl Courtesy of David Humphrey and Melinda Salinger; 187r LACMA, Purchased with funds provided by Lizabeth Scott; 188 PAM, Purchased with funds provided by Dorrie Braun Poole; 189al Courtesy of David Humphrey; 189ar PAM, Gift of Neptune Blood Smyth, III; 189b Courtesy of David Kamansky; 190l Photo by Alan McArthur; 190r LACMA, Gift of Dr. and Mrs. Pratapaditya Pal; 191 The Norton Simon Foundation,; 192l PAM, Gift of Union Bank; 192r The British Library, London; 193l LACMA, Purchased with funds provided by members of the Far Eastern Art Council; 193c PAM, Museum Purchase; 193b PAM, Gift of Mrs. Patricia Ayers Gallucci; 194a Copyright The Kelton Foundation 2005, Photo by Scott McClaine; 194b Courtesy of David Humphrey; 195l LACMA, Purchased with Museum Funds; 195r PAM, Gift of Mr. William Atwood in memory of Elaine Spaulding Atwood; 196 PAM, Gift of Lily Laub; 197l PAM, Gift of Gail Melhado; 197r PAM, Gift of Peter Ries; 198 LACMA, Gift of Mr. and Mrs. Harry Lenart; 199l PAM, Gift of the Nancy King Collection; 199c author; 199r Courtesy of Ruth Sutherlin Hayward; 200l author; 200r Courtesy of David Kamansky; 201a,b PAM, Museum purchase with funds from the Collectors Circle; 202 Courtesy of Yamataka Ryoun; 203l Courtesy of Luca Corona; 203r PAM, Gift of Mr. Charles Malchior ; 204 Courtesy of Ayomi Yoshida; 205l author; 205r Photo by Alan McArthur; 206 LACMA, Gift of James and Marilyn Alsdorf Collection in honor of Dr. Pratapaditya Pal; 207 LACMA, Gift of Mr. and Mrs. Harry Lenart; 208a LACMA, Mr. and Mrs. Allan C. Balch Fund; 208b Jennifer Jones Simon Art Trust; 209a Courtesy of Ruth Sutherlin Hayward; 209b PAM, Museum purchase with funds from Frank and Toshi Mosher; 210–111 Photo by Alan McArthur; 211r LACMA, Purchased with Harry Lenart Memorial Funds; 212 PAM, Gift of Dorrie Braun Poole; 213al PAM, Museum Purchase; 213ar PAM, Gift of Richard M. Cohen; 213b UCLA Fowler Museum of Cultural History; 214 PAM, Gift of Peter and Linda Zweig; 215 Victoria & Albert Museum, London, Purchased with the assistance of the National Art Collections Fund, the Vallentin Bequest, Sir Percival David and the Universities China Committee 216,217 LACMA, Purchased with Museum Funds; 218l PAM, Gift of Mrs. Arima Claypool; 218r PAM, Gift of Mr. Jacques Simon; 219 PAM, Gift of Margot and Hans Ries; 220 author; 221al LACMA, Gift of Mr. and Mrs. Harry Lenart; 221ar PAM, Gift from the Nancy King Collection; 221b Courtesy of Francesca Galloway Ltd.; 222l Photo by Alan McArthur; 222r author; 223 PAM, Gift of Mark Phillips and Iuliana Phillips; 224l author; 224r LACMA, Gift of Mr. and Mrs. Eric Lidow; 225l PAM, Gift of Margot and Hans Ries; 225r PAM, Gift of Hyatt Robert von Dehn; 226r Courtesy of Umakoshi Shohachi; 227 Photo by Rochelle Kessler; 228l The Norton Simon Foundation,; 228r LACMA, From the Nasli and Alice Heeramaneck Collection, Museum Associates Purchase; 229 LACMA, From the Nasli and Alice Heeramaneck Collection, purchased with funds provided by Mr. and Mrs. Allan C. Balch; 230 LACMA, Gift of Mr. and Mrs. Harry Lenart; 231l LACMA, Purchased with funds provided by The Smart Family Foundation in memory of Florence Smart Richards; 231r The Norton Simon Foundation; 232l LACMA, Gift of Anna Bing Arnold; 232r Norton Simon Art Foundation, Gift of Jennifer Jones Simon; 233 Courtesy of Francesca Galloway, Ltd.; 234a Photo by Alan McArthur; 234b PAM, Gift of Peter Sims; 235l LACMA, Gift of Mr. and Mrs. Harry Lenart; 235r The Norton Simon Foundation; 236l PAM, Gift of the Hon. and Mrs. Jack Lydman; 236r Norton Simon Art Foundation; 237a,b author; 238 Norton Simon Art Foundation; 239 Photo by Alan McArthur; 240l PAM, Gift of the Hon. and Mrs. Jack Lydman; 240ar,b Photo by Alan McArthur; 241a PAM, Gift of Barry and Louise Taper; 241b PAM, Gift of Mrs. Blanche Pope in memory of her husband Mr. Edkar Pope; 242 PAM, Gift of Johnson and Johnson, Merck Consumer Pharmaceuticals Co.; 243l PAM, Gift of the Hans Conreid Estate; 243r author

SELECT BIBLIOGRAPHY

GENERAL INTRODUCTIONS

Asiatic Art in the Rijksmuseum, Amsterdam, Amsterdam: Rijksmuseum, 1985

Clarke, Graham, *Symbols of Excellence: Precious Materials and Expressions of Status*, Cambridge: Cambridge University Press, 1986

Laplante, John D., *Asian Art*, Columbus: McGraw-Hill Humanities, 5th edition, 1992

Lee, Sherman E., *A History of Far Eastern Art*, 5th edition, New York: Harry N. Abrams, 1994

Leidy, Denise Patrick, *Treasures of Asian Art: The Asia Society's Mr. and Mrs. John D. Rockefeller 3rd Collection*, New York: The Asia Society Galleries, 1994

Penny, Nicholas, *The Materials of Sculpture*, New Haven and London: Yale University Press, 1993

REGIONAL INTRODUCTIONS: SOUTH ASIA AND THE HIMALAYAS

Asher, Frederick M. (ed.), *Art of India: Prehistory to the Present*, Encyclopedia Britannica, 2003

Craven, Roy C., *Indian Art: A Concise History*, revised edition, London: Thames & Hudson, 1995

Fisher, Robert E., *Art of Tibet*, London: Thames & Hudson, 1997

Harle, J. C., *The Art and Architecture of the Indian Subcontinent*, New Haven: Yale University Press (2nd edition), 1994

Huntington, Susan L., *Art of Ancient India*, New York: Weatherhill (first edition), 1985

Mitter, Partha, *Indian Art* (Oxford History of Art Series), Oxford: Oxford University Press, 2001

Pal, Pratapaditya, *Art of the Himalayas: Treasures from Nepal and Tibet*, New York: Hudson Hills Press, 1991

————, *Art of Tibet*: A Catalogue of the Los Angeles County Museum of Art Collection, expanded edition, Los Angeles: Los Angeles County Museum of Art in association with Mapin Publishing, Pvt. Ltd., 1990

————, *Art from the Indian Subcontinent* (Asian Art at the Norton Simon Museum, Volume 1) Pasadena/Princeton: Norton Simon Art Foundation in association with Yale University Press, 2003

————, *Art from the Himalayas and China* (Asian Art at the Norton Simon Museum, Volume 2), Pasadena/Princeton: Norton Simon Art Foundation in association with Yale University Press, 2003

————, *Art from Sri Lanka and Southeast Asia the Indian Subcontinent* (Asian Art at the Norton Simon Museum, Volume 3) Pasadena/Princeton: Norton Simon Art Foundation in association with Yale University Press, 2004

Weereratne, Neville and J. Robert Knox, *Visions of an Island: Rare Works from Sri Lanka in the Christopher Ondaatje Collection*, New York: Harper Collins, 1999

SOUTHEAST ASIA

van Beek, Steve, *The Arts of Thailand*, revised and updated edition, Singapore: Ibis, 1991

Brown, Robert, *Art from Thailand*, Mumbai: Marg Publications, 1999

Casal, Gabriel, Regalado Trota Jose Jr., et al, *The People and the Art of the Philippines*, Los Angeles: UCLA Museum of Cultural History, 1981

Jessup, Helen Ibbitson, *Court Arts of Indonesia*, New York: The Asia Society Galleries in association with Harry Abrams, Inc., 1990

Newman, Thelma R., *Contemporary Southeast Asian Arts and Crafts*, New York: Crown Publishers Inc., 1977

Noppe, Catherine and Jean-Francois Hubert, *Art of Vietnam*, New York: Parkstone Press, 2003

Soebadio, Haryati (ed.), *Art of Indonesia*, New York, The Vendome Press, 1993

Stadtner, Donald (ed.), *The Art of Burma: New Studies*, Mumbai, India: Marg Publications, 1999

Warren, William and Luca Invernizzi Tettoni, *Arts and Crafts of Thailand*, London: Thames & Hudson, 1994/San Francisco: Chronicle Books, 1996

EAST ASIA

Clunas, Craig, *Art in China* (Oxford History of Art Series), Oxford/New York: Oxford University Press, 1997

————, *Chinese Export Art and Design*, London: Victoria & Albert Museum, 1987

Goepper, Roger, and Roderick Whitfield, *Treasures from Korea*, London: The British Museum, 1984

Heibonsha Survey of Japanese Art, 31 volumes, New York/Tokyo: Weatherhill/Heibonsha, 1972–80

Hutt, Julia, *Understanding Far Eastern Art*, Oxford: Phaidon, 1987

Kakudo, Yoshiko, *The Art of Japan: Masterworks in the Asian Art Museum of San Francisco*, San Francisco: Asian Art Museum/Chronicle Books, 1991

Kim Won Yong, *The Art and Archaeology of Ancient Korea*, Seoul: Taekwong Publishing Co., 1986

Lee, Sherman E. et al., *Reflections of Reality in Japanese Art*, Cleveland: Cleveland Museum of Art, 1983

Mason, Penelope, *History of Japanese Art*, revised by Donald Dinwiddie, Upper Saddle River, New Jersey: Pearson/Prentice Hall, 2005

McKillop, Beth, *Korean Art and Design*, London: Victoria & Albert Museum, 1992

Murase, Miyeko, *Bridge of Dreams: The Mary Griggs Burke Collection*, New York: Metropolitan Museum of Art, 2000

Portal, Jane, *Korea: Art and Archaeology*, London: The British Museum, 2000

Rawson, Jessica (ed.), *The British Museum Book of Chinese Art*, London: The Trustees of the British Museum, 1992

Wilkinson, Jane, and Nick Pierce, *Harmony and Contrast: A Journey through East Asian Art*, Edinburgh: National Museums of Scotland, 1996

MATERIALS
CHAPTER 1: JADE

d'Argencé, R-Y. Lefebvre, *Chinese Jades in the Avery Brundage Collection*, San Francisco: the Asian Art Museum of San Francisco, 1972 (revised edition 1977)

Laufer, Berthold, *Jade: Its History and Symbolism in China*, New York: Dover Publications, 1974, revised 1989

Foster, Suzanne Haney, *Chinese Jade: The Image from Within*, Pasadena: Pacific Asia Museum, 1986

Hughes, Richard et al., *Burmese Jade: The Inscrutable Gem*, Part 1 & 2, www.ruby-sapphire.com, 2000

Keverne, Roger, *Jade*, New York/London: Lorenz Books, 1996

Kuwayama, George, *Chinese Jade from Southern California Collections*, Los Angeles: The Los Angeles County Museum of Art, 1976

Markel, Stephen, 'Carved Jades of the Mughal Period', *Arts of Asia* 17:6 (November–December 1987): pp. 123–130

Markel, Stephen (ed.), *The World of Jade*, Mumbai: Marg Publications, 1992

Palm Springs Art Museum, *Magic, Art and Order: Jade in Chinese Culture*, Palm Springs, 1990

————, and Ayers, John, *Chinese Jade throughout the Ages*, London: 1975

————, et al., *Chinese Jade from the Neolithic to the Qing*, Art Media Resources, 2002

Ward, Fred, *Jade*, Bethseda, Maryland: Gem Guides Book Company, 2001 (second edition)

Watt, J.C.Y., Chinese Jades from the Collection of the Seattle Art Museum, Seattle, 1989

Yang Jianfang, *Jade Carving in Chinese Archaeology*, vol. 1, Centre for Chinese Archaeology and Art, monograph series, 6, Hong Kong: Chinese University of Hong Kong, 1987

CHAPTER 2: SILK

Asian Art Museum of San Francisco, *Four Centuries of Fashion: Classical Kimono from the Kyoto National Museum*, San Francisco: Asian Art Museum of San Francisco, 1997

The Australian National Gallery, *Culture at a Crossroads: Southeast Asian Textiles from the Australian National Gallery*, Canberra: The Australian National Gallery, 1992

Burnham, Dorothy K., *Warp and Weft: A Dictionary of Textile Terms*, New York: Charles Scribner's Sons, 1980

Fraser-Lu, Sylvia, *Handwoven Textiles of South-East Asia*, Oxford/New York: Oxford University Press, 1988

Gillow, John and Barnard, Nicholas, *Traditional Indian Textiles*, London: Thames & Hudson, 1991

Gittinger, Mattiebelle and Lefferts, Jr., H. Leedom, *Textiles and the Tai Experience in Southeast Asia*, Washington: The Textile Museum, 1992

Green, Gillian, *Traditional Textiles of Cambodia: Cultural Threads and Material Heritage*, Chicago: Buppha Press, c.2003

Scott, Philippa, *The Book of Silk*, London: Thames & Hudson, 1993

Vaingker, Shelagh, *Chinese Silk: A Cultural History*, London/Brunswick, New Jersey: British Museum Press in Association with Rutgers University Press, 2004

Vollmer, John E., *Decoding Dragons: Garments in Ch'ing Dynasty China*, Eugene: Oregon Museum of Art, University of Oregon, 1983

————, *Silks for Thrones and Altars: Chinese Costumes and Textiles*, Paris: Myrna Myers, c.2003

Wilson, Verity, *Chinese Dress*, New York/Tokyo: Weatherhill and London: Victoria and Albert Museum, 1986

CHAPTER 3: PORCELAIN

Ayers, John, et al, *Porcelain for Palaces: The Fashion for Japan in Europe 1650-1750*, London: The Oriental Ceramics Society, 1990

Medley, Margaret, *The Chinese Potter: A Practical History of Chinese Ceramics*, 3rd edition, Oxford: Phaidon, 1989

Mikami Tsugio, (trans. Anne Herring), *The Art of Japanese Ceramics*, The Heibonsha Survey of Japanese Art, Vol. 26, New York/Tokyo: Weatherhill/Heibonsha, English Editions 1972

Pierson, Stacey, *Earth, Fire and Water: Chinese Ceramic Technology: Handbook for Non-specialists*, London: School of Oriental and African Studies, 1996

Scott, Rosemary, *Percival David Foundation of Chinese Art: A Guide to the Collection*, London: School of Oriental and African Studies, 1989

Singer, Robert, and Goodall, Hollis, *Hirado Porcelain of Japan*, Los Angeles: Los Angeles County Museum of Art, 1997

Stevenson, John, and Guy, John, *Vietnamese Ceramics: A Separate Tradition*, Chicago/Boulder: Art Media Resources/Avery Press, 1997

Vainker, S. J., *Chinese Pottery and Porcelain: From Prehistory to the Present*, London: The British Museum, 1991

Wilson, Richard L., *Inside Japanese Ceramics: A Primer of Materials, Techniques, and Traditions*, New York/Tokyo: Weatherhill, 1995

Wood, Nigel, *Chinese Glazes: Their Origins, Chemistry and Recreation*, London: A. & C. Black/ Philadelphia: University of Philadelphia Press, 1999

CHAPTER 4: LACQUER

Bourne, Jonathan et al., *Lacquer: An International History and Collector's Guide*, London: Bracken Books, published in Association with Phoebe Phillips Editions, 1984

Fraser-Lu, Sylvia, *Burmese Lacquerware*, Bangkok: The Tamarind Press, 1985

Hutt, Julia, *Japanese Inro*, London: Victoria and Albert Museum, 1997

Isaacs, Ralph and Blurton, Richard, *Visions from a Golden Land: Burma and the Art of Lacquer*, London: British Museum Press, 2000

Nguyen-Long, Kerry, 'Lacquer Artists of Vietnam', *Arts of Asia*, Volume 32, No.1, January/February 2002

Singer, Noel F., 'Myanmar Lacquer and Gold Leaf from the Earliest Times to the 18th century', *Arts of Asia*, Volume 32, No. 1, January/February 2002

Watt, James C. Y, and Ford, Barbara Brennan, *East Asian Lacquer: The Florence and Herbert Irving Collection*, New York: The Metropolitan Museum, 1991

CHAPTER 5: IVORY

Battie, David, et al., *Ivory: An International History and Illustrated Survey*, London: Bracken Books, published in Association with Phoebe Phillips Editions, 1987

Burack, Benjamin, *Ivory and Its Uses*, Rutland, Vermont/Tokyo: Charles E. Tuttle Company, 1984

Cutler, Anthony, *The Craft of Ivory*, Washington, D.C.: Dumbarton Oaks Research Library and Collection, 1985

Goodall, Hollis et al., *The Raymond and Frances Bushell Collection of Netsuke: A Legacy at the Los Angeles County Museum*, Los Angeles/Chicago: Los Angeles County Museum of Art/Art Media Resources Ltd., 2003

Hutt, Julia, *Japanese Netsuke*, London: Victoria and Albert Museum, 2003

Jose, Regalado Trota, *Images of Faith: Religious Ivory Carvings from the Philippines*, Pasadena: Pacific Asia Museum, 1990

Lapatin, Kenneth D. S., *Chryselephantine Ivories Statuary in the Ancient Mediterranean World*, Oxford: Oxford University Press, 2001

Oriental Ceramics Society/British Museum, *Chinese Ivories from the Shang to the Qing*, London: Oriental Ceramics Society, 1984

Stiles, Daniel, 'Ivory Carving in Myanmar', www.asianart.com, 2002
———, 'Ivory Carving in Thailand', www.asianart.com, 2003
Welch, Matthew, and Chappell, Sharen, *Netsuke: The Japanese Art of Miniature Carving*, Minneapolis: The Minneapolis Institute of Arts, 1999

CHAPTER 6: BAMBOO

Austin, Robert, Dana Levy and Ueda Koichiro, *Bamboo*, New York/Tokyo: Weatherhill, First edition 1970
Bess, Nancy Moore, *Bamboo in Japan*, Tokyo/New York/London: Kodansha International, 2001
Coffland, Robert T., *Contemporary Japanese Bamboo Arts*, Santa Fe/Chicago: Textile Arts Inc. and Art Media Resources, 1999
Cort, Louise Allison, and Nakamura Kenji, *A Basketmaker in Rural Japan*, New York/Tokyo: Weatherhill, and Washington, D.C.: Arthur M. Sackler Gallery, Smithsonian Institution, 1994
Cotsen, Lloyd, et al., *Masterworks of Form and Text: Japanese Bamboo Baskets*, Los Angeles; Cotsen Occasional Press, 1999
Farrelly, David, *The Book of Bamboo*, San Francisco: Sierra Club Books, 1984
Goldberg, Gale Beth, *Bamboo Style*, Salt Lake City: Gibbs Smith, 2002
Jenyns, R. Soame and William Watson, *Chinese Art: III*, New York: Rizzoli, English revised edition 1980
Kahlenberg, Mary Hunt and Mark Schwartz, *A Book About Grass: Its Beauty and Uses*, New York: E. P. Dutton, 1983
Lane, Robert F., *Philippine Basketry: An Appreciation*, Manila: Bookmark Inc., 1986
McCallum, Toshiko M., *Containing Beauty: Japanese Bamboo Flower Baskets*, Los Angeles: UCLA Museum of Cultural History, 1988
Otsuka, Ronald Y., *Selections from the Lutz Bamboo Collection*, Denver: Denver Art Museum, 1979
Tsien Tsuen-Hsuin, *Written on Bamboo and Silk*, Chicago: University of Chicago Press, 2nd edition, 2004

CHAPTER 7: PAPER

Bloom, Jonathan M., *Paper Before Print: The History and Impact of Paper in the Islamic World*, New Haven/London: Yale University Press, 2001
Buisson, Dominique, *The Art of Japanese Paper*, Paris: Terrail, 1992
Dawson, Sophie, *The Art and Craft of Papermaking*, London/Philadelphia: Quarto/Running Press, 1992
Gaur, A., *Writing Materials of the East*, London: The British Library, 1979
Hunter, Dard, *A Papermaking Pilgrimage to Japan, Korea and China*, New York: Pynson Printers, 1936
———, *Old Papermaking in China and Japan*, Chillicothe, Ohio: Mountain House Press, 1932
Miller, Bob, Meher McArthur, Wei Chen-hsuan, Sam Fogg, *East Asian Books*, London: Sam Fogg Rare Books, 1998
Mingei International Museum, *Paper Innovations: Handmade paper and handmade objects of cut, folded and molded paper*, La Jolla, California: 1985
Tsien Tsuen-Hsuin, 'Paper and Printing', Vol. 5, No. 1, *Science and Civilisation in China* Joseph Needham (ed.), Cambridge: Cambridge University Press, 1985
Alexandra Soteriou, *Gift of Conquerors: Hand Papermaking in India*, Middle Town, New Jersey: Grantha Corporation in association with Ahmedabad, Chidambaram, India: Mapin Publishing Pvt. Ltd., 1999
Wei Chen-hsuan, *Chinese Books*, London: Sam Fogg, 2000

CHAPTER 8: GOLD

Bunker, Emma C., and Julia White, *Adornment for Eternity*, Denver: Denver Art Museum, 1994
Engel, Erik, *Kinesiskt Guld och Silver / Chinese Gold and Silver in the Carl Kempe Collection*, Ulricehamn (Sweden): Ulricehamns Konst-o Ostasiastika Museum (The Museum of Far Eastern Antiquities in Ulricehamn), Swedish and English, 1999
Humphrey, David, 'Chinese Jewelry through the Ages', *Proceedings of The Santa Fe Symposium on Jewelry Manufacturing Technology*, Albuquerque, New Mexico, 2002
Kelley, Clarence W., *Chinese Gold and Silver in American Collections*, Dayton, Ohio: Dayton Museum of Fine Arts, 1984
Muzium Negara, *Gold Jewelry and Ornaments of Malaysia*, Kuala Lumpur, 1988
Singer, Jane Casey, *Gold Jewelry from Tibet and Nepal*, London: Thames & Hudson, 1996
Singer, Paul, *Early Chinese Gold and Silver*, New York: China Institute in America, 1972
Stronge, Susan, Nima Smith and J. C. Harle, *A Golden Treasury: Jewellery from the Indian Subcontinent*, New York/London: Rizzoli, Victoria and Albert Museum, 1988
Untracht, Oppi, *Traditional Jewelry of India*, New York: Harry N. Abrams, Inc., 1997
Zebrowski, Mark, *Gold, Silver & Bronze from Mughal India*, London: Alexandra Press in association with Laurence King, 1997

CHAPTER 9: WOOD

Bhirasri, Silpa, *Thai Wood Carvings*, Bangkok: The Promotion and Public Relations Sub-division, The Fine Arts Department, First edition, 1961, 5th edition, 1990
Clunas, Craig, *Chinese Furniture*, London, Victoria and Albert Museum, 1988
Ellsworth, R. H., *Chinese Furniture: Hardwood Examples of the Ming and Early Ch'ing Dynasties*, New York: Random House, 1970
Harris, Victor and Ken Matsushima, *Kamakura: The Renaissance of Japanese Sculpture, 1185–1333*, London: The British Museum, 1991
Heineken, Ty & Kuniko, *Tansu: Traditional Japanese Cabinetry*, 1st edition, New York/Tokyo: Weatherhill, 1st edition 1981
Kamansky, David (ed.), *Wooden Wonders: Tibetan Furniture in Secular and Religious Life*, Pasadena/Chicago: Pacific Asia Museum/Serindia Publications, 2004
Kates, George. N., *Chinese Household Furniture*, New York: Dover Publications, 1948
Koizumi Kazuko, *Traditional Japanese Furniture*, translated by Alfred Birnbaum, 1st edition, Tokyo/New York: Kodansha International, 1986
Larson, John and Rose Kerr, *Guanyin: A Masterpiece Revealed*, London: Victoria & Albert Museum, 1985
Michel, George (ed.), *Living Wood: Sculptural Traditions of Southern India*, Mumbai: Marg Publications for the Whitechapel Art Gallery, London, 1992
Moilanen, Irene and Sergey S. Ozhegov, *Mirrored in Wood: Burmese Art and Architecture*, Bangkok: White Lotus, 1999
Orientations, Volume 23, Number 1, *Papers from the Dr. S. Y. Yip Symposium on Classic Chinese Furniture*, Hong Kong, 1992
San Francisco Craft and Folk Art Museum, *Classical Chinese Wood Furniture*, San Francisco, 1992

Wang Shixiang, *Classic Chinese Furniture*, Hong Kong: Joint Publishing Co., 1986

Wright, Edward Reynolds and Man Sill Pai, *Korean Furniture: Elegance and Tradition*, 1st edition, Tokyo/New York: Kodansha International, 1984

CHAPTER 10: STONE

Fisher, Robert, *Buddhist Art and Architecture*, London/New York: Thames & Hudson, 1993

Ortner, John et al, *Angkor: Celestial Temples of the Khmer*, New York: Abbeville Press, 2002

Newman, Richard, *The Stone Sculpture of India: a Study of the Materials used by Indian Sculptors from c. 2nd century BC to the 16th century*, Cambridge, Massachusetts: Center for Conservation and Technical Studies, Harvard University Art Museums, 1984

Pal, Pratapaditya, *The Sensuous Immortals*, Los Angeles, Los Angeles County Museum of Art, 1977

————, *Light of Asia: Buddha Shakyamuni in Asian Art*, Los Angeles, Los Angeles County Museum of Art, 1984

————, *Indian Sculpture: 700–1800: A Catalogue of the Los Angeles County Museum of Art Collection*, vol. 2, Los Angeles: Los Angeles County Museum of Art in Association with University of California Press, 1989

————, *Indian Sculpture: Circa 500 BC–AD 700, A Catalogue of the Los Angeles County Museum of Art Collection*, vol. 1, Los Angeles County Museum of Art in Association with University of California Press, 1987

Rambach, Pierre and Susanne, *Gardens of Longevity in China and Japan*, New York: Skira/Rizzoli, 1987

Rooney, Dawn and Peter Danford, *Angkor: Cambodia's Fabulous Khmer Temples*, Hong Kong: Odyssey, 5th edition, 2004

Roveda, Vittorio, *Sacred Angkor: Carved Reliefs of Angkor Wat*, New York: Weatherhill, 2003

SOME USEFUL WEBSITES AND MAGAZINES

www.artsofasianet.com, *Arts of Asia*, Hong Kong
www.asianart.com
www.buddhanet.net
www.finestone.com
www.orientations.com.hk, *Orientations*, Hong Kong
www.ruby-sapphire.com
www.savetheelephant.org
www.thesculpturestudio.com

MUSEUMS

The following list (ordered alphabetically by place name) includes museums in North America, Europe and other regions with significant collections of Asian art, as well as some of the principal museums in Asia. There are many more museums, especially in Asia, with important Asian art collections; however, it is hoped that this list will give readers a sense of the great wealth of Asian art in the world's museums.

ASIA

AFGHANISTAN

Kabul Museum
Destroyed, but former collection can be viewed on the following website:
www.afghan-web.com/kabul-museum

BURMA

National Museum
66/74 Pyay Road
Rangoon/Yangon
Tel. (01) 282563 or 282608

CAMBODIA

National Museum
Corner of Street 13 and Street 178
Phnom Penh

CHINA

Imperial Palace Museum
Beijing

Hong Kong Museum of Art
10 Salisbury Road
Tsim Sha Tsui
Kowloon, Hong Kong
Tel. (852) 2721 0116
www.lcsd.gov.hk/CE/Museum/Arts

Shanghai Museum
No. 201 Ren Min Da Dao
Shanghai 200003
Tel. (021) 63723500
www.shanghaimuseum.net

National Palace Museum
221 Chih-shan Rd. Sec 2
Taipei, Taiwan, ROC 111
Tel. (02) 2881-2021
www.npm.gov.tw

INDIA

Prince of Wales Museum of Western India (Chatrapati Shivaji Maharaj Vastu Sangrahalaya)
159/61, M. Gandhi Rd, Fort
Bombay/Mumbai
Tel. (022) 284484
www.bombaymuseum.org

Indian Museum Kolkata (Calcutta)
27 Jawaharlal Nehru Road
Kolkata 700016
Tel. (033) 2249 9902

National Museum
Janpath, New Delhi 110 011
Tel. (011) 3018415
www.nationalmuseumindia.org

INDONESIA

Indonesian National Museum
Jl. Medan Merdeka Barat 12
Jakarta Pusat
Tel. (021) 3812346 – 3868172
www.museumnasional.org

JAPAN

Kyoto National Museum
527 Chayamachi
Higashiyama-ku, Kyoto 605-0931
Tel. (075) 541-1151
www.kyohaku.go.jp

Tokyo National Museum
13-9 Ueno Park
Taito-ku, Tokyo, 110-8712
Tel. (03) 3822-1111
www.tnm.go.jp

KOREA

Gyeongju National Museum
76 Inwang-dong
Gyeongju-si
Gyeongsanbuk-do
Tel. (54) 740-7518
www.gyeongju.museum.go.kr

National Museum of Korea
168-6 Yongsan-dong,
Yongsangu 140-026, Seoul
Tel. (02) 2077-9000
www.museums.go.kr

MALAYSIA

National Museum (Muzium
Negara) Malaysia
Jabatan Muzium dan Antikuiti
Jalan Damansara
50566 Kuala Lumpur
Tel. (03) 2282-6255
www.museum.gov.my

NEPAL

National Museum
GPO Box 21771
Thamel, Kathmandu

PAKISTAN

Lahore Museum
Shahrah-e-Quaid-e-Azam
Lahore
www.punjab.gov.pk/information/
institution_Museums.htm

PHILIPPINES

Ayala Museum
Makati Avenue/De La Rosa St
Greenbelt Park, Ayala Center
Makati City 1224
Tel. (632) 757-7117 to -21

National Museum
P. Burgos Street, Manila
Tel. (02) 527-1215

SINGAPORE

Asian Civilizations Museum
1 Empress Place
Singapore 179555
Tel. (65) 6332 7798
www.nhb.gov.sg/acm

SRI LANKA

National Museum
Sir Marcus Mawatha
PO Box 854, Colombo 7
Tel. (941) 695 366

THAILAND

Bangkok National Museum
Na Phrthat Rdm Phra
Borommaharachawang Sub-district,
Phra Nakorn District,
Bangkok 10200
Tel. (662) 224-1404, 224-1333
www.thailandmuseum.com/thai
museum_eng/bangkok

TIBET

Tibet Museum
No. 19 Norbu Lingka Road
Lhasa
Tel. (0891) 6835244

VIETNAM

Fine Arts Museum
66 Duong Nguyen Thai Hoc
Hanoi

AUSTRALIA

Art Gallery of South Australia
North Terrace
Adelaide, South Australia 5000
Tel. (08) 8207 7000
www.artgallery.sa.gov.au

The National Gallery
Parkes Place, Parkes

Canberra ACT 2601
Tel. (02) 6240 6501
www.nga.gov.au

Queensland Art Gallery
Melbourne Street
South Brisbane, Queensland
Tel. (07) 3840 7303
www.qag.qld.gov.au

Art Gallery of New South Wales
Art Gallery Road
The Domain
Sydney, New South Wales 2000
Tel. (02) 9225 1744
www.artgallery.nsw.gov.au

National Gallery of Victoria
PO Box 7259
Melbourne, Victoria 8004
Tel. (03) 8620 2222
www.ngv.vic.gov.au

EUROPE

FRANCE

Musée Cernuschi
7, avenue Velasquez
75008 Paris
Tel. (01) 45 63 50 75

Musée National des Arts
Asiatiques – Guimet
6, place d'Iéna, 75116 Paris
Tel. (01) 56 52 53 00
www.museeguimet.fr

GERMANY

Museum of East Asian Art
(Museum für Ostasiatische Kunst)
Takustraße 40
14195 Berlin
Tel. (030) 8301 382
www.smb.spk-berlin.de

Museum of Indian Art (Museum
für Indische Kunst)
Takustraße 40
14195 Berlin
Tel. (030) 8301 361
www.smb.spk-berlin.de

IRELAND

The Chester Beatty Library
Dublin Castle, Dublin 2, Ireland
Tel. (01) 407-0750

ITALY

Chiossone Museum of Oriental Art
Villetta Di Negro
Piazzale Mazzini, 4, Genova
Tel. (010) 542285
www.museochiossonegenova.it

National Museum of Eastern Art
Palazzo Brancaccio
Via Merulana, 248, Rome
Tel. (06) 4874415-4875077

Venice Eastern Art Museum
(Ca' Pesaro)
2076, Santa Croce, Venice
www.museiciviciveneziani.it

THE NETHERLANDS

Rijksmuseum Amsterdam
PO Box 74888
1070 DN Amsterdam
Tel. (020) 6747047
www.rijksmuseum.nl

RUSSIA

The State Hermitage Museum
2, Dvortsovaya Ploshchad
190000, St Petersburg
Tel. (Oriental Department)
(812) 110-96-68
www.hermitagemuseum.org

SWEDEN

Museum of Far Eastern
Antiquities (Ostasiatiska Museet)
Skeppsholmen, Stockholm
Tel. (08) 519-55-750
www.ostasiatiska.se

Museum of Far Eastern Art
(Ostasiatmuseum), Box 78
S-523 23 Ulricehamn
Tel. (0)321 150 90 or
(0)33-41 25 35
www.ostasiat.com

SWITZERLAND

The Baur Collection
8, rue Munier-Romilly
Ch 1206, Geneva
Tel. (022) 346 17 29
www.collections-baur.ch

UK

Museum of East Asian Art, Bath
12 Bennett Street,Bath BA1 2QL
Tel. (01225) 464-640
www.bath.co.uk/museumeastasianart/

Fitzwilliam Museum
Trumpington Street
Cambridge CB2 1RB
Tel. (01223) 332900
www.fitzmuseum.cam.ac.uk

Brighton Museum & Art Gallery
Royal Pavilion Gardens
Brighton, East Sussex, BN1 1EE
Tel. (01273) 290-900
www.brighton.virtualmuseum.info

The Royal Museum
Chambers Street
Edinburgh EH1 1JF
Tel. (0131) 247-4219
www.rms.ac.uk/royal

The Burrell Collection
Pollok Country Park
2060 Pollokshaws Road
Glasgow, G43 1AT
Tel. (0141) 287-2550
www.glasgowmuseums.com

Liverpool Museum
William Brown Street
Liverpool L3 8EN
Tel. (0151) 478-4399
www.liverpoolmuseums.org.uk

The British Library
St Pancras, 96 Euston Road
London, NW1 2DB
Tel. (020) 7412 7332
www.bl.uk

The British Museum
Great Russell Street
London WC1

Tel. (020) 7323 8299
www.thebritishmuseum.ac.uk

The Victoria and Albert
Museum
Cromwell Road,
London SW7 2RL
Tel. (020) 7942 2000
www.vam.ac.uk

The Ashmolean Museum
Beaumont Street
Oxford OX1 2PH
Tel. (01865) 278000
www.ashmol.ox.ac.uk

ISRAEL

Tikotin Museum of Japanese Art
89 Hanassi Ave., Haifa
Tel. (04) 8383554
www.haifamuseums.org.il

TURKEY

Topkapi Sarayi Museum
Sultanahmet, Eminonu, Istanbul
Tel. (212) 512 04 80
www.ee.bilkent.edu.tr/~history
/topkapi.html

NORTH AMERICA

CANADA

Montreal Museum of Fine Art
PO Box 3000, Station 'H'
Montreal, Quebec H3G 2T9
Tel. (514) 285-2000
www.mmfa.qc.ca

Royal Ontario Museum
100 Queen's Park
Toronto, Ontario M5S 2C6
Tel. (416) 586-5549
www.rom.on.ca

Vancouver Museum
1100 Chestnut Street
Vancouver
British Columbia V6J 3J9
Tel. (604) 736-4431
www.vanmuseum.bc.ca

EASTERN USA

Morikami Museum and Japanese
Gardens
4000 Morikami Park Road
Delray Beach, Fla. 33446
Tel. (561) 495-0233
www.morikami.org

Museum of Fine Arts, Boston
Avenue of the Arts
465 Huntington Avenue
Boston, Mass. 02115-5523
Tel. (617) 267-9300
www.mfa.org

Harvard University Fogg Art
Museum
32 Quincy St.
Cambridge, Mass. 02138
Tel. (617) 495-9400
www.artmuseums.harvard.edu

Peabody Essex Museum
East India Square
Salem, Mass. 01970-3783
Tel. (978) 745-9500
www.pem.org

Asia Society
725 Park Avenue at 70th Street
New York, NY 10021
Tel. (212) 288-6400
www.asiasociety.org

Brooklyn Museum of Art
200 Eastern Parkway
Brooklyn, New York 11238
Tel. (718) 399-8440
www.brooklynmuseum.org

China Institute (*no permanent
collection, but regular exhibitions*)
125 East 65th Street
New York, NY 10021
Tel. (212) 744-8181
www.chinainstitute.org

Japan Society (*no permanent
collection, but regular exhibitions*)
333 East 47th Street
New York, NY 10017
Tel. (212) 832-1155
www.japansociety.org

The Metropolitan Museum of Art
1000 Fifth Avenue at 82nd St
New York, NY 10028-0198
Tel. (212) 535-7710
www.metmuseum.org

Rubin Museum of Art
150 West 17th Street
New York, NY 10011
Tel. (212) 620-5000
www.rmanyc.org

Philadelphia Museum of Art
26th Street and the Benjamin
Franklin Parkway
Philadelphia, Penn. 19130
Tel. (215) 763-8100
www.philamuseum.org

Freer Gallery of Art/Arthur M.
Sackler Gallery
Smithsonian Institution
PO Box 37012, MRC 707
Washington, D.C. 20013-7012
Tel. (202) 633-4880
www.si.edu

The Textile Museum
2320 S Street, NW
Washington, D.C. 20008-4088
Tel. (202) 667-0441
www.textilemuseum.org

WESTERN USA

Asian Art Museum
200 Larkin Street
San Francisco, Calif. 94102
Tel. (415) 581-3500
www.asianart.org

Santa Barbara Museum of Art
1130 State Street, Santa Barbara
Calif. 93101-2746
Tel. (805) 963-4364
www.sbmuseart.org

Sherman Lee Institute of
Japanese Art at the Clark Center
15770 Tenth Avenue
Hanford, Calif. 93230
Tel. (559) 582-4915
www.shermanleeinstitute.org

Los Angeles County Museum of Art
5905 Wilshire Boulevard
Los Angeles, Calif. 90036
Tel. (323) 857-6000
www.lacma.org

UCLA Fowler Museum of
Cultural History
Box 951549
Los Angeles, Calif. 90095-1549
Tel. (310) 825-4361
www.fowler.ucla.edu

Pacific Asia Museum
46 North Los Robles Avenue
Pasadena, Calif. 91101
Tel. (626) 449-2742
www.pacificasiamuseum.org

Norton Simon Museum
411 West Colorado Blvd.
Pasadena, Calif. 91105
Tel. (626) 449-6840
www.nortonsimon.org

Phoenix Art Museum
1625 N. Central Ave.
Phoenix, Ariz. 85004
Tel. (602) 257-1222
www.phxart.org

San Diego Museum of Art
1450 El Prado, Balboa Park
San Diego, Calif. 92101
Tel. (619) 232-7931
www.sdmart.org

Mingei International Museum
1439 El Prado, Balboa Park
San Diego, Calif. 92101
Tel. (619) 239-0003
www.mingei.org

Denver Art Museum
100 W 14th Ave Pkwy
Denver, Colo. 80204
Tel. (720) 865-5000
www.denverartmuseum.org

Honolulu Academy of Arts
900 South Beretania Street
Honolulu, Hawai'i 96814-1495
Tel. (808) 532-8700
www.honoluluacademy.org

Seattle Asian Art Museum
Volunteer Park
1400 East Prospect Street
Seattle, Wash. 98112-3303
Tel. (206) 654-3100
www.seattleartmuseum.org

CENTRAL USA

The Art Institute of Chicago
111 South Michigan Avenue
Chicago, Ill. 60603
Tel. (312) 443-3600
www.artic.edu

Indianapolis Museum of Art
4000 Michigan Road
Indianapolis, Ind. 46208-3326
Tel. (317) 920-2660
www.ima-art.org

Minneapolis Institute of Arts
2400 Third Avenue South
Minneapolis, Minn. 55404
Tel. (612) 870-3131
www.artsmia.org

Nelson-Atkins Museum of Art
4525 Oak Street
Kansas City, Missouri 64111-1873
Tel. (816) 751-1278
www.nelson-atkins.org

New Orleans Museum of Art
One Collins C. Dibball Circle,
City Park
New Orleans, La. 70124
Tel. (504) 488-2631
www.noma.org

Kimbell Art Museum
3333 Camp Bowie Boulevard
Fort Worth, Tex. 76107-2792
Tel. (817) 332-8451
www.kimbellart.org

The Cleveland Museum of Art
11150 East Boulevard
Cleveland, Ohio 44106
Tel. (216) 431-7350
www.clevelandart.org

BUYING ASIAN ART

An increasing number of antique dealers, auction houses, art galleries, furniture and design shops and galleries sell Asian art of all ages and types, both for the collector and the decorator. For those interested in purchasing Asian antiques, there are many fine Asian art dealers who sell from their own shops, on the internet or at the various annual international Asian Art fairs. Probably the two most important centres in the Western world for purchasing Asian art are London and New York; international fairs are held in New York in March and in London in November. During these fairs, the leading auction houses, Sotheby's and Christie's, hold major sales of Asian art, art dealers from around the world (including Asia) set up booths at the fair, and local galleries and museums hold exhibitions of Asian art to appeal to the large number of Asian art collectors and enthusiasts who flock to the fair. (The list on p. 253 opposite introduces some of the most well established Western dealers in Asian art.)

For those readers looking to acquire Asian art objects in Asia, there are many dealers and galleries specializing in antiques in the major cities of Asia, most notably Hong Kong, Singapore, Bangkok, Hanoi and Tokyo. Many of these dealers are listed in local travel guides. However, perhaps a more exciting way of finding art objects is to visit local markets, such as Kyoto's monthly temple markets, the bustling night markets of Bangkok and Taipei, and craft fairs of Kuala Lumpur.

One word of warning is that, as in any other art field, the Asian art market consists of both genuine articles and very good quality fakes, and it can often be very difficult to differentiate between the two. If considering an expensive purchase, the most important point to consider is the object's history, or provenance. If the seller can provide adequate paperwork to defend the object's date (and hence the price), then the purchase is probably safe. However, if there is no proof of provenance, it may not be worth the risk, especially if purchasing far from home, when returning the object may not be an option. One safe way to buy Asian art is to avoid antiques and to buy directly from living artists who are either creating modern versions of ancient art works, or working in a completely contemporary style. Either way, you can feel safe in the knowledge that you are buying an original art work, and satisfied that you are supporting the continuation of Asian artistic traditions.

A SELECTION OF WESTERN DEALERS IN ASIAN ART

INTERNATIONAL AUCTION HOUSES

Christie's

8 King Street, St. James's
London SW1Y 6QT
Tel. (020) 7839 9060

85 Old Brompton Road
London SW7 3LD
Tel. (020) 7930 6074

20 Rockefeller Plaza
New York, NY 10020
Tel. (212) 636 2000

22nd floor Alexandra House
16–20 Chater Road Central
Hong Kong
Tel. (852) 2521 5396

Sotheby's

34–35 New Bond Street
London W1A 2AA
Tel. (020) 7293 5000

1334 York Avenue at 72nd St
New York, New York 10021
Tel. (212) 606-7000

5/F, Standard Chartered Bank
Building
4–4A Des Voeux Road Central
Hong Kong
Tel. (852) 2524 8121
www.sothebys.com

USA

WEST COAST

F. Suie One Company
1335 East Colorado Blvd
Pasadena, Calif. 91106
Tel. (626) 715-1335

Silk Roads Design Gallery
8590 Melrose Avenue
West Hollywood, Calif. 90069
Tel. (310) 855-0585
www.silkroadsgallery.com

Kagedo Japanese Art
520 First Avenue South
Seattle, Washington 98104
Tel. (206) 467-9077
www.kagedo.com

Tai Gallery/Textile Arts
616 Canyon Road
Santa Fe, New Mexico 87501
Tel. (505) 984-1387
www.textilearts.com

NEW YORK

R. H. Ellsworth Ltd.
960 Fifth Avenue
New York, NY 10021
Tel. (212) 535-9249

Flying Cranes Antiques Ltd.
1050 Second Avenue
New York, NY 10022
Tel. (212) 223-4600
www.the-maac.com

Kang Collection Korean Fine Art
9 East 82nd Street
New York, NY 10028
Tel. (212) 734-1490

The Tolman Collection of
Tokyo
350 West 50th Street
New York, NY 10019
Tel. (212) 489-7696
www.tolmantokyo.com

EUROPE

John Eskanazi Ltd.
15 Old Bond Street
London W1X 4JL
Tel. (020) 7409 3001
www.john-eskenazi.com

Sam Fogg
15D Clifford Street
London W1S 4IZ
Tel. (020) 7534-2100
www.samfogg.co.uk

Francesca Galloway
91b Jermyn Street
London SW1Y 6JB
Tel. (020) 7930-8717
www.francescagalloway.co.uk

Sydney L. Moss Ltd.
51 Brook Street
London W1Y 1AU
Tel. (020) 7629-4670

Jonathan Tucker Antonia Tozer
Asian Art
37 Bury Street, St James's
London SW1Y 6AU
Tel (020) 7839-3414
www.asianartresource.co.uk

Grace Wu Bruce
12A Balfour Mews
London W1Y 5RJ
Tel. (020) 7499-3750
www.grace-wu-bruce.com

Galerie Kevorkian
21 Quai Malaquais
Paris 75006
France
Tel. (01) 42 60 72 91

Gisele Croes
54 boulevard de Waterloo
1000 Brussels, Belgium
Tel. (322) 511 82 16

ASIAN ART DEALERS' ASSOCIATIONS

www.asianart.com

www.worldartantiques.com

Antique Tribal Art Dealers
Association Inc. (ATADA)
www.atada.org

Artline Art Associations
www.artline.com/associations

National Antique and Art
Dealers Association (USA)
www.naadaa.org

INDEX

Page numbers in italics refer to illustrations.

Abe Motoshi *141*
Angkor period *220*, 236–37
architecture: stone 228, 233, 242; wooden 210, 211, 217, 218, 219
Arita 84, 85
Ayutthaya period (1350–1767) 106, 190, 210

bamboo 13, 14, 20, 134–55; Chinese 136, *142*, 143–47; Filipino 152, *153*, 154; in garden design 155; growth of 137–39; Japanese *20*, 135, *138*, *139*, 148–51; Korean *143*, 147–48; Southeast Asian 152–55; techniques 139–43, 150–51
Ban Chiang culture (3600 BC–2nd cent AD) 41, 190, 235
basketmaking *20*, *134*, 140–43, *140–41*, 150–54, *150–53*
batik 52, 53
Begram Ivories 121–22
bi (discs) *24*, 33–34
blue and whites 68, 73–74, 80–83, 85, 89
Bombyx mori moth 46–47, 62
Bontoc people *152*, *153*
books: Chinese 144, 157, *163*, 164, 165; Indian *171*, *172*; Japanese 169; Korean 166–67; Thai 175
brocade *18*, *44*, 50, 60, *61*
Buddhist art: gold *178*, 180, 187, 190–92, 193–94, 195–97; ivory 122, *126*, *127*, 129–30; jades 35, 37; lacquer 108, 110; paper *163*–64, 166–67, *168*, 169, 174–75; silk brocades 60; stone carving 227–34, 235, *238*, 239–40, 241–43; wood *202*, 208–9, 211–12, 214, *216*, 217
Burma: bamboo 154; gold *23*, 192; ivory 132–33; jadeite 27–28, 32, 39, 40–41; lacquer 95, 96, 97, 108–10, *109*; silk 65; stone carving 234; wood 211–12

Cai Lun 159
calligraphy 158, 164–65, *166*, 167, *187*
Cambodia *220*, 222, 224, 235–36
carving: bamboo *142*, 143, 145–47, 151; ivory 116–19; jade 22, 28–30; lacquer

97, *97*, *99*, 98–100, 103, *103*; stone 226–27; wood 202–3, 209, 210–12, 217
casting, gold 179
celadon 22, 80
ceramics *see* porcelain
Champa period (AD 192–15th century) 239
Chenghua reign (1465–87) 74, *76*, 77
China: bamboo 136, *142*, 143–47, *146*; gold *179*, 181, 193–94; ivory *13*, *23*, *119*, 120, 128–31; jade 13, *14*, 27, 29, 30, *30*, *38*, *40*, 32–40; lacquer *94*, 95, *96*, *97*, *99*, 98–101, 144, 147; paper 157, 159, 161, 163–65; porcelain *8*, *11*, 67, 68, 69, 72–78, *73*, *76*, 77, *84*, *136*; silk *18*, 22, 46, 55–57, *54–57*; stone carving *13*, *224*, *225*, *226*, 241–43; wood *12*, *15*, 200–1, 214, *215*
Christian art: gold *188*; ivory *124*, *125*, 129, 132, *133*; lacquer *104*; wood carvings 213
cinnabar *21*, 94, *96*, *97*
CITES (Convention on the International Trade in Endangered Species) 115
clothes *see* garments
Confucian art, jade symbolism in 32
cong (cylinders) 34
Coromandel lacquers *94*, 100, 101

Daoist arts: ivory 130; jade symbolism in 32, 35; lacquer 110
Daruma *151*
dyeing techniques 48, 49, 52, 60

Eastern Zhou period (*c.* 770–256 BC) 34, 37, 214
Edo period (1600–1868) 84, 103–5, 131, 150, 170
elephants 114–16
embroidery: Chinese 22, 52–54; Indian 63; Japanese 60; Korean 58
enamelling 71, 77–78, *79*, 85–89
etching, lacquer 95, 98, 100

flower arrangement 149–50
'forbidden stitch' 22, 53–54
furniture: bamboo 148; ivory 122, 125; lacquered 94, 105; wooden 200–1, 203–4, 206–8, 209, 214, 219

gardens 155, 243
garments 55, *56*, 57–60, 63, 64–65, 197
glazes 70–71, 77–78, *79*, 80–83, 85–89
Goguryeo period (37 BC–AD 668) 166
gold *23*, 176–97; Burmese *23*, 192; Chinese *179*, 181, 193–94; in embroidery 54; gold leaf 18–21, *182*, *183*; Indian 184–87; Indonesian 188–89; Japanese *182*, *183*, 196–97; Korean 195–96; in lacquer 95, 96, 97, 98, 102, 107, *109*, 108–10; Nepalese *186*, 187; techniques 179–83; Thai *176*, *178*, *182*, 190, *191*; on wood carvings 204–5
Goryeo dynasty (918–1392) 80, 101–2, 214–17, 242
Gupta period (*c.* AD 320–mid-5th century) 122, 184, 228

Han dynasty (206 BC–AD 220) 35, 37, 55, 98, 144, 193, 241
Harunobu (Suzuki Harunobu, 1724–70) *170*, 219
Heian period (794–1185) 59–60, 102, 243
Hindu art: gold *188*, 189; ivory 122; stone carving 228–31, 236, 240; wood carving 205–6, 210–11
Hirado wares 87–89
Hokusai (Katsushika Hokusai, 1769–1849) *170*, 219
Honda Shoryu *141*
Hongshan culture 34
Hpakan (Burma) 27
huang (pendants) 34

igneous rocks 223
ikat 49, 52, *53*, 63, 65
Imari period and wares 85, 86
India: gold 184–87; ivory *112*, *113*, 120, 121–22, *123*, *125*; jade 30, *31*; lacquer 95, 111; paper 159, 171–73; silk *18*, *44*, 47, 62–63; stone carving 227–33; wood *207*, 205–8
Indonesia: gold 188–89; ivory 132, *133*; stone 239–41; wood carving *203*, 212–13
inlays: ivory 119; jade 42; lacquer 95–96, 102, 107; wood 204, 208
inro 105, *113*, 131, 151
Islamic art 41–42

ivory *23*, 112–33; Burmese 132–33; Chinese *23*, *119*, *120*, 128–31; Filipino 132, *133*; Indian *113*, 120, 121–22; Indonesian 132, *133*; Japanese 117, 131; Nepalese 127; Sri Lankan *126*, 127; techniques 116–19; Thai 132, *133*; Tibetan *126*, 127

jade 13, 24–43; Burmese 27–28, 32, 39, 40–41; Chinese *14*, 24, *33*, *38*, 32–40; Indian 31, *41*–42; jadeite 26, 27, 28, 27–28, 30, 39, 40–41; nephrite 26–27, *26*, *30*, *31*, 32, *33*, *34*, *35*, *38*, 39, *40*, 39, 41; techniques 22, 28–30

Japan: bamboo *20*, *134*, *135*, *138*, *139*, *140*–*41*, 148–51; gold 22, 182, *183*, 196–97; ivory 117, 131; lacquer *14*, 95, 96, 102–6; paper *16*–*17*, 22, 156, *157*, 159, 160, 161–63, 168–69, *168*–*71*; porcelain 67, 68, 69, 84–89; silk *18*, 48, *59*, 60, 59–61, 182; stone *226*, 243; wood *15*, *202*, 205, 218–19

japanning 92

Jin (Jurchen) dynasty (1115–1234) 36–37, 214

Jingdezhen 69, 71, 73, 74

Joseon (Yi) dynasty (1392–1910): bamboo 147–48; lacquer *101*, 102; porcelain 80, *81*, *83*; silk garments 58; stone carvings 242; wood carvings 217

Kajiwara Koho 135

Kakiemon Sakaida (1596–1666) *66*, 85

Kakiemon wares 67, 85–86

Kamakura period (1185–1333) 102, 103, *169*

Kandy period (1592–1815) 127

kaolin 69

Kashmir 111, 122

kesi (cut silk) tapestry 51, *51*, 55

Khmer 235–36

Khotan 27, 32, 39, 41

kilns 71, 72, 84

Kim Sun Wuk, see Sun Wuk Kim

kimono 59–60, 197

Koetsu Honami (1558–1637) 103–5

Konbuang period (1752–1824) 192, 211, 234

Korea: bamboo *143*, 147–48; gold 195–96; lacquer 101–2; paper 166–67; porcelain 69, 80–83; silk 58, *58*; stone 242; wood 214–17, *216*

Korin (Ogata Korin, 1658–1716) 105

Kutani wares *67*, 86–87

lacquer 15, 21, 90–111; Burmese 95, 96, 97, 108–10; Chinese *94*, 95, *96*, 98–101, 144, 147; Indian 95, 111; Japanese 95, 96, 102–6; Korean 101–2; techniques 93–97, 108–10, 183, 204–5; Thai *93*, 96, 97, 106–7; Vietnamese *90*, *91*, *96*, 110–11

lai rot nam technique 96, 97, 107, 182

legends: about papermaking 159; about porcelain 69; about silk 47, 55; about wood 201

Liangzhu culture 33–34

Liao (Khitan) dynasty (907–1125) 36–37, 193, 214

maki-e 96, 97, 102, 183, 197

Mandalay period (1857–85) 110, 132–33

manuscripts *see* books

marble 225, 231–33

marquetry 204, *205*

'medicine lady' 129

Meiji period (1868–1912) 131

metamorphic rocks 225

Ming dynasty (1368–1644): bamboo *142*, 145; gold 194; ivory 128–29, *130*; jades 37, 39; lacquer 100; porcelain *67*, 73–74, 77, *84*; printed books 165; wood *201*, 214

Momoyama period (1574–1615) 103

Mon-Dvaravati period (6th–11th century AD) 235

Mongols 37, 73

mother-of-pearl 95–96, 98, 102, 106–7

moulded decoration, lacquer *97*, 110

Mughal period (1526–1857): architecture 233; gold 183, 187; ivory *122*, *124*, 125–27; jade 30, 41–42; paintings 172, 180; silk *63*; wood 208

Muromachi period (1333–1573) 102–3

Musavi, Abul Baqa al- *187*

Nabeshima wares 87

Negoro lacquers 102

Neolithic Period (*c.* 5000–1500 BC) 32–33, *34*, 143

Nepal: gold *186*, 187; ivory 127; paper 173–74

nephrite *see* jade

netsuke 117, 131, 151, 218, *219*

Nguyen Gia Tri (1908–93) 111

Northern Song dynasty (960–1127) 72–73, *73*

Ogawa Haritsu, see Ritsuo

origami 21

Pagan period (1044–1287) 108, 192, 211, *211*, 234

painting: on ivory 120; lacquer 94–95, 110–11; on paper 158, 169, *172*, 173; on silk 54, 55; on wood carvings 204–5

paper 21, 22, 156–75; Chinese 157, 159, 161, 163–65; Indian 159, 171–73; Japanese 22, *157*, 159, 160, 161–63, *167*, 168–71; Korean 166–67; Nepalese 173–74; Southeast Asian 159, 174–75; techniques 160–63, 168; Tibetan 173–74

Philippines: bamboo 152, *153*, 154; gold *188*; ivory 132, *133*; paper 175; wood carving 213

porcelain 15, 22, 66–89; Chinese 67, 68, 69, 72–80, *72*–*80*, *84*, *136*; Japanese 68, 69, 84–89, *84*–*88*; Korean 69, 80–83, *81*–*83*; techniques 70–71; Vietnamese 88–89, *89*

printing, movable-type 166, *167*; *see also* woodblock printing

puzzle balls 118

Qianlong Emperor 9, 30, 40, 42, 78, 100–1, 147

Qing dynasty (1644–1911): bamboo *145*, 147; gold 194; ivory 130; jades 30, 39–40; paper 165; porcelain *67*, 77–78, *79*, 80; wood 201, 214

resist-dyeing 52, 60

Rhus verniciflua 91, 92, 93, 101, 102

Ri Sanpei 84

rice paper 21, 159

Rikyu, Sen 149

Ritsuo (Ogawa Ritsuo or Ogawa Haritsu, 1663–1747) 105, *105*

robes *see* garments

rubbings *164*, 165

Ryukyu Islands 105, *106*

Sakaida Kakiemon, see Kakiemon

Satsuma wares 89

schist 225, 231

sculpture *see* carving

sedimentary rocks 223–24

semi-precious stones 226, 242

sericin 47

Shang dynasty (1500–1027 BC) 34, 98, 128, 144

shell inlays 95–96, 102, 107

Shibata Zeshin, see Zeshin

Shi Yengje *136*

Shokansai, Iizuka *150*
silk 44–65; Burmese 65; Chinese 22, 46, 55–57; Indian 47, 62–63; Japanese *48, 59–61, 182*; Korean 58; legends of 47, 55; techniques 46–54, 65, 182; Thai *48, 49*, 65; Vietnamese 65
'Silk Road' 46
silk-making moth 46–47
Six Dynasties (265–589) 35
soapstone 225, 242
Song dynasty (960–1279): bamboo carving 145; jade 36, 37; lacquer wares 98; paper 164; porcelain 72–73; silk 55; see also Northern Song, Southern Song
Southeast Asia: bamboo 152–55; gold 188; ivory 132–35; paper 159, 174–75; silk 64–65
Southern Song dynasty (1127–1279) 73
Sri Lanka: ivory *126, 127*; stone carving 233–34
stone 21, 220–43; Cambodia *220, 222, 224*, 235–36; China *224, 225, 226*, 241–43; India 227–33; Indonesia 239–41; Japan *226*, 243; Korea 242; Sri Lanka 233–34; techniques 226–27; Thailand 235–36; Vietnam *238*, 239
Su Dongpo (1036–1101) *136*
Sukhothai period (1238–1368) 190
Sun Wuk Kim *166*

Suzuki Harunobu, see Harunobu
symbolism: of bamboo 13, 14, 136; of gold 180; of jade 13, 32, 34, 35; motifs on porcelain 80

Tang dynasty (618–906): bamboo 144; gold 193; ivory 128; jade 35; lacquer 98; paper 163; porcelain 72; silk 55; stone Buddhas 241
tea ceremony 149
Thailand: bamboo 154; gold *176, 178, 182*, 190, *191*; ivory *132, 133*; jade 41; lacquer *93*, 96, *97*, 106–7; paper 175; silk *48, 49*, 65; stone carving 235–36; wood 210–11
Tibet: gold *187*; ivory *126*, 127; paper 173–74; wood *203, 208*, 209
tie-dyeing 49, 52
'true' lacquer 92
tsuikin ('piled-up brocade') 105–6
tsujigahana 60
tussah silk 47, 60

Umakoshi Shohachi *226*
Unified Silla period (668–935) 242

Vietnam: bamboo 154; lacquer *90, 91*, 96, 110–11; paper 174–75; porcelain *88–89, 89*; silk 65; stone *238*; wood 212

Wada Waichisai III *150*
Warring States dynasty (475–221 BC) 98
weaving: bamboo 140–43, 150–51; silk 49, *50–51, 64*, 65
wood 21, 198–219; Burma 211–12; China 200–201, 214, *215*; India 205–8, *207*; Indonesia *203*, 212–13; Japan *202, 205*, 218–19; Korea 214–17, *216*; Philippines 213; techniques 202–5; Thailand 210–11; Tibet *203, 208, 209*; Vietnam 212
woodblock printing 164, 165, 166–67, 169–70, 204, 219

Xuande reign (1426–35) *67, 74, 76, 77, 78*

Yamataka Ryoun *202*
Yi dynasty, see Joseon
Yoshida, Ayomi 204
yu (Chinese jade) 32
Yuan dynasty (1279–1368) 37, 73, *74*, 98–100, 128
yun technique 108, *108*

Zeshin (Shibata Zeshin, 1807–91) *105*
Zhou dynasty (1050–221 BC) 128; see also Eastern Zhou period